Praise for *Vocational Astrology*

Faye brings a rare combination of insight, hands-on experience and astrological verve to her work on vocation. She can walk clients through a process that touches both outer necessities and inner calling. A valuable resource.

– Lynn Bell, author of *Planetary Threads*

Faye Blake's excellent book is practical, very interesting, and fun to read. I am sure that many others will appreciate it as well.

– Mary Plumb in *The Mountain Astrologer*

It's not only a terrific and much-needed resource from an expert in both fields – astrology and career guidance – it's also a great read! I've taught for 20 years now and there's been nothing like it for intelligence and usability.

– Kim Farley, author of *Mind Maps*

A most useful insight into the ways in which a counselling approach can be dovetailed with astrology. The style is lively, thoughtful and undogmatic.

– Garry Phillipson, author of *Astrology in the Year Zero*

Faye's excellent book is tremendously well-conceived and full of good information. I really like her structured approach and thoughtful analysis.

– Christina Rodenbeck, The Oxford Astrologer

Thought-provoking, fascinating and wonderfully readable.

– John Green in *The Astrological Journal*

This book gave me a lot to think about on several levels, a real rarity among astrology books. The author's ideas about structuring the consultation are worth the price of the book even if you aren't interested in doing vocational astrology, but odds are you'll find that vocation is an exciting possibility for your work as an astrologer after reading it. I highly recommend it.

– Armand Diaz, author of *Integral Astrology*

The book is authentic, it is Faye speaking. I really recognize the positive approach she has, which contributes so much to her style of astrology.

– Elizabeth Hathway in the *Astrologie Blog*

Faye, you've written one of the most useful and intelligent books I've seen on vocational astrology. What I especially appreciate is that you don't provide a cookbook approach but really delve into the process work that people need to do to find the occupational path that's right for them. I also find your writing style fluid, engaging, original, and highly expert. I am learning a lot studying your important text.

– Greg Bogart, author of *Planets in Therapy*

A terrific resource for astrologers and counselors interested in supporting clients to live their authentic career. Cossar offers a pragmatic strategy in assessing a person's natural orientation to a public contribution … She brings many years of experience to this work, and writes in a witty and engaging style. This book is not only an enjoyable read for the astrologically-minded, it will help strengthen the tools to be an effective counselor.

– Eric Meyers, author of *The Astrology of Awakening*

When professional career advisors alight on this book it may inspire them to start using astrology in their work when they see how swiftly it delivers information about a client's character qualities, aptitudes and blockages.

– Phoebe Wyss, author of *Inside the Cosmic Mind*

The book reflects (Faye's) knowledge, skills and expertise. It contains a wealth of information and its contents aim at personal development as much as career development.

– Ghislane Adams in *Conjunction*

An innovative, practical and creative book presenting a skillful model of vocational astrology.

– Margaret Gray in the *ISAR Journal*

Faye Blake sets out a powerful and comprehensive strategy for identifying core factors essential to job satisfaction as well as for writing effective CVs to showcase unique abilities and personality traits to prospective employers. Her book also provides a deceptively simple but effective tool for choosing words and images for websites, marketing and other promotional material that authentically reflect the individual … Invaluable for astrologers who offer vocational counselling and anyone looking to clarify and polish their public profile.

– Jane Ridder-Patrick, author of *A Handbook of Medical Astrology*

Full reviews at www.fayesbook.co.uk

Vocational Astrology

Finding the Right Career Direction

Faye Blake

Flare Publications
The London School of Astrology

The London School of Astrology

Original 2012 edition: *Using Astrology to Create a Vocational Profile*

This edition published in 2017 by Flare Publications
in conjunction with the London School of Astrology
BCM Planets, London WC1N 3XX, England, UK
Tel: 0700 2 33 44 55
www.flareuk.com and www.londonschoolofastrology.co.uk
email: admin@londonschoolofastrology.co.uk

A CIP catalogue record for this book is available from the British Library

ISBN: 978-1-903353-46-2
ISBN: 978-1-903353-47-9 (ebook)

Cover Illustration: Klaartje Berkelmans, www.klaartjeberkelmans.nl

Cover Design: Karin Kerremans from Strut Your Stuff,
www.strutyourstuff.nl

Author Photo: Cristina Stoian Portraits, www.cristinastoian.nl

Text editing: Jane Struthers, Frank Clifford
Diagrams: Craig Knottenbelt
Charts: Solar Fire (Esoteric Technologies)
Additional images: shutterstock.com, dreamstime.com,
freedigitalphotos.net and kozzi.com

For Zelda
whose warm, generous, loving and encouraging
Leo heart helped birth this book

My heartfelt thanks to:

Sue Tompkins
For your Aquarian wake-up call. Attending your insightful, eccentric, laughter-packed classes back in 1984 in London helped me find my vocation (not to mention a friend) and literally changed the course of my life. Having you write the foreword to my first book feels like coming full circle.

Frank Clifford
For your, as you put it, 'gentle (Aries) kick' to get me started on writing a book at all. Your help with this, the publishing (with your beady Virgo eye) and running training at the London School of Astrology are deeply appreciated. It's nice to be so well looked after.

My example client Jackie (You know who you really are!)
It was fun working with you on this project and I appreciated the time you put in to finish the homework — an achievement for an Aries. Your writing adds greatly to the book and I am so glad you are heading towards your true calling now.

My clients
Without you I simply would not have learned so much about astrology or had so much fun along the way. Thanks for your trust.

CONTENTS

FOREWORD

The issue of work is so important that it demands that the *whole* horoscope be involved. So, good vocational advice requires much, much more from the astrologer than merely looking at the tenants and rulers of the 2nd, 6th and 10th houses. Given that an understanding of the entire area of vocation and employment is so essential to every astrologer's toolkit, any help they can receive has to be a good thing. In *Vocational Astrology: Finding the Right Career Direction*, readers are taken gently through this whole process by Faye Blake, who is as well versed in non-astrological vocational models as she is in astrology.

Expertise in the areas of work and vocation is possibly the most important specialism for astrologers to have under their belt. This is because the principal areas that clients bring to astrologers concern either their career or their love life. To be human is to be concerned – even consumed – with matters of work and/or relationship. And even where an individual says they only want to talk about spiritual matters – or the meaning of life, their kids or their health – frequently there will be add-on questions regarding work.

For those with a strong sense of vocation, the *choice* of employment isn't an issue. Their unconscious, if not conscious, self knows what they want to do and they follow their chosen path like a sniffer dog that's picked up a scent. In such cases, the chosen vocation is usually pretty obvious to see in the horoscope. Such individuals may not need to discuss their choice of vocation but, as with everyone, there will inevitably be issues that arise from *doing* the actual job. For who among us has mastered *all* the skills necessary to do what we do and to work alongside colleagues, bosses and employees? Inevitably a degree of self-confidence and self-esteem informs everyone's capacity to be effective in the workplace and justly remunerated.

It will come as no surprise that an individual's entire psychological state can affect matters of work and vocation. One's work is usually the best way of working through and making use of one's psychological difficulties. For instance, imagine that, for whatever reason, you are a touchy person, one who feels easily threatened and exhibits an argumentative, militant attitude. No doubt these traits will have a history attached to them and might be ameliorated by therapeutic help – but that is not the issue here. Such traits may not make for easy personal relationships anywhere, but these qualities could be ideally utilized if your job were that of a trade union official engaged in defending workers' rights. Work so often offers a socially acceptable outlet for psychological issues.

While some people say they follow a vocation, many more say they just 'do a job'. Either way, whatever the individual does with him- or herself all day – even if it's unpaid or not traditionally called a job – it should connect as many aspects of the individual's psyche as possible. Ideally, each person should be doing whatever it is that makes their heart sing, even if it is in their spare time. Following their inner self as much as possible contributes hugely to both their inner psychological health and outer physical health.

This book does not assume that the astrologer should know everything. What I like about Faye's work is that it is client-centred, as arguably all astrological consultations should be. The astrologer is in control of the actual *process* of the discussion but the client must always feel in control of the *content* of that conversation. In terms of vocation, most people (even those who don't have a strong sense of which direction they want to pursue) know somewhere deep inside them what they want or need to be doing with their lives. What is sometimes more elusive is the *name* of that pursuit or the confidence or wherewithal to actually pursue it. A job may require a range of skills and at times we may have *some* of those skills but not all of them. However good we may be at our job, there are usually areas where we are stronger and others where we are weaker.

The topic of vocation isn't just about the kind of work a person might pursue or even about which set of skills or qualities they personally may bring to their particular work table. It is about the journey of getting there and, having arrived, how to thrive and move forward. A clichéd line that is often linked to the success of a shop or a restaurant is 'Location, location, location'. For success generally, I would say, 'Preparation, preparation, preparation'. Success tends to come through preparing oneself adequately for a given role, coupled with the opportunity of that role presenting itself. Astrology is a tool for highlighting future opportunities as well as offering clues to an individual's particular strengths and weaknesses. Weaknesses can be overcome and strengths can be celebrated. When it comes to personal growth, becoming more conscious of both can only be of benefit to us.

Sue Tompkins, April 2012

INTRODUCTION

Is that what they call a vocation, what you do with joy as if
you had fire in your heart, the devil in your body?
                                          Josephine Baker

My belief is that if we can hold our nerve and pursue what we love,
we will be happier, more successful, develop our true talents and
feel more fulfilled. Success for me is 'doing your horoscope' in the
most positive and creative way possible. It has never been, is not,
and never will be, about money!

The book's title begs the question: What is a vocation? The
Oxford Dictionaries Online (www.oxforddictionaries.com) states it
to be:

- A strong feeling of suitability for a particular career or
  occupation
- A person's employment or main occupation, especially
  regarded as worthy and requiring dedication
- A trade or profession

I prefer Josephine Baker's words above – they imply an engagement
of the heart *and* the body for a true calling. As an Aquarian, I might
also add that the mind needs to be fed, too.

The word 'vocation' has its roots in the Latin *vocare*, which
means 'to call'. Originally one was 'called' by God. Later, career
advice came from ancient priests or religious leaders who could
interpret the heavenly signs and state what an individual should
do. Through time, the source of this advice changed, resulting
in parents or teachers being the ones to provide guidance. Now,
as well as parents and teachers, we have career counsellors and
student advisory services. And of course astrologers.

Since Shirley MacLaine's book *Out on a Limb* (1983) was made
into a television series in 1987, the image of her repeating 'I am God'
has affected the way many seek advice. In a paper I once wrote on
this topic, I referred to this change through the ages as going from

'outside-in' to 'inside-out'. Perhaps it was easier when the decision of career was made for us and there were fewer professions. Now, there are so many options, it becomes very difficult to know what we really want to do with our working life. And the responsibility is clearly with the individual. We seem to be caught in the struggle of trying to follow our heart (inside) and fitting in with what the workforce (outside) is asking. This book is my attempt at solving this dilemma.

Some time ago, when I was a board member of the Dutch Astrological Association, which promotes education and quality in astrology, I was given an idea for a training course. I jumped at the chance to teach this course with two colleagues. One, who had suggested it, was an astrologer and the other was a career counsellor who knew nothing of astrology. I had seen the need for a course of this kind – one that took the knowledge acquired during the basic astrology classes and put it to use to help clients find their true calling and assist them with all manner of career questions.

Since those early days in 2001, the course has been run many times and different career counsellors have been involved. The content has developed substantially and, after much feedback and many enthusiastic responses, the method has proved to be a very worthwhile way of presenting this material.

This book is the result of these years, using a framework which has essentially been borrowed from the career advisors' world. In Holland, and I imagine in other countries too, this area has a large market. Career advisors are very successful, being employed both in-company and out. They are often used in long-term outplacement situations where companies pay to help redundant staff members find work. In this case, clients have the advantage of several sessions with an advisor. These advisors have many clients, so they must be doing something right!

There were many things that I learned from working with career counsellors, but two stand out. One is that when you are dealing with questions relating to work, jobs, vocation – whatever you want to call it – you *must* get the client involved. The client has to take responsibility for the process and put in the necessary work. If they want to find a job, change jobs or set up their own enterprise, it must be the client who embraces the idea and puts in the effort to get there. It's not that I didn't know this, but the model I use in this book assumes that the client does all the writing, note-taking, research and anything else required. Generally, I am of the opinion that:

ASTROLOGERS DO TOO MUCH WORK
FOR THEIR CLIENTS!

The second lesson I learned is that as astrologers we have an absolutely wonderful tool for this kind of work. Again, it's not that I didn't know this already, but the career counsellors I have worked with were flabbergasted by how easily we can get information from a chart. They have to prise information out of clients with questionnaires and other forms of exercises. They all commented on what a fantastic tool astrology is and expressed a wish to learn more in order to make their lives easier.

So this book takes a framework and shows you how to get a result – a vocational profile (VP) – by using the horoscope. For each part of the profile, it offers a way of looking at the chart as well as giving some suggestions for getting your client involved. It also provides examples and case studies. The chart opposite is for Jackie, who is used as an example throughout the book. We did the whole process together and at the end of the book you will see the Vocational Profile she created.

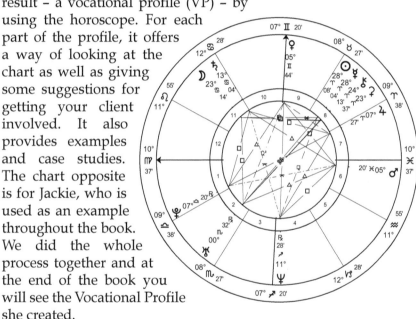

At this point in the book, I believe I should state my philosophy and beliefs about career, vocation and work. In my view, most people are not fulfilling their potential. Many are just doing a job to fund the rest of their lives. They don't have the confidence to dare to go for what they love, they believe it is too late or they think it isn't even possible. They haven't thought that a job could or should be something they love to do.

My hope is that this book will be a practical guide to working with career questions of all kinds and assist you in making the most of your astrology in this field. Along the way, you can encourage your clients to be who they truly are.

Faye Blake, July 2017

CHAPTER 1
WHY THIS BOOK?

The power to question is the basis of all human progress.
Indira Gandhi

One of the problems astrologers have, particularly when they are just beginning to work with clients, is where and how to start. There is so much information that can be found in a horoscope and usually a lot of time has been invested in preparing for any possible question that may arise. There is never enough time in a single session to cover every interesting thing you have discovered during the preparation phase. As I said, we work too hard. What is needed is a structure.

The beauty of the framework that career counsellors use is that it gives us a place to start and, more importantly, it has an end result. We know where we are heading and we know when we have arrived. The result is a vocational profile, also known as a PCP – a personal career profile. Well, that end result is as far as we can go as astrologers. Career advisors actually take it a step further and help to make appointments for interviews. They may also have contacts in the employment market. Career advisors have other skills. However, as astrologers, we have better tools for defining the three questions that this model is based on:

Who am I?

What can I do?

What do I want?

These are the areas we can help to define. I believe encouraging your client to clarify these three questions will help in any career or job question they might throw at you.

'PCP' is a term given in a very useful book (among others) by Gerald Sturman. In English it is called *If You Knew Who You Were, You Could Be Who You Are,*[1] and is a self-help book. However, it provides exercises that are useful for you to give to clients, enabling them to get involved in the VP process. The other main way to get clients engaged, which astrologers don't do often enough, is in a dialogue.

The power of the question

We need to ask the client, before they arrive, what their question actually is. Why are they coming and what are they expecting? By doing this we can manage expectations and can prepare what is necessary. During the session we can also ask clients, particularly when it comes to career areas, many questions regarding their working life. An astrologer 'getting it right' by identifying the current career or work area is not really adding much to the client's knowledge or giving them much insight. So in the chapters that follow, I encourage you to use dialogue often with clients. Someone searching for help in their working life knows far more about their life and their situation than you ever will as an astrologer.

However, this doesn't mean you can just listen and offer a few good suggestions. It means that you need to be able to listen with an astrological ear and translate what you hear back to the chart, so you can see how an area of the horoscope works. This takes practice, but the reward is that the horoscope can offer up suggestions that help the client to use the chart's gifts more positively. You can and should be able to offer advice to clients who have job questions, but this needs to come from the chart, not from your own views. And remember the client is free to not take your advice. What they do after seeing you is always their responsibility.

I wanted to offer something very practical in this book, something that can help guide you through one of the pitfalls of working with clients: having too much information. When preparing a chart, and while working with clients, many topics can be covered. If you have ascertained that a client is coming for a career session, a framework is helpful for keeping your client from digressing into other areas. It will also help you to prepare in a more focused way by studying each section. Of course other topics can be discussed, and having a way of grouping issues together allows you to address these later in the session or during another appointment.

Another reason for writing this book is that, in my search for information on this topic, I found many astrology books to have good information on career/vocation, but they all start with the chart and go through the zodiac signs and the houses. Often there's an emphasis on the MC or the so-called 'work houses'. Many astrologers give career advice by looking at forecasting techniques such as transits and progressions. This provides suggestions as to **when** you can progress in your chosen profession. These methods are all valid. However, this book features the birth chart only. It's not that forecasting techniques can't show the timing of events or help with career questions – they can. But first you must know what fits the client.

More and more it has become obvious to me that as astrologers we need to go back to the birth chart to really look at vocation. Vocation will unfold through life and may take twists and turns, but the theme of the calling doesn't change. So this book offers a model to help you, as an astrologer working with any career questions, to **get a result**. It begins with a non-astrological model – the vocational profile – a result that you are trying to achieve. And for this, you need to let go of the idea of starting with the chart. Instead, start with the idea of defining vocation and putting the client in the centre. Only then should you start looking at the chart to find the answers. This book also provides suggestions for getting the client involved in the process. Another benefit in using this method is that you will learn a lot of astrology. I hope that by working with astrology in this way, and being able to offer a concrete and tangible product, the image that astrology and astrologers have will be improved. More importantly, your clients should be a step closer to their true calling.

---

1. *If You Knew Who You Were, You Could Be Who You Are,* Gerald M Sturman, Bierman House, 2010.

CHAPTER 2

HOW TO USE THIS BOOK

It is nothing short of a miracle that modern methods of instruction have not yet entirely strangled the holy curiosity of inquiry.

Albert Einstein

Before I start with the actual process of working with clients, I want to give a few suggestions as to how to use this book. The structure follows one that some career advisors use. It is divided into three sections:

- Who am I?
- What can I do?
- What do I want?

This process,[1] which can be set in motion extremely well using the horoscope as a tool, is a means (divided into practical sections) of getting to know who you are so you can express your true self in your (working) world.

The 'work' chapters in my book are as follows:

Chapter 3   The start: using the biography

Who am I?
Chapter 4   Finding vocation and motivation
Chapter 5   Recognizing style and drive
Chapter 6   Expressing an authentic image

What can I do?
Chapter 7   Discovering talents and ways to make money
Chapter 8   Defining communication skills
Chapter 9   What can't I do? Clarifying blocks

What do I want?

The rest of the book puts it all together and suggests the next steps to take.

The Full Monty?

One way to use this book is to follow the whole trajectory, beginning with Chapter 3. You can then go through each chapter in any order to create a vocational profile and help your client make a new CV or website. However, most clients will not want or need every section. Although you should not automatically assume this, they probably won't be prepared to pay for all the sessions that this would involve. Secondly, and more importantly, you will only need to use some parts of the process to solve their presenting problem. Be aware, though, that the presenting problem discussed in the initial contact may not be the real issue. In working with the example client I introduce throughout the book, you will see I have spent more time on some parts of the VP than others.

I suggest you try out all the steps for yourself to improve your own publicity material and clearly define who you are and what you want as an astrologer. And practise it on your friends. By doing this you will not only have a better website or brochure, you will also understand how the process feels for your clients.

Doing only a few sessions with a client

Chapter 3 describes how to use a client biography. If the client is prepared to come to you for more than one appointment, I suggest you ask the client to produce a bio. It is a valuable tool and gives you insight into the point the client has reached in their life. It also provides information about the expertise they have already built up.

All the chapters from 4 to 12 can be used in a stand-alone way, as each one describes a different part of the VP, such as talents or style. So you can work with one or maybe two chapters in a session, depending on how long your consultations are. I make appointments of approximately two hours. Any more than this is too long for most people to take in information.

Unless they specifically ask me not to, I always record discussions for clients to listen to again as no one can absorb all that is discussed in one go. Also, I have noticed that it is very valuable for a client to hear what they have said. Most people answer their own questions. It is our task to frame those answers in a way that helps our client to gain clarity on a particular issue.

Most popular sessions

The parts of the VP that I have worked through most frequently with clients are those that define vocation and motivation, talents and, particularly, blocks, although I don't usually do blocks as a stand-alone element. As these issues can be quite challenging or painful, I like to work with a client in a session or two before tackling this area, although this does depend on the level of the client's self-awareness.

My techniques… but use yours, too

In these chapters I offer you my techniques, but I stress throughout the book that you can use your own favourites. If they fit in with the structure, then please use them. You will probably find that you end up with your own way of working, with bits added and subtracted. This is my ideal outcome for you. There are many good techniques in astrology but some will speak to you more than others. What I want to get across is the structure involved in creating a VP. It doesn't matter how you get there, although I hope you will try some of my ideas. With years of experience in both astrology and therapy behind me, I have found them to be really useful in providing a framework and, more importantly, in helping clients.

Typical questions and possible scenarios

Clients visit astrologers for myriad reasons, but career issues are some of the main ones. You need to decide for yourself which questions you want to handle. Clearly, the whole VP process is useful for everyone but, in case you don't have the luxury of having several appointments with each client, here are some suggestions for sessions using a few typical presenting issues.

I have just finished studying but I am not really sure what I want to do. What would suit me?

This question usually comes from someone who is just finishing school and needs to choose a university (or further study) program, or someone who has completed their study and now needs to start applying for jobs. In this case, the vocation session is the only one I usually do, as it provides the opportunity to discuss various areas that have been studied already. It also provides confirmation and encouragement of what the student loves to do and might be good at (as opposed to what the parents might want). This helps to narrow down the choices that need to be made.

I am unhappy in my job but don't know what I want.

This is a very broad issue but I would suggest a strategy that will first highlight whether the problem lies in the type of work your client does or whether it's the environment that is unsuitable (and this can be the wrong country, company or people). I would ask for a bio and a CV first if the client is open to having at least two sessions with me. If not, I would do a vocation session. Usually it will become obvious to the client in this session where the problem lies.

I am at a crossroads in my life – what should I do?

This is similar to the question above but usually this type of question comes from someone who has looked at a few options. The vocation session, with the matrix I describe in this chapter, is a good place to start. There will often be issues other than work hidden in this question.

I have been made redundant and am not sure what I want.

People who have been made redundant are usually very worried about the future and feel very vulnerable. They need encouragement and someone to talk to about why they were made redundant. Clients often feel that somehow it is their fault, even though this is not usually the case. A blocks session is very worthwhile, but not as a first consultation. You may need to reframe the client's question and turn it into a session about how they can make money/develop their talents, with a bit of vocation work thrown in. Often these clients need to feel financially secure before embarking on a journey of self-discovery. The other potentially good thing here is that companies often have a budget for outplacement. If your client wants to come to you, they may be able to apply for some of those funds to pay for you. You can suggest this to clients facing redundancy.

I have had kids and am ready to get back into the workforce but am not sure how to go about it.

Women often ask this question once their children are at school or are old enough to look after themselves. One of the things I do is to get mothers (they are usually the ones asking this question, rather than fathers) to write up a biography that includes their skills. What I *don't* want is a bio or CV that shows gaps in their working experience. The first thing potential employers seem to ask at an interview is what happened during gaps in employment. I like clients to be prepared for this by being able to quote skills they have gained while being in unpaid jobs, too. You can help your clients to get started by doing a talents session. Their write-up will include skills they have used at work but, most importantly, it will highlight skills they use daily simply by being mothers. Project management, budgeting, organizing, running an after-school swimming group – all of these things show valuable expertise. The fact that they are unpaid is irrelevant. Whatever these women are good at and have experience of should be included in their work experience. Mothers are better than a lot of people (probably most!) at managing input from several directions. And often mothers do many unpaid jobs, such as sitting on committees or fund-raising. This is all beneficial experience. Highlighting these talents makes mothers feel more valuable to the workforce. After going through that I would try a vocation session if only one more session is planned. That is always a good standard.

I have just lost my partner and need to earn more – but doing what?

With this type of question, this major issue must to be attended to first. Clients want to talk about their lost husband/wife/ partner. And, as many people these days rely on two incomes, they need to talk about finances with someone who can be objective. There may, of course, be a lot of sadness here but, most of all, there is fear. And there's often an urgent practical problem that needs to be sorted out. What I would do with this is try to gauge if the client is ready to look at the kind of job that really suits them. But I might simply need to listen and suggest a way of getting over any practical problems first. After that, the question becomes similar to any of the others.

I am self-employed but that is difficult in the current climate. Should I take a salaried job?

At the time of writing I can certainly understand this question myself, as we are all in the middle of tricky economic times. This is a different kind of question, with the answer depending somewhat on your philosophy of life. I always state my philosophy (do what you love and what is authentic for you – and success will follow) to clients as I think it is relevant in this instance. Clients are always responsible for what they choose to do but my philosophy is to encourage people to hold their nerve if being self-employed fits their birth chart. The question stems from uncertainty. Helping your client to define his calling, using the vocation session, can often help. I would also do a mission and goals session plus the image one, if time allows, as this will help with any promotional material.

I really want to start my own business but am too scared.

This is really the same issue as above but stated in a different way. My strategy is the same: I would encourage clients to go for what they love and help them define their talents and money-making options, as well as offer them advice on PR material. If being self-employed is indeed a good idea I also look at the client's blocks to see what might be holding them back.

I have noticed a pattern in my behaviour at work but don't know how to change it.

I would offer a general session, spending a little time on each of the individual sections, and then use any remaining time to look at blocks. The question implies a certain amount of self-awareness. So dealing with blocks is often where this sort of client needs to focus. You can help to define what these patterns might be, guiding your client towards pursuing this area either with you (if you have the skills) or, if necessary, with a therapist.

More sessions
I want to add a note about doing more than one session. As astrologers we are often used to giving only a single consultation. This is a pity, for many reasons. One is that we don't get any feedback so we don't know how useful our sessions are (unless we send out questionnaires – which is a good idea but another topic

altogether). Another reason is that we try to fit too much into the time available, so a lot of the good advice we can give gets buried or is skipped over.

On a business level it is far easier to get existing clients to come for more sessions (unless they disliked you) than it is to get new clients. So we need to learn to promote ourselves better. I have a client who refers her friends to me, telling them that 'they should get it done'. This implies that once they have had a 'reading' they will have done what is necessary and all will then miraculously be OK! It sounds like having your teeth out, but I know she is joking. On a serious note, many people don't understand that astrologers could offer more sessions. I'm not suggesting we get pushy and persuade people to spend a lot of money on appointments they don't need. I believe that what is needed in the astrological field is to educate our clients about the possibilities of what astrology can offer. Clients often love to come a few times but they feel that it might not be 'the done thing'. One of the offers I make is to give a good discount if a client pays up-front for five sessions. Many clients love this.

This book offers a way of structuring more than one session. You will probably find you need more than five sessions when you get going. Don't underestimate the value of a listening ear for clients. We don't need to talk at them for a full two hours! When they trust you, they will come back to you with all manner of questions.

Once you have carried out some sessions or have achieved what can be done with your expertise, you will find it useful to have tried-and-tested people in your network who you can recommend to clients. These might be career counsellors who take the steps to help get someone a job. They might be therapists or body-workers who can work with any deeper issues that need solving. They might be logo designers, website builders or communication experts who can write a good CV. In my opinion you need to have this type of network around you, and it has the added advantage of operating as a source of potential clients for you through recommendations.

Number of sessions – summary

Because you can get into therapeutic territory, the table below makes it clearer who can do what. It is good to be aware that there is a strong coaching movement aimed at all levels within organizations. This is your competition although, in my view, many (executive) coaches do not have the required skills for dealing with career counselling – especially for handling blocks.

This book is intended mainly for use by astrologers with client experience, although others may learn a lot from it too. If you are going to fully embrace this work, I recommend that you get some sort of counselling training as you can then offer a better service.

Number of available sessions	Astrology/Therapy	Possible service
1	Astrology	Strong points and/or Calling and/or Mission and/or Talents and/or Image
1–5	Astrology	Vocational profile Parts of the profile Information about blocks
More	Astrotherapy	Same as above plus deeper work on blocks
More	(Executive) Coaching – a term that is very badly defined! In my view, therapy and coaching are very different but some coaches attempt to give therapy without recognized qualifications	Total career counselling with/ without astrology

Two special services
Because I have a practical approach, I like working with a set 'product', which works well for my own marketing. Clients know why they are coming and what they will get. There are two parts of the VP that operate extremely well on their own. The first one is image and is described in Chapter 6. This service works for individuals and companies as either *personal or corporate branding*. I cannot overemphasize what a useful and fun service this is. At the time of writing I am working with a logo and website designer to help create a house style that reflects an authentic image for both my client personally (for a website and blog) and for her company (website and publications). It is a very creative process, and since we started doing this the designer has seen the benefit that astrological archetypes provide in enabling discussion on images. She will now recommend me to others in a design project.

The second service you can offer is one of the things I describe in Chapter 14, 'What next?' Every time one of my friends goes for a new job they get me to look at their CV. This 'feedback session' is a great service to offer, especially if you like writing. I work on this with a text writer. I have good contacts in my network with people who can write professional English and Dutch text. What I can offer is a quick scan of a *CV or website and provide suggestions for improvement* in line with the authentic nature of the client. Again, this is such a useful service that you can offer. Clients love it and it can be very quick once you get the hang of it. So, Chapter 14 tells you how to go about doing this.

I hope you enjoy this way of working with your clients. I have found it very rewarding and, in the process, I have learned a great deal more about astrology. I am very grateful to all my clients for the descriptions of astrological themes they have provided throughout the years and for their trust in me.

Now, down to work...

---

1. These questions sound more punchy in Dutch: *Wie ben ik? Wat kan ik? Wat wil ik?* However, the title of the book by Gerald Sturman that I mentioned earlier, which puts this idea of Adriaan Hoogendijk's into practice, sounds better in English. Adriaan Hoogendijk is a well known figure in the career coaching world in the Netherlands. He is the author of several books, has given hundreds of lectures and now runs an organization that coaches at all levels. He has also trained many coaches to use his methodology. He is a member of many advisory boards that are concerned with career development and coaching. In case you have the English version of Sturman's book, the structure of the Dutch book I use as a basis here has been modified slightly in the English version. In Dutch the title of Sturman's book translates literally as 'Wanted: a job that fits me'. The English title, *If You Knew Who You Were, You Could Be Who You Are,* actually better describes the process used in his book.

CHAPTER 3
THE START: USING THE BIOGRAPHY

An autobiography is an obituary in serial form with the last instalment missing.

Quentin Crisp

The first thing I do when asked to give advice on career is to ascertain whether the client wants a quick fix, a one-off consultation or a longer version. If what is required is simply a horoscope reading with career as a focus, then this is usually clear in the initial contact and we make an appointment. I also tell the client that I can offer further sessions, as many who visit astrologers have no idea about this possibility. As already mentioned, my view is that we need to market our services better. If more than one session is an option, I offer a free intake appointment. The goal of this is threefold:

- To ascertain whether what I do fits the expectations of the client – including costs

- To make a plan with an outline for the required number of possible sessions

- To determine whether I want to work with this client

The last point is not unimportant, as we cannot be all things to all people, and to do our best work we need to feel comfortable with any contract we enter into. We should know it is feasible. I find a 'contract' (this can be verbal) very important so we both know where we are going with the work and we understand the desired result. After we have thought about it and agreed, the client must get to work.

The first exercise, before they come for the first session, is for them to write the biography. In truth it is autobiographical, as the client writes it about themselves, but everyone seems to use the term 'bio' these days, which I will do throughout this book. This is the information I give to the client:

Biography exercise

When you ask, 'What should I do about my career?' or 'How can I find a job that really suits me and that I love?', then the past becomes really important.

How did you get to your current situation? What has contributed to your career in a positive or negative way? By answering a few questions, you can write a short biography. To help you discover what the patterns are in your career path, it is important for you to highlight themes and turning points in your career and in your life.

The following are questions that will help you do this. These are suggestions, but please use your own ideas and include what is important for you. Don't make the story too long. Three A4 pages will suffice.

Your home life

What was your family like? What sort of relationship did you have with your parents? What sort of atmosphere was there at home? What role did you have? Were you the eldest? Youngest? What was your relationship like with your siblings? How did you get on with friends and classmates?

What sort of relationships have you had with partners and what is the situation now? Which roles do your partner, family and/or children play in your working life?

Your schooling

What was it like at primary school? What were the best and the worst experiences? What about high school? How did you choose subjects to study in your higher education? Which subjects were you good at when you were at school? What did you enjoy? What were your dreams? Did you have a role model? Was there someone you wanted to be like in terms of career or achievements?

Your working life

Make a note of the jobs you have had – both paid and non-paid. What are your hobbies or other interests? Where can you 'lose yourself'? What was great and not so great? What were you good at? What were important decisions? Why did you leave a job or stop a hobby? What have you learned about yourself at work? What have you learned as a parent?

The client is asked to send their bio to me at least a few days before the first session. Many will have a CV but, if not, I ask them to write one. There are numerous suggestions on the Internet about how to do this. This may seem like a lot of effort but, if a client is really looking for work or wanting to change direction or get back into the workforce, then commitment is VERY important. Astrologers offer far too much information that may never be used – a pity, as we can give very valuable insights. Career counselling, vocational profiling or guidance – whatever you want to call it – is very much a joint effort. The client must be involved and must take responsibility for the outcome. Students will hear me say this often: as astrologers, we work far too hard for our clients. For this service to be valuable to the client, it is important that we change the 'consumer' attitude. OK, I'm off my soapbox.

Why is a biography important?

Career advisors need to get a feel for the client and their history, and the bio is the advisor's reference when making a list of questions to start a discussion. Intuition plays a role when reading the stories that clients give us. As astrologers, we can of course start a discussion by using the chart – and I often tell clients that their horoscope is my questionnaire. But a bio is extremely useful to us, too. It creates involvement, as I have already stated. But it also offers an insight into how the client has used their chart until now. Their history is vital if we want to discover their possible 'futures'. By studying their bio we can highlight patterns, which we can use later when explaining a particular aspect. We can see where there might be blocks (these will be covered later when defining and identifying issues that may need work). Perhaps even more importantly, we can see what is absent from the stories, and here I think we have the advantage over others who do not use astrology. I have often looked at a chart while reading the bio and thought, for example, 'Where is all this Aries energy being used?', as there may be no sign of it in the client's text. This is a warning light for me. What I am doing when reading the bio is matching it to the horoscope. You'll have to find your own way of doing this but I will attempt to show you how I do it by using a real-life example throughout this book.

Introducing my client

My client, who I will call Jackie, is a single woman with no children. She was 35 years old at the time of the sessions and was in a job with which she was very dissatisfied. She wanted to change but stayed in her job because it was safe (I hear that a lot!) and it was paying her salary (ditto). She is a foreigner in the Netherlands, with a varied background, and had realized that she needed help in order to take the next step forward and follow her calling. However, she was unsure of how the things she loves to do could offer a good financial reward (also a common complaint). Unlike many of my clients, she *did* have an idea of where her passion lies.

We agreed to do six sessions after the intake, which in my experience is a little too short but this still offers the chance to create a vocational profile. You will find Jackie's later on in this book. Note that **the resulting profile should be a tool that is valid for the rest of your client's working life**. Jackie saw the benefit of these sessions not only in the creation of a VP, but also in the insights she would gain along the way about herself and her calling. The question of 'Why am I here and do I have a calling?' is often implicit in the original idea of going to an astrologer for career advice. Jackie was amazed to discover how much information can be gained in this field from a horoscope.

It is fascinating to see how clients approach their bios. They are all so different and interesting and, of course, we can tell a lot from the style and the tone of the writing before any further analysis. Here's Jackie's bio:

I'm a first generation American, born to a Kenyan mother and Tanzanian father. I'm also a redundant, second-born girl, middle child to boot. I was never as bright a star as my older sister and nowhere near as adorable as my baby brother. My mother ran the show like the Mafia, dishing out our orders. When my father's embassy post was up and he had to return to Tanzania, she gave the call to split the family in the name of her children's education. Daddy went back by himself. We saw him once a year for a couple of months, which was just fine because he was really, really bad at being a father. Mommy was the Alpha and the Omega.

Early on she told us kids she wanted a lawyer, doctor and an engineer. She thought I had an aptitude for electronics because I took apart the VCR (didn't put back together, mind) and assigned me the engineer role. Doing well in school was her primary focus, which naturally became ours as well. Compared to American kids we were well behaved, respectful and quiet. When we went back home the Kenyans saw us as spoiled American brats.

Because we were close in age – my sister one year older and brother two years younger than me – we got on well at times and fought like hell other times. My sister and I used to bully my poor brother like crazy, until he grew taller. Big sis and I would fistfight and wrestle over clothes. We created and performed mini-musicals together, entertaining the aunts and uncles that lived with us while growing up. My mother enrolled us in an after-school performing arts programme and even took us to an audition for a TV commercial. I think she wanted actors as well as scholars. My sister was the smartest and the do-right-est, amply filling the first-born's shoes. From first breath, my brother could do no wrong even when he did do wrong. I was someone my mother could count on, responsible enough to handle household duties early on. I was there to be of service; it was hard to get noticed otherwise.

My mother was away a great deal, first to acquire her PhD and then for work. We weren't a 'tell me how your day was' family. Us kids were alone a lot and sorted ourselves out for dinner. Later Mommy would return from work and then go off to her room to decompress as we watched TV. She took us to the movies on the weekends, which was our family thing. We loved going to the movies, once we saw three in one day. She took us out to eat a lot, cooking not being her thing. We learned to communicate via movies and food. Oh, and she bought us things.

At school, I was a super-shy and insecure kid. My friends usually ran the show; I followed and waited to be asked to participate. Early school started out fun, I guess, but soon turned to crap. Maybe because I was one of six black kids (including my brother and sister) in an all-white primary school in the 80s, I got teased and taunted a lot. It probably didn't help I was chubby and taller than all the boys. I don't think my siblings had a tough time of it; they always had more friends than me. I remember being really quiet and intensely sad. Remembering all this now is agony. I'm finding it hard to recount without feeling the residual yuck that presided over my childhood. I was bullied and made fun of throughout school. Not so much as to totally alienate me but enough that I started to believe I deserved it. My good friend went away during our sophomore year so I ate lunch in the bathroom because I couldn't bear the social angst of the cafeteria.

I dreaded the social part of school but found refuge in the classroom: the first presentation I ever liked giving was in Mr Butler's Contemporary History class. I marvelled at how Mr Baskerville fit African History in one semester. Music in primary school was a delight, despite the teacher's overproduction of saliva. Our psychology teacher looked young enough so he tricked us and sat at a desk among us on the first day of class – clever. I really enjoyed Human Anatomy, Calculus and every English class. High school studies came easy, my mother's hard stance on education paid off.

Most of my dreaming took place when the lights dimmed in a movie theatre. I used the movie to ignite my imagination. I wasn't shy any more, I was as big and loud as the characters on the big screen. I didn't want to be an actor per se, I couldn't go against mother's wishes. I wanted to really exist in the 2-hour-and-15-minute dream. Maybe I applied to engineering schools in Los Angeles for a reason. One reason for sure was to escape my lonely and quiet sadness. In LA, no one knew me, the sun shone every day and high school would never happen ever again.

My first job as a teen was as an office assistant at a photography studio run by a father-daughter team. Earl was the photographer all the soon-to-be brides wanted; the others were good but Earl was the star. He was full of good old stories he would recount as I assembled wedding albums. I loved learning the story of the wedding through the photos. I could feel the merriment of the day in every picture. My most favourite-ist thing was embossing photos with the studio's name. I got a little rush each time I applied heat to that gold leaf and stamped each photo.

I once had to do community service with an organization of my choosing. The Clean Water Fund needed someone to make fund-raising calls for its annual ball. I absolutely hated disturbing people in the evening begging for money. No matter how nice and apologetic my voice sounded, most times I was received with nastiness, which I could understand.

I don't even know if you would call this next one a job. This cutlery company recruited a bunch of high school kids to *peddle their high-end knives. We went through this selection process that I felt special for getting through. I realized later they were filtering out those of us who couldn't afford the knife set we needed to demo the product. I made one half-hearted pitch to a friend's family and dreaded every bit of it. You needed confidence to sell. At least we had a good set of knives.*

Luckily (or not), I only had to work on my electrical engineering degree while in college. My first job out was in the missile lab of a defence company in Massachusetts. The coolest thing about it was the top-secret clearance and the interview with the nice FBI agent who just needed to make sure, because of the Tanzanian passport I held, that my allegiance belonged to the US of A in all matters concerning missiles. For the rest of it, I was locked in a secure room all day running missile flight simulations using a computer program. I was monumentally bored.

After a merger, our missile lab moved to Arizona. I didn't follow but instead went back home, deluding myself into trying for a master's degree in electrical engineering. Three weeks of that and a chance meeting with a primary school friend inspired me to shut the door firmly on the engineering life. The clouds opened up when I took a degree in film studies. I had honest-to-goodness genuine fun while studying film; no class was ever a chore. During my studies I worked at a production company servicing the advertising market in metropolitan DC. These were excitable moving times with everything new: I PA'd on commercial sets, location scouted, did a spot of editing, worked with interesting characters with dynamic stories and laughed a lot. I didn't know work could be something fun to do.

After a couple of gigs in post-production, I landed a job with an English production company transplanted to DC to shoot a reality show for the Discovery Channel. It was a hellish project, horribly managed with super-long hours, but I so thoroughly enjoyed spending all that time with the Londoners. These are the folks that planted the first 'move to Europe' seeds.

Finding work in Amsterdam wasn't as easy as it had always been in the States. The lack of proper permits made employing me unfavourable, well, that's what I told myself, anyway. I got a couple of freelancing jobs doing voice-overs, acting in a video game and babysitting, etc. I finally got a permanent position marrying my engineering and film degrees: working in the interactive department of a cable TV provider. I rejoined the working force in a big way and for the most part it was rewarding, but lost its lustre a year or so on. I work in entertainment in a sense but not the content side and I do time for the Man in a typical corporate job where creativity does not reign.

I usually stop a job when I've learned all the aspects of it, when it stops challenging me, when it turns into boredom. I get most of my stimulation in life outside of work: on stage doing improv comedy, shaking my booty on the dance floor, writing my heart out, meeting new people, hanging out with kids, falling in love with music festivals, reading people at the poker table and trying everything. I start a lot of things but don't usually follow through. I stopped tango lessons because I realized it would take ages for me to be dazzling and my impatience won out. I almost gave up snowboarding for the same reason but the need to glide beat out impatience. I've learned I sizzle when I'm kept active, when enough of my senses and talents are engaged that I feel fulfilled. I don't want to communicate with the computer all day; I need human interaction.

I'm conscious I haven't written anything about romantic relationships, probably because I didn't want to depress myself further. Writing things out makes everything look stark, my 'boyfriend' situation is a bit lacking: I'm 35 and my longest relationship is 10 months. 'Boyfriend' is in quotes because I'm not sure some of the guys I've been with qualify for the status. I've got trust and intimacy issues up the wazoo. I'm starting to get the whole 'why it's nice to have a partner' thing and am currently trying to recalibrate to attract someone accordingly.

Jackie already had a CV which was the standard sort of model. I will comment on this in a later chapter. I include it here for completeness. You also get a feel for the client from their CV.

PERSONAL INFORMATION
Date of birth: 18 April 1975
Place of birth: New York, New York, USA
Citizenship: American
Marital status: Single
Interests: Writing, travel, music, dancing and laughing

EDUCATION
Master of Arts, Film and Video, March 2005
American University, Washington, DC, USA
Bachelor of Science, Electrical Engineering, August
1997
University of Southern California, Los Angeles, CA,
USA

EXPERIENCE
TV Production – Product & Online Media Group
UPC Broadband, Schiphol Rijk, Netherlands (July
2008–present)
   Produce storyboard and functional specification for
   interactive applications such as TV Guide and TV
   Search. Create customer-facing text and manage
   affiliate translations.

iTV Operations
Chello Interactive, Amsterdam, Netherlands (March
2007–June 2008)
   Supported the deployment and management of
   interactive TV services for digital TV platforms.
   Coordinated with both internal and external clients
   to ensure successful broadcast of (enhanced) TV
   projects.

Self-employed
engagemedia, Amsterdam, Netherlands (June 2006–
present)
   A business established to exploit talents in
   production, post-production, improvisational acting
   and writing. A business dedicated to engaging
   communication.
easylaughs Improvisation – cast member (Jan 2007–
present)

Mob. Handers Radio Pilot – cast member (Nov 2009)
Fate By Numbers – 'Rosie Denton' (February 2007)
Six Sigma Business CD-ROM – VO (February 2007)
Fascinatio – VO (November 2006)
Walki Talki Tours – VO (September 2006)

Freelance Post Production Coordinator
Post-Op Media, Arlington, VA, USA (May 2004–
November 2004)
Post-production house whose clients include Time
Life Music and National Geographic. Scheduled
sessions in audio, narration, online and offline
suites. Managed elements and deliverables for each
session. Coordinated with client to execute post-
session needs.

Post Production Coordinator
Leopard Films USA, Washington, DC, USA (October
2003–March 2004)
US branch of British-based production company.
Productions include *Cha Ching! Money Makers*
(Discovery Channel), *Cash in the Attic* (BBC1, BBC
America) and *Thunder Races* (Discovery/Channel 4).
Coordinated between production team, editors
and contracted post house for 14 programs of the
Discovery Channel series *Cha Ching! Money Makers*.
Relayed daily progression of each edit session to the
executive production team.

Production/Post-Production Assistant
Engine Pictures, Washington, DC, USA (March 2001–
October 2002)
Clients include CableOne, AOL and National
Institute on Drug Abuse. Assisted on commercial
shoots in camera, production and art departments.
Conducted research on vendors and locations;
loaded and edited location scout and casting tapes;
organized and distributed DP reels.

Missile Systems Engineer
Raytheon Systems Company, Tewksbury, MA (Sept
1997–Jan 1999)

Conducted computer analysis to adhere to missile
system requirements. Upgraded and integrated
simulation code for missile model functions.

SKILLS
Production: Sony PD100/PD150
Editing: AVID Media Composer/Express/DV Express
Pro, Multimedia: Photoshop 7.0, After Effects 4.0
Word Processing: Microsoft Office Suite, Final Draft
Operating Systems: Macintosh OS X, Windows XP
Languages: English (native), Dutch (conversational)

Here is Jackie's horoscope, cast for 18 April 1975, 15:33 EDT, New
York, NY (40n43, 74w00). The aspects I use are shown in Table 1
of the Vocation section (Chapter 4). I use the Koch house system
– you'll see why later in this book. But you should use whichever
house system and aspects you are comfortable with.

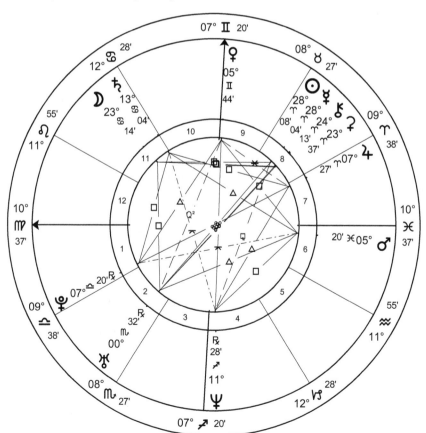

Next step
The next step you take cannot really be put into a clear structure, so I will give my ideas here on what I want to investigate more deeply and under which sessions I might place certain questions/ observations. With Jackie, my six sessions (each two hours long) were as follows:

1   Vocation and motivation
2   Style
3   Image, goals and norms and values
4   Talents and how to make money
5   Blocks
6   Environment, summary and bringing it all together in a VP (vocational profile).

After the last session there should be contact between the astrologer and the client to finalize the profile and to give and receive feedback.

Questions, thoughts, observations about my client arising from the biography and CV

General
She likes writing. I enjoyed reading it. Even though it is painful, it is witty. She is aware of some of the things she loves and is pretty self-aware generally. Below I summarize where I have 'parked' my thoughts.

Vocation session
(see Chapter 4, pages 49–85)

As you will see in the Vocation chapter, I use the Sun to explore vocation and calling.

Sun opposite Uranus
'Redundant second-born girl.' Father gone. 'Taller and chubbier than boys.' 'All-white primary school.' 'Teased and taunted.' 'Bullied and made fun of.' 'Social angst.' 'Felt special' for getting through a selection criteria. 'Trust and intimacy issues.' But reading between the lines, she does want to be 'dazzling'. She works with technology but says 'I need human interaction'.

I want to delve further into all of these. For me these are mostly negative expressions of Uranus – being singled out and teased for being different. Becoming terrified of not fitting in. Developing a strategy of non-bonding. A feeling of abandonment? Of being unwanted. Having a missing father often results in having no role model for what our heart wants. Her father left, showing the 'break' side of Uranus, but this is also a form of abandonment.

I want to find out how terrified she is of standing out and being special. The pattern of fear seems to have started early. Her 8th House Sun might mean that it is dangerous to be noticed. But as a Sun Aries with an aspect to Uranus, she will want to be special, to be noticed and to be different. What comes out of this will go into the blocks session. I will try to help her turn negative Uranus energy into a positive, quirky, special one.

Sun conjunct Mercury

I want to see how this related to her father. She mentions Mercury words in her CV: 'storyboard', text', 'improvisational acting' and 'writing'. A business dedicated to engaging communication. Interests: writing. In her bio she says 'I was a super-shy kid'. This doesn't sound like Sun conjunct Mercury in Aries – I want to delve here, too. She writes quite a lot about her brother and sister (Mercury) – the only role for her seems to be the good girl. 'Sister smartest, brother – do no wrong' – that must have been difficult for an Aries child. I want to explore that more. Sun–Mercury seems to be resulting in (from her point of view) siblings getting all the attention. There is not a lot of Mercury in her bio, except for the outside work – 'Writing my heart out, meeting new people' – although she has done voice-overs and PA work where she met 'interesting characters with dynamic stories'. She seems to see her love of writing as something she has to do outside of work. For me, this aspect must become part of her vocation.

Sun sesquiquadrate Neptune

Her biography is a good example of why sesquiquadrates are useful. The bio is littered with Neptune! It works both positively and negatively. Missing father – no contact really. Men who disappoint? Music, dancing, TV, film all over the place. But she also filled the role of being of service, in particular to her mother. I want to see if this happens with everyone – whether she is a caretaker and helps everyone. Her strategy for handling pain is to escape. As Neptune also picks up Mercury, of course, this explains her 'shyness'. More like avoidance, perhaps. She needs a very creative job where her imagination can be seen and valued.

Sun square Moon

This is often the signature of a writer, which is an activity she obviously loves. Her bio doesn't really highlight the need to belong except where she says she wants human interaction. This is a dilemma for her with her background. I would like more discussion on this theme. How can she use her 'feeling and caring' for people in a way that is positive for her?

Sun conjunct Ceres and Chiron

I think the possible wound from Chiron is obvious: can she follow her heart? I want to discover whether she recognizes the positive sides of these two bodies and if they could form a part of her vocation. I felt that neither of their themes showed up in her bio.

Aries Sun

One of the major points here is the lack of Aries in her work. Yes, she fights with her siblings. Yes, she sounds enthusiastic about some things. Yes, she was bullied. But she hated disturbing people. She had a hellish project and I really had to laugh that she had worked selling knives ('at least we had a good set of knives') and in a missile lab! You *can* see the positive side of Aries in her bio but, again, it is mostly expressed outside her working life. My focus will be to help her get all these things into her work: 'big and loud, shaking my booty, starting a lot of things', being allowed to be impatient – the other side of which is taking action and leading. Being an initiator. Being active and moving – Aries doesn't do well in sit-down jobs. Her Sun is in the more private 8th House though, so how does this work?

Style session
(see Chapter 5, pages 87–101)

I'll be looking at Mars here. Mars is in Pisces with a square to Neptune, so we can see this theme as a repeat of the Neptunian issues with her Sun. The way she approaches something (Mars) will have some overlap with her heart's desires (Sun), e.g. she likes taking care of people and reading people, and that will be seen in her approach to getting what she wants. I want to find out how aware she is of this. She is working to make the world better, perhaps – how might this happen? How does being 'of service' affect her in her work? She also has an aspect between Mars and Venus – I see this in her coordination roles on the CV. Her style might be one of discussion and needing feedback. Saturn and

Pluto also aspect Mars: a trine from Saturn and a quincunx from Pluto. The Saturn comes across quite clearly in her bio. The way she operated had to be responsible, she also picked up a strong work ethic from her mother. She also 'waited to participate'. She 'hated disturbing people'. Pluto can be seen in the bullying, both by her as the bully when young and later being bullied herself.

This needs a reframe, as reading her bio makes me think these aspects act more as blocks: being bullied and having to be so responsible. There are questions relating to how these aspects work. Is she jealous? Too compliant with others' rules in her approach to getting things done? How does that work with a Mars–Uranus trine, which would suggest a style of wanting to do something her own way?

Image and goals session (see Chapter 10, pages 187–92)

Venus is prominently placed on the MC, which I see as representing goals and reputation. How does this work in Gemini? The writing is pretty obvious, but what has that given her in her career? When has she worked in a Gemini environment (10th House)? She mentions a couple of occasions in her bio. For me, Venus must be part of her reputation – but is it? How does she think she comes across? Can she see the Aries and how does she feel about that? For me, our image is a mix of Sun, Ascendant and MC. So, can she see the Virgo part of herself? The service-orientated theme is again highlighted, but how does she feel about that and how can we use it to promote her image?

Norms and values session (see Chapter 11, pages 193–205)

This will probably be a repeat of themes already mentioned – Jupiter (her beliefs) is in Aries and Venus (values) is in Gemini, which resonates with the Sun–Mercury conjunction. This will just be a discussion about her norms and values.

Talents and how to make money session (see Chapter 7, pages 117–28)

What she loves is obvious to me from her bio. The question seems to be: why not at work? 'I get most of my stimulation outside of work.'

I hear this a lot from clients. It is not that they don't know what they love. The problem is usually a block (or several!) that needs to be addressed in that session. But, in my experience, it is very important to confirm talents to clients. Venus, a major focus in this part of the VP, is right at the top of the chart, so this is an important planet for her. Some of the aspects to Venus repeat themes already covered (Venus square Mars, Venus opposite Neptune) and she has a Venus bi-quintile (which I see as a natural talent) with Uranus. However, she has two other Venus aspects as well, so I will address these in this session. Her 2nd House spans Libra and Scorpio, with Uranus featured again and in the sign of Scorpio. The two extra themes here are Venus trine Pluto, which I don't see at all in her working life, and Venus sextile Jupiter, which we could get more ideas about in this session to make the most of this theme.

Blocks session
(see Chapter 9, pages 145–84)

The idea behind a VP is to define the blocks, not to work on them. Defining them means they are clear and can be addressed by you if you have the skills, or by a therapist, who ideally is someone you like and can recommend to your client. Often stumbling blocks and heavier issues are very clear from the bio, as they are in this case: Mommy, to name an obvious one. As well as the Uranus issue and aspect with the Sun mentioned above, and the fact that her father 'was really, really bad at being a father', the Moon also picks up Uranus, so the aloneness/abandonment issues will have to be discussed again in this session. We need to add the Moon–Saturn conjunction, as this is mentioned several times in the bio. Actually, this conjunction is a bit wider than I would normally use but I can't help thinking it works here, so I let the chart–client combination speak. 'Mother dished out orders.' 'She wanted us kids to be a lawyer, doctor and engineer' (assigned engineer). 'I was someone my mother could count on, responsible enough to handle household duties early on.' 'Insecure kid.' 'Social angst of the cafeteria' (what about eating problems?) 'My mother's hard stance on education paid off'(!) 'I couldn't go against my mother's wishes.' 'Lonely and quiet sadness.'

These comments all point to someone who will have trouble setting their own goals and feeling authoritative. The pattern is probably to wait for orders and be given instructions. A real dilemma for an Aries. The Moon is in Cancer, so the need to belong will be strong, which goes completely against the desire to stand out. In Jackie's case, this is probably a very deep and painful part of the chart. The block here will probably be fear of 'going for it' for fear of being totally alone. The pattern might be: have fun and do what you love at movies, etc. when you are allowed time off, but otherwise 'you do as you're told'.

Note that we will not cover relationship issues in any depth here, as the goal of the sessions is to create a vocational profile. The blocks are covered in regard to what is holding Jackie back at work, but of course there will be an overlap with any parent or relationship issues mentioned in the bio.

> **Environment session**
> (see Chapter 12, pages 207–220)

This session is to determine where and with whom she feels comfortable, and it includes environment, bosses and colleagues. Some of the environments Jackie likes can be inferred from the bio but I want to explore this more. Here's a start. Places with stories: 'Earl the photographer ... feel the merriment ... coolest thing was top-secret clearance ... genuine fun studying film ... excitable times with everything new ... interesting characters with dynamic stories ... time with Londoners ... meeting new people ... I sizzle when I am kept active ... I need human interaction.' Her preferences for bosses and colleagues need exploration, which I will do in this session.

So now I have an outline structure for what I want to cover in each of the sessions. In each of these, my goal is to set Jackie the task of writing up each discussion so that it will form part of the VP. I need to make clear what I am expecting. The way you do this and the way you work with clients will vary according to their nature. The client's horoscope will give you tips on how to work with them, especially as you gain more experience. And, of course, your own working style can be determined from your own horoscope. You can add your own ideas as you get more practised at using the bio.

An extra: a career counsellor's exercise
Some clients respond well to visual tools. Below is an exercise I have adapted that can be used to add to the discussion on vocation and also later in the Blocks section. It's called the Life Panorama.

Draw a horizontal line representing your life from birth to the age you are now, and divide it into phases of six years.

0-----6-----12-----18-----24-----36-----42-----48-----54-----60-----

Choose three colours. Each one represents a line for

- Your health
- Your work
- Your emotions

Draw the three lines with high and low points – above and below the horizontal line – to represent your experience of these three themes. Don't think about it too much, just draw spontaneously, using a different colour for each theme.

Make it a real panorama by adding symbols, words or pictures to the high and low points, as a way of showing what happened at each of these peaks and troughs. This creation can be any size from A4 to a huge painting – as long as the client can carry it! They can bring it with them to start the discussion. This is a great exercise to give together with the bio exercise for visually-orientated clients.

Now it's on to the first session.

WHO AM I?

FINDING VOCATION AND MOTIVATION
RECOGNIZING STYLE AND DRIVE
EXPRESSING AN AUTHENTIC IMAGE

CHAPTER 4

FINDING VOCATION AND MOTIVATION

*Working hours are never long enough. Each day is a
holiday, and ordinary holidays are grudged as enforced
interruptions in an absorbing vocation.*
Sir Winston Churchill

Following the light of the sun we left the Old World.
Christopher Columbus

One of the main questions I am asked is 'Am I in the right job?' It
may not be worded quite like this, but the real question is 'What
should I be doing?' There seems to be an unspoken idea that we
each have a calling – that there is a perfect job for us if only we
could identify it and then find it. I am often asked 'How can I find
my passion?'

With my astrologer's hat on, I can look at the chart and find
what someone loves to do. But I need input from the client to see
how this works in practice – clients are far more creative in using
their skills than any astrologer can ever be in guessing their
profession.

Vocation means looking firstly at the Sun and starting with the
real basics: the Sun sign. I agree with Liz Greene, who takes the Sun
as the vocation, the calling. If you can discover this in other ways,
then use your own methods. Some astrologers take the North Node
into account and many look to the 10th House. As long as you can
use the client's words to define and agree upon their vocation,
it doesn't matter how you get there. The end result should be a
definition of vocation and motivation. This chapter describes how
I do this using the Sun.

Why the Sun?
Following your heart makes you happy. The Sun represents the heart
and what we want in life. I think astrologers can underestimate the
Sun sign, and I spend quite some time with clients to clarify what

their sign can mean for them. Sometimes a whole session can be taken up just on the Sun in terms of vocation, and of course it is revisited in later sessions in other ways.

The Sun sign

There can be confusion between the signs and the houses. Often astrologers describe houses when what they are really referring to are the signs. The sign of the Sun (or any planet) shows the HOW. In the case of the Sun, *how* can we feed our heart's desire? How can we be happy? How can we express what our heart wants? The basis of this is the Sun sign. In Table 1, I present some ideas for the signs so you can use these if your clients can't come up with something themselves. These are very brief and there are many good books you can use to make your own lists (see the bibliography for some of my favourites). I also give a few examples of questions you can ask to start a dialogue, and I encourage you to add your own. There are of course some generally useful questions such as 'Which jobs have you enjoyed the most and why?' The whole point of this is that **together with your client**, you can discover what the Sun sign means for them and how your client wants to shine and be recognized. This sign is part of the calling, with the aspects playing another important role.

Frequently, clients will recognize Sun sign characteristics. However, these will often be the negative qualities of a sign, which is not what you want here. The client may need to work on some of these issues (and I will discuss these in Chapter 9 on blocks), but what you are trying to do is find words and expressions that will become part of the vocational profile and will eventually be used in a CV. The words must describe positive qualities that can be used at work. Remember, this is your goal in the discussion.

Let's look at a few examples of Sun signs.

Aries can describe someone who is always having conflicts at work. Someone who believes that there is always a struggle to get somewhere. However, this person has learned how to defend themselves or others. Another characteristic that Arians will probably recognize is impatience. In fact, they often say, 'Yes, I need to learn patience.' No, they don't! They can't. By going along with this you are throwing out the positive sides of impatience: action, starting something impulsively. People who work in emergency situations need these qualities. Courage, guts; doing things without thinking can be very useful. Aries is usually good at this. Enthusiasm is another quality that Aries can offer. What the client often needs is a reframe – helping to see the positive side of what they view as a negative characteristic. Examples of questions here for your client include: *How have you used your impatience to obtain a positive result? Where has your ability to act quickly been useful – in which situations and in which jobs? When has having guts resulted in a benefit?*

The most maligned sign is **Scorpio:** jealousy at work, too dominating, too controlling. Yes, that can all be true. The 'why' of this can come later, we don't want to get too psychological here when exploring vocation. What Scorpio Suns often love to do – and do well – is research, digging deeply into an issue. They often love office politics or at least are good at seeing what is going on. They can operate in life-or-death situations and are not afraid of 'heavy' topics that many cannot deal with, such as death, abuse and life-threatening situations. They need something to get their teeth into and take control of. Some example questions: *Where have you used your power for good? In what jobs did you have to really go for something in a passionate way? Where did 'digging' have a result? In what job was it beneficial or useful when you took control?*

And a last example, one that often gives problems for astrologers, is **Pisces:** too sensitive, chaotic, no boundaries – these are often the ideas that Pisceans have about themselves. Again, these can all be true. But Pisceans are very useful at work and are frequently well liked because they are so service-orientated. That is a very helpful quality for many jobs where *care* is paramount. However, Pisceans often suffer for this. They help everyone and often stay late at work. They can never say no and can then feel victimized. What they really need is a job where chaos and creativity are rewarded – where daydreaming has a use. Where they can dream up concepts such as advertising campaigns. They need to be able to be lost in something creative and be part of building a better world. They are intuitive and are excellent at creative concepts. Often where they have been at their best is not in a paid job. But that doesn't mean they should only do volunteer work. The skills learned in these situations should be included in the skill sets that will form part of the resulting profile. Not all the qualities we have will show up at work, but that does not mean they are not valuable skills. Many things are learned, for example, by being a parent! Questions to create dialogue are clear here: *Where have you felt you were involved in helping the world? When have you been creative, and how? In which job was caring for people and helping others rewarded and valued? Have you ever created a concept that has been useful? Has art of any kind played a role in your life?*

Table 1 shows some positive and negative qualities of each sign. Too much of one usually leads to the other, e.g. too much speed = foolhardy; not sticking to a goal = creative ideas. I have also offered a few questions to start a dialogue about the Sun sign. Remember, you are looking for positive key qualities *in the client's own words* that will be used in any promotional material such as a CV or website.

Table 1: The Sun through the signs

Sign	Positive quality at work/ what is desired/ should be used in vocation	Negative quality	Examples of questions to ask
Aries	Speed, action, pioneer, initiating (not finishing), guts, bravery, encouraging people, defending, challenging, leadership qualities.	Not thinking first, always starting something new, impatient, foolhardy, daredevil, fighting, creating conflict, being aggressive, selfish.	How have you used your impatience to obtain a positive result? Where has your ability to act quickly been useful – in which situations and in which jobs? When has using your guts resulted in a benefit? When has challenging something been worthwhile?
Taurus	Stable, practical, common sense, calm, finishes projects, stays on the path, follows routine, physically strong, good in a 'physical' crisis, solution-orientated, good with the land/ plants, good with money, wants to build.	Stubborn, stuck in the mud, allergic to change, slow, 'it's all about the money'.	When has your stubbornness led to the right result? In which job did you come up with the solution to a practical problem? When have you been in a situation where staying calm has helped? Do you ever use your physical strength at work? Where have you felt valued? What have you built?

Gemini	Generating ideas, quick thinking, curious, communicative, good in a crisis where ideas can help, questions things, networks, linking things together, can deal with many things at once, busy situations.	Lack of commitment, too many ideas, jumps from one thing to the other, talks too much, asks too much, chatting, gossips, can't stick to one goal.	When has your quick-thinking been an asset? When has your love of talking to people and being curious been useful? In which jobs did being good at networking give a result? Has writing or speaking been beneficial to you?
Cancer	Patriotic, creating good atmospheres, caring, cooking, feeling, good in emotional situations, motherly, inclusive, ability to belong, respects traditions.	Emotional, too inward-focused, family more important than work, moody, too attached.	When have you cared for someone at work? Have you ever created a team? When has your ability to nurture or look after the emotional needs of a group been an asset? In which jobs have you felt at home? Has respecting tradition or protecting something been useful to you?
Leo	Generous, creative, playful, leadership qualities, can delegate, lucky speculator, good in the spotlight, good presenter, fatherly, loves children or childlike activities.	Attention-seeking in a disruptive way, self-absorbed, plays king, over-speculates.	What do you want recognition for? When have you loved your work? When have you been in the spotlight or got recognition for something? When did you feel most creative? Has your willingness to take a risk resulted in something positive?

Virgo	Service-orientated and practical, eye for detail, ordered, helpful, analytical, information-orientated, fastidious. Understands health and body-mind connection.	No overview, worrier, over-critical, too much information, works too hard for others.	When has your love of making a list proved worthwhile? Has your ability to notice small things been helpful? Have you ever enjoyed putting something in order? Have you ever been praised for your ability to find information? Do you know a lot about, or have an interest in, health or nutrition?
Libra	Dialogue, feedback, looks at all sides, focused on the other (e.g. customer or patient), partnership, works well with others, harmony, balance, mediation.	Can see everyone's viewpoint so it's difficult to have own viewpoint, requires too much feedback and discussion, too outward-focused, making comparisons with others.	Has balance ever been an important part of your work? When has your ability to discuss and give or accept feedback been useful? Has your enjoyment of listening to others given you a result at work? Have you ever mediated between two parties?
Scorpio	Passionate, willpower, 'goes for it', digs deep, researcher, can take control, can work with taboo subjects and keep a secret, can handle political environments.	Vindictive, possessive, control-freak, dominant, too black-or-white, jealous.	When have you been in control and had success at work? When have you had to go deeply into something or literally dig in your job? Have you ever worked in areas that others might fear? Does survival or life and death mean anything to you in your working life? When has your passionate approach got you somewhere?

Sagittarius	Strategic, leadership qualities, 'big-picture' thinker, optimistic, entrepreneur, business risk-taker, has vision, good with patterns and meaning, has faith, traveller, adventurer.	Over-optimistic, no eye for detail, plays God, overestimates ability, 'all talk and no trousers', arrogant. Gambler and opportunist.	Have different countries or cultures (including company cultures) played a role in your working life? Have you ever started your own enterprise? Has being involved in strategy or 'big-picture' thinking been useful or rewarded? Can you easily see patterns?
Capricorn	Responsible, structured, teaching ability, mentor, authoritative, good management skills, goal-orientated, ambitious.	Tunnel vision, strict, disciplinarian, blames self or others, over-responsible, hard, stuck, fearful, fear of failure.	Have you ever been in an advisory or teaching capacity? Does part of your job ever include mentoring in any way? Do you enjoy working with structures? When have you had responsibility for something that led to a result? Do you enjoy planning and managing things at work or at home?
Aquarius	Mental agility, future-orientated, independent, generates 'out of the box' ideas, questions stupidity, good with technology.	Know-it-all, mentally stubborn, too geeky, no patience mentally, thinks too much, needs too much explanation, too independent, rebellious, cold and unemotional.	Does your ability to be future-orientated help you at work? Which technological skills have you used to great effect? When has a wacky idea been useful? How does your independence help you at work? Has being 'an outsider' ever been useful?

| Pisces | Creative, conceptual, imaginative, emotionally service-orientated, compassionate, intuitive, artistic, ability to stand in others' shoes. | Chaotic, escapist, can't say 'no', addictive, no borders and boundaries, helps everyone. | When have you enjoyed daydreaming and been allowed to be creative at work? How has your helpful nature been of value when you have enjoyed it? Have you trusted your intuition and been proved right at work? When have you worked with concepts? Do the Arts or art of any kind play a role in your life? |

Once you have a list of words that fit the client's Sun sign and the client has made a note of them, you can go on to the next step – the houses.

The Sun's house position

Many astrologers use the ruler of the Sun and its house placement to look at vocation. By all means use this. My style is to go for simple techniques and spend time deepening the understanding of the client (and gaining knowledge myself in the process). If you have an accurate birth time you can simply look at the house placement of the Sun. Note that the other techniques I employ for finding vocation can be used without a very accurate birth time (assuming you have a birth date), which is why I like them so much!

The house placement shows the 'where'. The house of the Sun shows the area of life in which you can shine, where you want to be seen and recognized, where your heart is, where there is a focus on what you love to do. It is the area into which you can pour your heart. This can also literally relate to which area of a company you might find appealing. For instance, the Sun in the 7th House might highlight someone who would be good in the customer relations area; the 10th House might be someone who shines in management; the 3rd might show someone who is at home in the communications department.

Table 2 shows some examples of the Sun through the houses and gives examples of world leaders with this placement. The charts of public figures give some idea about reputation, but to really know *what drives them* is trickier. In Table 2, I also offer a few examples from my practice that give a better idea of what motivates someone. The Sun *sign* will show *how* they do this. The *house* position shows *where*.

As I mentioned above, I find that astrologers sometimes interchange these. Of course there are links between Aries and the 1st House, Taurus and the 2nd House, etc. So, perhaps an example will explain my focus. What would the difference be between someone who has a Scorpio Sun in the 4th House, such as Prince Charles who I mention below, and someone who has the Sun in Cancer in the 8th House?

As a Scorpio, Prince Charles *wants* to show his passion. He wants to have influence and control and perhaps loves research. He also has a reputation for interfering in matters of politics and business, often winning his particular battle. He could do all of these things in many different places, but the *areas* he is active in (the astrological house) concern preserving and protecting tradition (the 4th House). For instance, he writes copious letters about architecture, expressing his desire to keep many historic buildings. He also wants to protect the purity of plants and food, and is active in organic farming. We know him because of his family ties, the reason for his being in the spotlight (Sun in the 4th House). Not only is he known for his family line but mother and child, those Cancerian themes, also gain attention in the form of his mother, Queen Elizabeth II, and his son, Prince William. If he were anyone else, we would hear much less about his work.

In his book *Julian Assange: The Unauthorized Autobiography* (Canongate Books, 2011), Assange gives the time of his birth as 'around three in the afternoon'. He is a Cancer Sun and this would put the Sun in the 8th House. (An earlier given time of 2 p.m. puts the Sun just in the 9th.)

Now, a person with a Cancerian 8th House is not going to be easy to know. Assange's Uranian side (he has the Sun square to Uranus) is much more obvious than his Cancerian side: his book reveals his love of technology and the breaks with his father. I noticed that he had done a lot of family research. He knows more about his family than I would expect from someone coming from Australia, as this involves much searching in different countries. What he is known for might be an argument for the 8th House Sun birth time being correct: the areas of his work with WikiLeaks deal with privacy (and the lack of it) and hacking – definite 8th House connotations. But I wonder if he really is seeking to belong, as are many Cancerians. And I wonder what he feels about all the other Cancerian themes.

His combination of Cancer/8th has a very different feel to Prince Charles's Scorpio/4th, although there are similar themes, such as scandals involving sex.

I have done my best to check the birth times of the people given in the examples, as this ensures the accuracy of the house placings. Be warned that many celebrity birth times given on the web are contradictory, are not substantiated or (worse, in my view) have been rectified by astrologers! The best sources for birth times are *The Astrologer's Book of Charts* by Frank C Clifford (Flare Publications, 2009) and www.astro.com/astro-databank/Main_Page (Astro-Databank is the online database started by the late Lois Rodden).

Table 2: The Sun through the houses

House	Areas/comments	Example
1st	A 1st House Sun produces someone who wants to be known for who they really are. This is usually someone who is noticed for their personality and image. As far as work goes, a job where they can use the force of their personality to gain recognition is important. It is interesting to note that both David Cameron and Silvio Berlusconi have the Sun in Libra but with different rising signs – Cameron is a double Libra, while one birth time gives Berlusconi Virgo rising. It is obvious at the time of writing that Cameron is setting up his reputation as someone with Libran qualities of fairness and decency. Berlusconi comes across as someone who is far more egotistical, which can be a result of a more negative 1st House Sun.	David Cameron, Silvio Berlusconi, Pope Benedict XVI People I know: Self-centred individuals but very enthusiastic and positive about work; among them a lawyer and various consultants.
2nd	Interestingly, I found it difficult to find a world leader with the Sun in the 2nd but I'm sure there are some. Karl Marx is not a very clear example as he also has a Taurus Sun and Moon, so his chart would have a Taurean feeling anyway. However, he is known and recognized for the Communist system, which has at its heart the idea of values: that everyone should share in the wealth of the nation. The 2nd	Karl Marx People I know: Presenters, body-workers, a nurse, people with a focus on the basic senses.

	House shows how we can make our money (I will look at this in detail later). With the Sun in the 2nd House, you want to earn a living through being centre stage. Marx certainly got attention for his life's work. Other areas for this placement might be such things as a focus on values, being in the spotlight (the sign may show the way in which this happens), lecturing, or work in valuing the body or the earth.	
3rd	Both Queen Elizabeth II and Churchill are known for their wit and extensive knowledge. It is an unusual person who hasn't heard Churchill's voice or doesn't know some of his quotes. He won a Nobel Prize in Literature in 1953. The Sun in the 3rd House gives a 'heart' that loves ideas, and someone who would like to be known for their ability to communicate, which Churchill clearly was. In her role as monarch, the Queen often has to address the public, and her words are taken very seriously. Rumour has it that she loves her email. Work areas could be places where getting the word out or linking ideas together plays a role. A busy environment where keeping up with new ideas might be vital. As the 3rd House has siblings and short transport in its domain, it could be worth exploring whether these themes are relevant in terms of previous work or loves.	Sir Winston Churchill, Queen Elizabeth II (Sun exactly on 3rd House cusp) People I know: Communications and marketing people, ideas (too many, sometimes) people, brainstormers and writers.
4th	The Sun in the 4th House denotes some form of family ties. In the Huber Age Point system the 4th House represents the process of leaving home and building your own nest, and this will be a necessary focus for people with a 4th House Sun. However, one of the drives seems to be protection of some kind. Prince Charles is an avid protector of tradition, particularly in	Prince Charles, Indira Gandhi People I know: An older man acting as a mentor to staff for a young manager. A body-worker who uses her intuition. A boss

	terms of architecture. He is deeply committed to protecting the planet. Indira Gandhi, although a controversial figure, also had an influential family background and attempted to address poverty – protecting the poor and needy. Work environments need to feel like home. There is a need to 'belong' to a firm. The Sun in the 4th can also indicate a sort of parent-figure who supports young people to develop their own strengths.	of a family business. Two astrologers who see their work as honouring and protecting old traditions and history. An astrologer who is chairman of an astrological group aiming to improve the quality of astrological work.
5th	There is a certain amount of 'me' in a 5th House Sun. Fifth House people suffer in an environment where their creativity and playfulness cannot be unleashed. A bit of drama now and then doesn't go amiss and in fact the theatre could be a good place for a 5th House Sun to shine. Recognition for the products of their work makes them happy. Work should be fun. But there is also a need for some kind of prestige, such as involvement with important people. Nicolas Sarkozy seems to love being in photos with famous people; he likes being at the centre of events. Franklin D Roosevelt was a controversial figure but, despite his constant health and personal difficulties and taking office at a very difficult time during the Great Depression, he is the longest serving president of the US. After his presidency the constitution was changed to prevent such a long term in office. Although he is very much an Aquarian Sun, which is obvious from any reading of his biography, the 5th House Sun shines through. This is what others have said of him: 'Thanks to his flair for drama, he acted as if never in all history had there been times like our own' (Clinton Rossiter); 'Conspicuous courage, cheerfulness, energy and resource' (Sir Ronald Lindsay, British	Nicolas Sarkozy, Franklin D Roosevelt People I know: Teachers in creative areas, one in theatre skills for children. A personnel consultant for top management. An entrepreneur setting up a new type of care home for the elderly that honours their life and individual needs. A banker working with futures (the Sun in the 5th House loves a risk).

		ambassador to Washington); 'Radiating an infectious zest, he did the most important thing a President can do: he gave the nation a hopeful, and hence creative, stance toward the future' (George Will). At the end of his term he had set the US on the world stage as a military power, after an isolationist approach by his predecessors. The Pentagon was born and dealings with the press were changed forever. He had strong leadership qualities.	
6th		The first idea that comes to mind for the Sun in the 6th House is service – the practical kind, as opposed to the emotional kind of the 12th House. A quote from Barack Obama: 'We need to usher in a new spirit of service and sacrifice and responsibility.' He believes he should serve, as should all Americans. The Universal Service plan says it all ('helping all Americans serve their country'). Interesting too is that his first challenge as President involved the 6th House topic of health reform.	Barack Obama, Helen Clark

6th — The first idea that comes to mind for the Sun in the 6th House is service – the practical kind, as opposed to the emotional kind of the 12th House. A quote from Barack Obama: 'We need to usher in a new spirit of service and sacrifice and responsibility.' He believes he should serve, as should all Americans. The Universal Service plan says it all ('helping all Americans serve their country'). Interesting too is that his first challenge as President involved the 6th House topic of health reform.

Helen Clark, as the first female and longest serving Prime Minister of New Zealand, had many impressive achievements during her leadership. Among them are many 6th House issues including health and the workplace: four weeks' annual leave; more affordable primary healthcare, including cheaper doctors' visits and prescriptions; the biggest upgrade of New Zealand's public health services ever undertaken; the Employment Relations Act, increasing the minimum wage every year; free meningitis vaccinations; increasing surgical funding for key operations, such as hip and cataract; rebuilding the school dental service; targeting obesity and related diseases; and increasing funding for sport and recreation. She wanted to be known for her dedication to the job.

Barack Obama, Helen Clark

People I know: An animal communicator. A catering manager at a major airline. An astrologer who loves to help others even though she is a Leo. An astrologer involved in the alternative medical world who adores animals. A manager at a council department dealing with unemployment.

	Sixth House people can do many things to serve but key among their wishes is to offer something practical, helpful and useful. Areas you might like to explore are jobs involved with working conditions, work with animals, health, areas of body-mind connections and nutrition.	
7th	There are very different examples here. Of course Princess Diana was not a world leader but her 7th House Sun shows that she was known because of her partner. Later she developed her own agenda to help others – a strong focus for the 7th House. Many therapists, counsellors, mentors and aura readers have the Sun in the 7th House. So what about Hitler? I suppose you could say he was obsessed with 'the other' – those who were not part of his chosen group. He is also known for his long relationship and control over his mistress and eventual wife, Eva Braun. Seventh House people want to pour their energy into matters concerning partnerships or where the opinions of others are important. PR, focus groups and market research all come to mind. Jobs where different opinions are relevant are also good environments. Peace deals, negotiations, conflict resolution, improving relationships and the lives of others are relevant, as in therapy or human rights. Life needs to have a sense of fairness, which means that an ability to compare could be a topic for discussion with these people.	Adolf Hitler, Diana, Princess of Wales People I know: A fighter for patient rights. Counsellors, mentors, therapists. A project manager (generally going for the goals of others). A teacher.
8th	John F Kennedy is known for his efforts leading to further innovation in the Moon landing. He had the passion and drive to go for it. Organized crime was another area that was tackled during his short tenure, although there were allegations about the people with whom he mixed. He also had a reputation for sexual exploits, most famously with Marilyn Monroe. So the	John F Kennedy People I know: Therapists, astrologers. A genealogy researcher. A consultant working in big political organizations.

	8th House shows here, too. However, his life showed extraordinary struggle and courage – his serious health problems being kept quiet until after his death. Probably the best known fact about JFK is that he was assassinated – an 8th House reputation, perhaps. Death might be something that is a fascination for 8th House people – such as an interest in reincarnation or working with people who are dying. There is a need for a deep experience. At the other end of life, some with this placement may work with birth situations. There is a love of making a difference in the world (in the area shown by the Sun sign). For example, Kennedy's words live on – he was a Gemini. A 'real', in-depth experience is what is craved. Passion needs to be part of the vocation and possibly working with issues of control and power – such as in therapy (for example, with abuse) or in a dangerous or political environment. The 8th House could also show a preference for a research organization, such as one with a scientific or forensic interest. There is usually a fascination with the unseen. Banking, pensions, inheritances and mortgages – anything with 'big' money relating to life's big decisions – are also part of the 8th House's domain. Some 8th House people feel at home in these environments.	
9th	Ninth House people often seem to end up in politics. But here it is more about a love of political vision than about having control. There's a wish to address laws and belief systems. The search here is for meaning. There is a certain amount of entrepreneurship in the 9th House and a love of philosophies. Higher education, in particular, can be of interest. Travel and expansion leading to overseas	Benito Mussolini, Jacques Chirac People I know: Consultants who have also dabbled in politics – one now a City Council member. A cook who has worked in several countries.

	businesses can bring happiness and recognition. Ninth House people need freedom in the working environment. Looking for patterns can be a talent, such as in demographic studies or where an ability to see the big picture is needed. Work in strategy departments could be fulfilling. But perhaps the 9th House can also bring delusions of grandeur and a sort of 'playing God' mentality, the positive side of which is a 'go for what you believe in' attitude. Mussolini was known as the Great Dictator. A violent man who had an interesting, if somewhat contradictory, relationship with religion, which is often a 9th House theme. Although he declared himself an atheist after his Catholic upbringing, he tried to appear to be a good Catholic in public for political gain. He compared himself to Christ and God and reportedly stated that there was no room for him and the Pope in Rome. His legacy of the Fascist system lives on in part today in Berlusconi's right wing party. Most of the information written on Chirac focuses on his downfall and the allegations of wrongdoing. But clearly politics was always in his blood. He studied it at university and his subsequent career was in politics. As he is also a Sagittarius with the Moon and Mercury in this sign too, it is difficult to isolate the house from the emphasis on this stellium.	An entrepreneur/ teacher who has brought her vision of safe workspaces to a large company. A director of personnel for an overseas branch of a big company. An astrologer who brought new concepts to the art. A founder of a new political party.
10th	I was always surprised when I started studying astrology that all world leaders did not have the Sun in the 10th – after all, that should show someone who is in the world's spotlight, right? Someone who has a reputation for leadership can have this placement. However, it seems to me to be more about wanting to be seen and recognized for your work in society.	Harold Wilson, Prince Albert of Monaco People I know: Teachers (also in astrology). Business consultants. An owner of a hairdressing

It is, I think, more descriptive of a good manager than a leader, depending on the Sun sign. Respect for hard work is craved here, as are recognition and reward for efforts. The aim is towards gaining authority in the area shown by the Sun sign. Ambition should also be present and taking responsibility should be no problem – in fact, 10th House people often flourish in situations that give them responsibility. They are not afraid of a bit of hard work to achieve their goals. There can also be a love of teaching as, of course, this is a position of authority. Environments linked to structures might be favoured, such as accounting practices or architects' offices. Often there is a penchant for planning and goal-setting. There can be a focus on business itself, perhaps in an advisory capacity. Tenth House people love to shine in their chosen work and be honoured for it.

Harold Wilson was known as a very down-to-earth politician. He was in touch with the 'working man' and appreciated the simple things in life. Although his lasting reputation is mixed, during his leadership he was valued for his strong management skills and 'indicative planning'. He was an economist who loved statistics. He was also one of the youngest Members of Parliament in the 20th century, which perhaps highlights his ambition.

Prince Albert of Monaco is also known as a down-to-earth leader. Although his father represents the more authoritarian, strict leader concerned with the reputation of his country, Albert is an ambassador for Monaco's business interests. He is one of the few ruling monarchs with very wide powers of decision-making over his subjects. His ambition has been focused on sport, in which he has been very successful. His other interest seems to

business. A business developer for a city.

	reflect his Pisces Sun, as he works with environmental issues, particularly water. At the time of writing, he has just married and has yet to produce a legitimate heir to the throne, although there are illegitimate ones. The 10th House often gives a slow but steady approach!	
11th	I've always found the 11th House a bit confusing as it covers all manner of things: friends, groups, the clan, hopes and wishes. The Sun in the 11th indeed produces leaders of particular groups. A sort of spokesperson for a particular '-ism' or some special cause. A team-leader. A focus on like-minded people might describe this better. But I think that an 11th House word is 'authenticity'. People with the Sun here want to be who they really are – to be accepted for themselves and what they know. As the opposite of the 5th House, which is where you want to be known for what you create, the 11th wishes to be known for the true self despite the group or society. Perhaps that's why they feel comfortable with like-minded people – it's easier to be authentic with support. Eleventh House people often don't lead without a team behind them, although the sign of the Sun may alter this. Margaret Thatcher is really better known for her Saturnian qualities – 'The Iron Lady'. And indeed Saturn is on her Ascendant in the sign of Scorpio, so that would need to be included in her VP as one of her vocational 'qualities'. There are various schools of thought as to her qualities and legacy. The 11th House can suggest an Aquarian 'I know best' type of role within a group; a sort of mental arrogance as a leader. However, she was a spokesperson for a particular vision. In fact, an article I read by Germaine Greer suggests she was merely a spokesperson who was told	Margaret Thatcher, Bill Clinton People I know: A leader of an orchestra. An owner and manager of a community theatre and restaurant business. An owner of a group of real-estate businesses. An owner of an astrology school. A joint owner of a corporate branding company. A publisher.

	what to do by others. She was an advocate for the big idea of the 'free market', which could be an 11th House theme. It is often said that Thatcher took credit for the ideas of others, perhaps a negative characteristic of this placement. She went her own way though, whether others liked it or not, and in that regard you could see her as authentic. And she was the leader of a group with particular ideas. The PR that Bill Clinton had while he was President highlights his Leo Sun more than the 11th House. However like Thatcher, free trade was a topic that he tackled while in office (the North American Free Trade Agreement). Clinton also appointed several women and minorities to significant government posts throughout his administration – the 11th House can give a focus on equality. Also within its domain are humanitarian causes, with which Clinton was, and still is, heavily involved.	
12th	It is perhaps surprising that there are many world leaders with the Sun in the 12th House. Astrologers often see this house as a private or spiritual house – definitely not one that likes the spotlight. They look to explain this as being a difficult placement linked to the relationship with the father. However, what is needed when looking for vocation is a different focus. Twelfth House people often look for the 'spiritual': Bush and Blair have both been in the news for their religious views and Gandhi is, of course, seen as a spiritual leader. To me, 12th House people have an intuitive grasp of the interconnectedness of everything. The problem is, though, that 12th House people can be chameleon-like and we don't see their inner world or who they really are. They can be good actors. The 12th House person wants to offer emotional service and support.	Gordon Brown, Tony Blair, Mohandas Gandhi, George W Bush People I know: Astrologers who are deeply intuitive. Body-workers who create a sense of peace. People who have sacrificed their own careers to support their partners. Musicians. Performers.

	Spirituality and otherworldly pursuits might interest them. There is often a talent for tuning in to the dreams or wishes of others. In terms of vocation, what is needed is an environment away from normal daily life, such as hospitals (where one can serve emotionally), prisons or such quiet places as libraries, museums and churches. A place where quiet contemplation is possible. However, with a positive expression of this placement, the basic drive can be to help make the world a better place.	

My main tool: aspects to the Sun

I am a big fan of using astrological aspects and by the end of this book you will either be sick of hearing about them or you will (hopefully) be inspired to use them more. Like Bruno and Louise Huber, the Swiss astrologers who founded a psychological astrology school, I start in the centre of the horoscope. The Huber method draws a horoscope with an empty circle in the middle showing the 'Inner Being'.[1] Moving outwards from the centre of the chart we meet the aspects and planets, showing the drives of the person in this life. Lastly, the signs and houses show the environment. My belief is that the planetary aspect pattern (not including aspects to the Ascendant and the MC axes – these are different and show our connection with the environment) forms a sort of individual 'crystal' shape. At birth, it gets locked into the cross of matter (the four angles) and that gives the 'crystal' its orientation (the twelve houses being part of this). My work with relocation has clarified the fact that we take that crystal aspect pattern – i.e. our drives – with us when we move around the planet but our orientation alters, meaning that we focus our drives in a different area of life. This is why I find aspects more important than house placements, as they describe an inner motivation or drive. However, if a question from a client concerns moving to another country, then looking at the house placement of the Sun in both the current location and the projected location is a very useful tool. (See the section on the Sun's house position, above.)

Table 3 shows the aspects and orbs I use. In Holland, where I live, many astrologers do not use out-of-sign aspects, but I have found them to be extremely accurate and useful. I also use many types of aspects that others don't, such as the quintile and the sesquiquadrate. Most astrology software allows you to set up the aspects and orbs you wish to use. The point here, though, is to check what works for the client. If you normally don't use all these aspects I would encourage you to try them out with the client and see whether they recognize what those aspects say about them. Not only does this give you more information when compiling the career profile, but you will learn a lot of nuances for each of the aspects. Asking questions of my clients has been *the major way* I deepened my astrology.

I am often asked what the difference is between the types of aspects e.g. a sextile and a square. The answer to that is probably 'I don't know'. A lot of the material I have read takes a traditional stance, such as squares = bad, trines = good. In all my years of working with clients, this is *not* my experience. I don't think you know how an aspect truly works until you ask your client. For me, their answer depends on how much self-knowledge the client has and also on their background. My conclusion is that the more shocking or negative the upbringing, the less likely it is that a client can use an aspect positively, be it a square or a trine. A supportive upbringing results in a more positive use of aspects, but we all still have our quirks and issues. The combinations formed by the aspects definitely show themes, and by investigating each aspect we can offer advice on how a negative can become a positive. In my opinion, this is an under-used tool in astrology.

Table 3: Aspects and orbs

Degrees	Aspect	Orb either side
0–8	Conjunction	8°
43–47, 313–317	Semisquare	2°
56–64, 296–304	Sextile	4°
70–74, 286–290	Quintile	2°
82–98, 262–278	Square	8°
112–128, 232–248	Trine	8°
133–137, 223–227	Sesquiquadrate	2°
142–146, 214–218	Bi-quintile	2°
148–152, 208–212	Quincunx	2°
172–188	Opposition	8°

The Sun aspect matrix
I love the description Liz Greene once gave in a lecture when she talked about aspects to the Sun. She said that as you follow your

life path, you need to have the planets that aspect the Sun walking beside you, too. These planets add to our vocation in life.

This matrix is one of the main tools I use for career questions, particularly if the client is coming for only one session. It is a way of getting the client involved and thinking about what they are good at and what they love to do. It also results in a matrix that forms the basis of all future job decision-making. I cannot emphasize enough how much clients benefit from using it.

It is a very simple tool. I start with one column with the heading 'Attribute/Role' and then note (along with keywords) the Sun sign, its house position and aspects from other planets. I will take Barack Obama as an example as, although I have yet to have him as a client, he has only a few aspects with the Sun and I can illustrate how to create the matrix without you having to read pages of aspects (and my having to write them!) I'm going to assume I have had a long conversation with him and we have agreed the words that *he* will write down. Here's the first column:

Attribute/role
Sun sign – LEO
In the spotlight Leading role Fun at work 'Heart' in what I do Presentation skills 'Father' role 'Yes, we can' – positivity …

Next, let's add some words from the house position of the Sun:

6th House
Being of service Working in the health area Exercise Staying healthy …

The next task is to do the same for each planet making an aspect to the Sun. I do this by suggesting keywords for each planet. Sue Tompkins' book *Aspects in Astrology* is an excellent resource for this. I have also included a list of words in Appendix 1, which shows each planet's role in the vocational profile and also what effect each planet will have when aspecting another. I explain to the client that this adds a kind of 'sauce' to the original Sun sign. To me, the type of aspect doesn't matter, but the flavour and, more importantly, what the client recognizes in it, does. If the client doesn't recognize the theme, I leave it out. *You need to use the client's own words here.*

Obama has the following aspects with the Sun:

- A wide conjunction to Mercury – which I would definitely use for him, knowing his capacity for rhetoric and his addiction to his BlackBerry
- A square to Neptune
- And, whether you use her or not, there is a square to Ceres

After discussing each aspect with him, he will have an understanding of how each aspect applies to him. He can then add his descriptions to the matrix. We can add these to the first column:

Attribute/role
Planet 1 – NEPTUNE
Compassion Acting ability Creative imagination, dreams Intuition – ability to stand in others' shoes Global – interconnectedness Spiritual element Higher purpose Glamour Good at creating concepts …

Attribute/role
Planet 2 – MERCURY
Communication ability Dialogue Networks Quick thinking Linking ideas Social media …

```
Attribute/role

Planet 3 – CERES

Environment
Agriculture
Purity (e.g. food)
Valuing older women
…
```

Once you have completed the first column of the Sun aspect matrix, you can add any other qualities that you might have missed by looking at any emphases in the chart. You should then have the 'red thread' of the vocational aspirations.

The 'red thread'
The Dutch have a great expression, the *rode draad*, which literally means the 'red thread'.[2] There is no good translation, but it means something like 'common themes or threads' in a story. Astrologers can read a client's biography and find pieces of the story that naturally go together – parts that are different expressions of the same planets or aspects. Career counsellors have to find the red thread without the aid of a chart, so they need to spend more time analysing the biography. We have a great advantage here for structuring what we see and hear. Often a chart will show an emphasis on a sign or a house, perhaps through a stellium or planets clustered around the MC/IC and ASC/DSC axes. There may be a strong aspect pattern that cannot be ignored. These clusters or patterns will form an important part of the strengths that a client has, and will often be obvious threads in their biography. Using the bio shows the client's experience of how these threads work. Even if it does not involve the Sun, any biographical (and chart) theme you feel has a strong influence in the client's life must be investigated to see how it has worked, or could work, for the client. Are any of these qualities in this new dialogue missing from the vocation/motivation list? Again, the client's words and terms are the important key here. The client must 'own' the result.

Adding the stars
I am currently investigating the fixed stars for inclusion in the VP with the help of Bernadette Brady's fascinating program Starlight. The stars add another dimension to a horoscope. If you wish to use them, you can add them to the first column of this matrix. I am still only using the Sun here and, in particular, stars that make a paran

to the Sun. A paran to the Sun forms when, at some time during the day of birth, the Sun is on one of the four angles (i.e. rising, setting, culminating or anti-culminating) *at the same time* that a star is also on the horizon or the meridian. This is not the same as an aspect, as the stars form a whole backdrop to the zodiac circle and the picture formed with parans is three-dimensional. The stars are part of a *fixed* backdrop and perhaps represent more fixed parts of our character. My feeling is that we can negotiate more with the planets but the stars to us are immovable. They appear to add very specific qualities that cannot always be seen in a standard horoscope, and my research so far shows them to be amazingly accurate. So I'm not sure if we can help the client to make them more positive, as they seem to be just 'there', but we can use them to help clients become more aware of their calling. Like many things in a horoscope, stars provide confirmation of a client's feelings about who they really are.

To give a few examples, which speak for themselves:

- Barack Obama has the star Zuben Eschamali (aren't they lovely names?), a star in the constellation of Libra, setting when the Sun is on the IC.

  Brady's interpretation: 'The ability to influence society through one's work. Social reform and social justice, politics and the law... that improves the helper's personal power.'

- Britain's Prime Minister David Cameron has the star Spica in the constellation of Virgo setting together with the Sun.

  Brady writes: 'A gifted or talented person, bright ideas and new solutions.'

And a couple for our famous women:

- Margaret Thatcher has Facies, the eye of Sagittarius, culminating at sunset.

  Brady: 'A possessive dedication to one's goals. Penetrating vision with no regard for others. A great leader or a fearsome and ruthless dictator.'

- Thatcher also has Alhena, a star at the heel of Pollux, on the nadir at the same time.

  Brady notes: 'A person with a desire for a mission, a "Marcher".'

- Queen Elizabeth II has the star Acubens in Cancer, rising when the Sun is on the MC.

Brady: 'A person who sees life as sacred. A protector.'

The final step

So far, we have one column, but sometimes, if there are some ideas for specific jobs, I now go further and create a matrix. The beauty of this matrix is that it visually highlights what type of work fits the client. So let's see how a few other roles 'fit' Obama's Sun profile.

Table 4 is the completed matrix for Obama, as he might fill it in, but with too many qualities. I would suggest weeding out the less important ones. Here, we are providing the answer to two questions: 'Does the job fit the quality?' and 'Can I use this skill in this role?' Sometimes it is an obvious 'yes' or 'no', but sometimes it will depend on the specific job, hence the question marks. When clients complete this matrix, one job or role often clearly stands out. Sometimes it is work that a client is too afraid to do, but would really love to try – that's where the chapter on blocks comes in. This role or job is a good reflection of the client's skills and desires, and I usually try to encourage clients to 'go for it'. That has to do with my own belief, which may not be yours, of 'follow your heart and success will follow'.

Table 4: Obama's matrix

Attribute/role	President	Lawyer	Stay-at-home father
Sun sign – LEO			
In the spotlight	✓	✓	x
Leading role	✓	✓	✓?
Fun at work	✓	✓	✓
'Heart' in what I do	✓	✓	✓
Presentation skills	✓	✓	x
'Father' role	?	?	✓
'Yes, we can' – positivity	?	?	✓

Attribute/role	President	Lawyer	Stay-at-home father
6th House			
Being of service	✓	✓	✓
Working in the health area	?	?	✓?
Exercise	?	?	✓
Staying healthy	?	?	✓
Planet 1 – NEPTUNE			
Compassion	?	✓	✓
Acting ability	✓	✓?	?
Creative imagination/ dreams	✓?	x?	✓
Intuition – ability to stand in others' shoes	✓	✓	✓
Global – interconnected-ness	✓	?	x
Spiritual element	?	✓?	?
Higher purpose	✓?	✓?	?
Glamour	✓	?	x
Good at concepts	✓	?	x
Planet 2 – MERCURY			
Communication ability	✓	✓	✓
Dialogue	✓	✓	✓
Networks	✓	✓	✓
Quick thinking	✓	✓	?
Linking ideas	✓	✓	?
Social media	✓	?	✓
Planet 3 – CERES			
Environment	✓	?	?
Agriculture	✓	?	?
Purity (e.g. food)	✓	?	?

Attribute/role	President	Lawyer	Stay-at-home father
Stars – Parans			
ZUBEN ESCHAMALI			
Social justice	✓	✓	?
Politics	✓	x	x
Social reform	✓	✓	?

You can see that being President literally ticks a lot of Obama's boxes.

Jackie's example

To see how it really works in practice, below is a real matrix filled in by my client Jackie, whose bio was in the previous chapter.

Here's her chart, showing only the Sun and the aspects we shall be looking at.

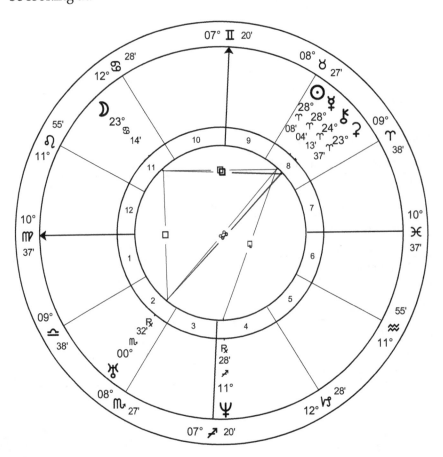

Vocation session

To serve as a reminder, I have repeated the notes that I made for each astrological factor when I read the biography. These were the themes to be discussed. The goal of the vocation session is, of course, to get enough information in the client's own words to help them create their own matrix. In order to do this, I go through each part and discuss it in depth. What always comes up are blocks, which will be defined more clearly later, so we don't want to get too side-tracked by these. You will also have to get the client to 'own' their qualities, and the time taken for this will depend on the client. In this case, what Jackie needed to hear was the fact that all her talents could be used at work as well as at play. So I started with the Sun in Aries, and here are my notes. At the end of all the parts, you will see her matrix.

What's missing? Aries

> My notes: One of the major points here is the lack of Aries in her work. Yes, she fights with her siblings. Yes, she sounds enthusiastic about some things. Yes, she was bullied. But she hated disturbing people. She had a hellish project and I really had to laugh that she had worked selling knives ('at least we had a good set of knives') and in a missile lab! You *can* see the positive side of Aries in her bio but, again, it is mostly expressed outside her working life. My focus will be to help her get all these things into her work: 'big and loud, shaking my booty, starting a lot of things', being allowed to be impatient – the other side of which is taking action and leading. Being an initiator. Being active and moving – Aries doesn't do well in sit-down jobs. Her Sun is in the more private 8th House though, so how does this work?

What happened?
She recognized 'fiery', 'don't finish', 'excitable', 'lots of energy' and 'going for it', but she said 'but I'm not always like that. It is good when it happens – being enthusiastic.' She didn't immediately recognize being an initiator, so I asked her to think about where she has ignited or started something. She acknowledged being competitive but hates that about herself. She recognized how she wants to be direct but stops herself. She saw that she wants to, and should, defend people in certain situations, but doesn't.

It was clear to her that she is not using much Aries energy in her current job. I think she loves improvisation so much because it's fast and of the moment. It's gutsy and she can get into the flow without thinking too much. Improvisation means you have to act – in both senses of the word. Also, she can express things that she might normally keep to herself, because having an 8th House Sun makes her quite private. We spent a lot of time seeing how she might be able to use these qualities in her work.

Much of this session with clients is often doing what I call a reframe. For example, in Jackie's case, thinking about how impatience has a positive side. How is it useful to be direct? Some jobs need Aries energy. This required a big mind-shift for her, which she could see and understand. She thought that defending the underdog or speaking up was too 'big', too 'good'. This needs more analysis in the blocks session.

Sun opposite Uranus

My notes: 'Redundant second-born girl.' Father gone. 'Taller and chubbier than boys.' 'All-white primary school.' 'Teased and taunted.' 'Bullied and made fun of.' 'Social angst.' 'Felt special' for getting through a selection criteria. 'Trust and intimacy issues.' But, reading between the lines, she does want to be 'dazzling'. She works with technology but says 'I need human interaction'.

I want to delve further into all of these. For me these are mostly negative expressions of Uranus – being singled out and teased for being different. Becoming terrified of not fitting in. Developing a strategy of non-bonding. A feeling of abandonment? Of being unwanted. Having a missing father often results in having no role model for what our heart wants. Her father left, showing the 'break' side of Uranus, but this is also a form of abandonment.

I want to find out how terrified she is of standing out and being special. The pattern of fear seems to have started early. Her 8th House Sun might mean that it is dangerous to be noticed. But as a Sun Aries with an aspect to Uranus, she will want to be special, to be noticed and to be different. What comes out of this will go into the blocks session. I will try to help her turn negative Uranus energy into a positive, quirky, special one.

What happened?

This is indeed a big block. Chiron is close to the Sun so there are big blocks on every aspect of doing what Jackie really loves. She recognized the themes such as 'I don't like doing what others do', but she experiences this as being alone. This is a common problem when Uranus is involved. She recognized that she needs to do her own thing and that it is her dream: to do something funky and different and special. But that seems such a long way off. Uranus, of course, gives her technical ability, too, but she needs to embrace the idea of being very quick-thinking and being able to think out of the box as well. And, in particular, she needs to grasp that her ideas are good ones. The pain here is in not feeling understood, so she doesn't speak up. She has a huge dilemma here of wanting to fit into a team (the Moon in Cancer squares the Sun) and wanting, in a good way, to be an outsider. We ended up with some words she could own but this is a very painful part of her chart.

Sun conjunct Mercury

My notes: I want to see how this related to her father. She mentions Mercury words in her CV: 'storyboard', 'text', 'improvisational acting' and 'writing'. A business dedicated to engaging in communication. Interests: writing. In her bio she says 'I was a super-shy kid'. This doesn't sound like Sun conjunct Mercury in Aries – I want to delve here, too. She writes quite a lot about her brother and sister (Mercury) – the only role for her seems to be the good girl. 'Sister smartest, brother – do no wrong' – that must have been difficult for an Aries child. I want to explore that more. Sun–Mercury seems to be resulting in (from her point of view) siblings getting all the attention. There is not a lot of Mercury in her bio, except for the outside work – 'Writing my heart out, meeting new people' – although she has done voice-overs and PA work where she met 'interesting characters with dynamic stories'. She seems to see her love of writing as something she has to do outside of work. For me, this aspect must become part of her vocation.

What happened?

She 'likes to have cool information'. She recognized her love of linking things together, being a network hub. Giving information, being curious, stories. She doesn't let herself create and write enough, though. The fact that she could earn money as a writer was 'too big a goal for me to be allowed to have that'. This is another big block. Most clients *do* know what they want and love although there is often a 'yes, but…' She writes at work, so I asked her to find out what her boss thinks of her in that role. She said 'Yeah, good', as she had just had an appraisal, but she couldn't put into words what was good. Getting feedback from others is often a way of hearing what is good about you – what you do well.

Sun sesquiquadrate Neptune

My notes: Her biography is a good example of why sesquiquadrates are useful. The bio is littered with Neptune! It works both positively and negatively. Missing father – no contact really. Men who disappoint? Music, dancing, TV, film all over the place. But she also filled the role of being of service, in particular to her mother. I want to see if this happens with everyone – whether she is a caretaker and helps everyone. Her strategy for handling pain is to escape. As Neptune also picks up Mercury, of course, this explains her 'shyness'. More like avoidance, perhaps. She needs a very creative job where her imagination can be seen and valued.

She recognized this aspect in wanting to help old people, wanting to volunteer to help kids who are troubled, and wanting to support people who need help at work. Having the Sun in the 8th House seems to make her a natural psychotherapist. Her strategy now, though ('I'm in me mode'), is not to be close to people. 'I can't do this a little bit.' This is a struggle for her: Aries Sun, wanting to do things for herself, and the Neptune, wanting to help everyone and be sensitive to their needs. I think she has overdone the 'helping' as a child and is now trying to find a balance. She recognized the need for some kind of emotional bond at work, but how *not* to get swamped with others' problems is the dilemma.

She can see the positive side of it when she is 'in the zone' reading people, and life flows naturally. But she is worried it might overwhelm her. One of her talents is to combine fantasy and painting pictures with writing. She's a good listener. With the 8th House focus, she is not afraid of the deeper subjects. As with other Neptunian clients, I suggested that she do some voluntary work. She had done volunteer work in the past and found it too easy, so that wasn't 'good' enough. Obviously, a discussion ensued from this statement! I always say that Neptunian people should use this energy at work, then they don't have to look after everyone in their spare time!

Sun square Moon

> My notes: This is often the signature of a writer, which is an activity she obviously loves. Her bio doesn't really highlight the need to belong except where she says she wants human interaction. This is a dilemma for her with her background. I would like more discussion on this theme. How can she use her 'feeling and caring' for people in a way that is positive for her?

The need to belong is strong in Jackie, and she is very sensitive. Again, we have a dilemma here. She cannot, in my view, be happy working in a company where there is not some emotional attachment. There must be some protective and caring quality to her work. It was more difficult for her to see how she could use this quality to make money, although she could see it in her love of being involved with children and old people. One suggestion we discussed was her writing stories that she might collect from different cultures and traditions or from elderly people that she volunteers to help in the future.

Sun conjunct Ceres and Chiron

> My notes: I think the possible wound from Chiron is obvious: can she follow her heart? I want to discover whether she recognizes the positive sides of these two bodies and if they could form a part of her vocation. I felt that neither of their themes showed up in her bio.

We discussed Chiron in terms of blocks (see later). We also discussed whether this part of her could be used for healing others in some way, but this was not immediately recognizable. I think Chiron can only be embraced when some blocks are dealt with on a personal level. I think, however, that Jackie could heal with her words.

She resonated with the ideas I have about Ceres, such as having some involvement with the environment, food, purity or women's issues (to name a few). I gave her homework to read about the myth of Ceres and Chiron so she could see whether any of it was relevant to her vocation. Chiron spoke to her the most and she liked the idea of healing. She said, 'Yes, I do have a sense of wanting to "fix" everybody so that we can all be happy. Like, imbed subliminal messages in my performances and writing that would unlock some... something.' Do we sense the strong 8th House here?

Adding the stars

Jackie has the Sun in paran with Sirius – culminating at sunrise, and Capella, rising with the Sun.

Brady on Capella[3] – a star linked to Artemis: freedom and independence will be important. The embodiment of action and movement. 'The free agent takes centre stage.' The sentence from Brady, 'The need to balance the desire for independence with matters of personal responsibility,' really spoke to Jackie. As I have already mentioned, the stars provide confirmation of the main themes, and this can be very helpful.

Brady on Sirius[4] – one of the brightest stars, known to the Egyptians as the 'shining one' or 'scorcher', and linked to burning. An association with Isis. With the Sun: 'Sudden success that can burn'; 'A person who can be sacrificed to the larger need. A vocation that overrides the normalness of one's life.' Jackie said of this, 'I can't really relate to this, although sudden success would be nice.'

She also has another star in paran with the Sun, with a slightly wider orb. She felt this one more. It is Sualocin in the Dolphin constellation. This is a fun, trickster energy.

Brady: 'The talented long-shot takes centre stage,'[5] and she gives Charlie Chaplin as an example. He is one of Jackie's favourite people. Role models can offer useful information in this process.

Here's the matrix that Jackie made after the session. They are her words!

Table 5: Jackie's matrix

	Interactive TV Production	Acting	Writing	Improvisation
ARIES				
Fiery, enthusiastic, ARGGHH!!!		✓	✓	✓
Initiative	✓	✓	✓	✓
Challenge	✓	✓	✓	✓
Competitive, going for it		✓		✓
Acting quickly				✓
Direct			✓	✓
Jumping in, throwing myself at it		✓		✓
Real deep experience (8th House)		✓	✓	✓
MERCURY				
Communication, talking, writing	✓	✓	✓	✓
Observant, curious	✓	✓	✓	✓
NEPTUNE				
Getting lost	✓	✓	✓	✓
Creative, imaginative	✓	✓	✓	✓
URANUS				
Rebellious		✓	✓	✓
Unique		✓	✓	✓
Innovative	✓	✓	✓	✓
MOON				
Feeling of belonging	✓	✓		✓

Working with emotions and feelings		✓	✓	✓
Stars – Parans				
CAPELLA	✓	✓		✓
SIRIUS			✓	
SUALOCIN		✓	✓	✓

There could, of course, be more ways, which are not mentioned here, to use all these qualities in other jobs. This type of matrix can be used in different ways. As well as being a quick reference when checking whether a job suits you (obviously, in Jackie's case, not her current job), it will form the backbone of any promotional material in which these words can be used. I suggest that clients use these terms in their CVs or websites, and also that they include in their CVs the tasks they have undertaken in order to highlight these qualities. Clients can consider removing anything in their promotional material that doesn't highlight these talents, e.g. an old position that no longer reflects who they are. The idea is to get a CV or website that is in line with who you really are. If you do this, you are more likely to attract a job (or clients) that supports your true calling.

Last comment

Most people tend to use some of their innate qualities in each of the jobs they do. No experience is ever wasted and each job usually fulfils part of the chart. The trick is to eventually find a job in which everything is satisfied. This is no easy task and usually takes a long time. The way I see it, astrologers can help clients *not* to stray from their path. In other words, we can help clients to focus on their mission and support them in making career steps that progress towards their true vocation. Jackie's chart probably means that she will eventually want to work for herself. But that doesn't have to happen now. Each job needs to act as a stepping stone to something more in tune with who you are. And it should potentially give you the experience that will help you to get where you eventually want to be.

So now it's on to the next part of the VP, one that forms part of the 'Who am I?' section – style.

Books to use for this section (see the bibliography for further details):

Star and Planet Combinations, Bernadette Brady
Linda Goodman's Sun Signs, Linda Goodman
The Luminaries, Liz Greene and Howard Sasportas
Horoscope Symbols, Robert Hand
LifeClock, Bruno and Louise Huber
The Twelve Houses, Howard Sasportas
Aspects in Astrology, Sue Tompkins
The Contemporary Astrologer's Handbook, Sue Tompkins

---

1. The Huber method of drawing a chart is described in their book *LifeClock* (HopeWell, 2006). Pages 303–304 describe the four levels of man, which are drawn around an inner core and go from inside to outside. The aspect structure is the first level, followed by the planets, signs and houses.

2. In Greek mythology, Theseus found his way out of the labyrinth of the Minotaur by following a red thread, given to him by Ariadne, who had fallen in love with him.

3. *Star and Planet Combinations*, Bernadette Brady, The Wessex Astrologer, 2008, pp. 139–40.

4. ibid., pp. 229–30.

5. ibid., p. 236.

CHAPTER 5
RECOGNIZING STYLE AND DRIVE

He has found his style, when he cannot do otherwise.

Paul Klee

My favourite way of finding our style or a particular approach from the horoscope is to use Mars. It's certainly not the only way and I will comment on another possibility – the elements – later in this chapter.

Why Mars?
Style is defined in many ways. What I'm referring to is best described as 'how something is done or how it happens'. Mars describes how something is done. It tells us about our approach, how we go about getting what we want. It has to do with direction in the short term – our aim towards a particular result. Longer-term goals require more of a strategy, so we might look at Jupiter. Mars also describes how we fight for something or how we defend ourselves. In a working environment (or anywhere else, but here we are looking specifically at vocation), our Mars is needed to stick up for ourselves and get what we want.

The working environment is still fairly competitively orientated. This is changing, but the best, the fastest and the boldest are still valued. 'He who dares wins' is still a very common concept in many companies. These masculine values are highly rated and there is nothing wrong with that, as companies would be lost without them. But it is out of balance with Venusian qualities (another story!) However, looking to Mars to help your client recognize how they defend themselves, get what they want and how they argue, can be helpful in defining the type of position and environment that will best suit them.

Career counsellors define style, as they find it an important element in a vocational profile. Not every personal style is suitable for every job, and frustration can result if the approach you are required to use is incompatible with your own authentic style.

(How annoying are help desks that have a set approach to asking questions?) Not being able to use your normal Mars makes you lose enthusiasm and creates a feeling of impotence in your function.

The tool I use for this is similar to the one for vocation: helping the client to recognize their style by discussing Mars' sign, house position and aspects, and sometimes by doing an exercise with the client (more on this later).

Mars – his sign and house

The sign, of course, describes *how* you get what you want. You can use Table 1 (see page 52 in the Vocation chapter) to get ideas about how each sign works. Similarly, ideas for Mars in each house will have similar themes to the house ideas in Table 2 (see page 58). Mars through the houses shows in *which area of life* we will defend and fight our battles. Here again, we need to discuss these themes with the client to see what they recognize. Many clients don't appreciate their Mars. This is connected with the way we value Mars as a society. Some aspects of it are valued, such as the competitive aspect and the kind of 'manliness' it can show. But fighting our corner, getting angry at work or showing frustration at inaction is frequently viewed negatively, especially if it's a woman doing the fighting. There is an unwritten code in most companies I know to keep calm and be reasonable. This is cultural, of course. For example, in Holland there is far more directness than in the UK or New Zealand, where I have also worked but, on the whole, we are still a bit scared of some Mars topics, in particular anger. So it feels good when our style is accepted in the workplace, as we can then use Mars positively by showing our enthusiasm and taking action – our way of doing things is valued and we can simply get on with it.

By using Tables 1 and 2, it is fairly straightforward to grasp the meaning of Mars through the various signs and houses, but I have given a few examples below. Questions with which to start discussions with clients are: 'Do you ever get angry at work – and, if so, what about?' 'What are you enthusiastic about in your job?' 'How do you stick up for yourself?' I sometimes suggest clients ask others to give them feedback on how they are seen. Mars is often very visible to others and this feedback can be a real eye-opener. Here are some real-life examples…

Examples of Mars by sign and house

A high-level consultant with Mars in Capricorn in the 6th House
A style that highlights responsibility in the workplace. If an

agreement is made it cannot be changed. Very goal-orientated. A bit of a workaholic (but you wouldn't put this in the VP). Strict approach to project management. Adheres to the goals and wishes of the person giving the contract. This placement can make it difficult to work in an environment where flexibility and chaotic meetings are the norm. Anger at work has got him into trouble on many occasions.

An author and counsellor with Mars in Scorpio in the 3rd House
Someone who passionately attacks her research on a chosen topic. A vehement defence of ideas. Seeks the phrase or word that perfectly describes what she wants to say. She has fixed but well researched opinions. It can be difficult for her to work in a group with ideas that are different from hers. She is much happier when working alone or one-to-one.

An author with Mars in Virgo in the 12th House
Her style is to tackle problems and bring them into the public domain in a very quiet way. She frequently uses participative research for her books about patients' rights and problems in healthcare, accompanying patients to meetings with doctors and interviewing families, patients and consultants. Her research areas are geriatrics and the terminally ill. She is quiet in meetings but takes in everything and mulls it over in her own time. It is difficult for her to define what she wants for herself. She has a very intuitive style, but has yet to always trust her intuition (again, not what you want on the VP). Her interviewees feel safe about giving her information.

An owner of a fitness club and sports instructor with Mars in Aries in the 1st House
His style is very enthusiastic and encouraging. He confronts, argues, and goes for what he wants and can be experienced as selfish. After years of doing other work, this is a role that suits him well and he can get the best out of others. He loves competing and is a very good and very fit sportsman.

A language teacher with Mars in Aquarius in the 6th House
Her style is unconventional. She approaches teaching in a very unorthodox way – for example, she goes shopping with her students and expects them to have fun in their lessons. She has a quirky sense of humour and has many innovative teaching ideas. She would not fit well into a conventional company.

Feeling that such a company would stifle her ideas, take away her independence and freedom in the way she wants to work, she set up her own company.

Mars and aspects

As usual, aspects to Mars are my main tool for defining style. The information gleaned from discussing each of these is added to the standard house and sign ideas above. I will go a little deeper into this technique: using astrologers as an example, I offer some ideas on how aspects might translate into a description in their publicity material of their style. Remember, ending up with a definition is your goal. In Appendix 1, there is a table showing how each planet is used in a vocational profile. The aspecting planet (also in Appendix 1) offers some ideas on how the style might be affected, e.g. the table for Jupiter has these suggestions: *Strategic, big picture, overview, philosophical, vision, entrepreneurial, risk-taker, adventurous, confident.* So the style of someone with a Mars –Jupiter aspect might be described as strategic, showing someone with an entrepreneurial style who starts a task by beginning with an overview; a top-down approach. Below are a few examples…

Mars in aspect to the Sun
Defending quality

In my experience, many astrologers tend to interpret this aspect as Mars colouring and adding description to the meaning of the Sun. Interpretations include conflict with the father and a sporting father who loves competition. I also use it in this way when talking of vocation (e.g. someone who might want a pioneering job). All good. But this, and in fact all aspects, can be taken both ways: Mars describing the style and the Sun adding flavour to that. It is comparable to Mars in Leo. So what this aspect might suggest is a style (Mars) that gains recognition (Sun), a style that attracts attention – perhaps a drama queen or someone with a theatrical style. It might suggest a generous or regal approach, or describe a good speculator. Someone very playful, perhaps, or even arrogant. Someone who fights for quality. This placing will not usually belong to a shrinking violet. Whatever work this person does, they need to be recognized and given a pat on the back for their **approach**.

Here is an idea for publicity material for an astrologer with this aspect: 'My approach is to use role play or astro-drama to help you gain insight. Sessions are fun and I create a space where you can express your problems. I encourage you to get to know your heart.'

Mars in aspect to the Moon
Defending the emotional
The same comment applies here: we often use this Mars aspect to describe the mother (Moon), but we can also give Mars the flavour of the Moon. So this might be a nurturing style, a protective or a very emotional style. It will describe someone who perhaps sticks up for children or women. Tears may be used as a fighting tool. It can also show someone with a changeable style that depends on the mood or the circumstance. It is similar to Mars in Cancer and can describe someone who finds it difficult letting go of something emotional. But, again, that's not what you want for the profile. The question is: what's the positive side of Mars being aspected by the Moon in a work sense? Someone who always has the tissues ready!

   Astrologer idea: 'I find creating a safe space, where my clients can express feelings, to be very important. I like nurturing people so that they feel good about going for their potential.'

Mars in aspect to Mercury
Defending ideas or order
Using the table in Appendix 1, we can expect a curious, chatty, inquisitive or quick-thinking style. This is somebody who can be very spontaneous with ideas. They might love going to networking events or company drinks parties. They have a rational, if somewhat jumpy (from topic to topic), style. They can do several things at once. The Virgo–Mercury individual can take a very detailed list-type approach, one that offers practical help, whereas the Gemini-Mercury type with Mars will offer ideas. A busy environment is often appreciated.

   Astrologer idea: 'My way of working is through dialogue and asking you questions, which encourages you to come up with your own answers. I love suggesting new ideas for helping you find your true vocation.'

Mars in aspect to Venus
Defending harmony or common sense
This is a style that uses feedback and dialogue; someone who can listen well and cite many examples of people with similar issues, which can offer a different perspective. A kind, fair approach. A style that can make someone feel valued. This aspect can also produce the peace-maker at work, or the one who makes the office look beautiful. The Taurean side to Venus will give a very down-to-earth, practical style. One that wants concrete results. A Mars-Venus person is happier when there are few conflicts.

> *Astrologer idea: 'My style of working aims to get your life more balanced. By having a sounding board, you can gain clarity about where your vocation might lie.'*

Mars in aspect to Ceres
Defending plants, the environment, nature's cycles or women

Although I have yet to gather substantial evidence for this, I recognize this aspect in someone with a 'green' style, driven to know the source of products used. There is respect for the earth and environment and an attempt to champion women. There is also an approach that favours purity, getting to the essence of something and not diluting the original concept. I have seen this aspect in people who are very in tune with the seasons. How this might inform your working life might be in how you set up your physical environment. Are you a recycler? Do you only buy 'responsible' products for the office? Do you bring in your own food? Or in another way: Do you protect or defend other women at work?

> *Astrologer idea: 'The way I work takes account of the seasons and the many astrological cycles. I can explain where you are in a particular cycle and how you can take advantage of the phase you are in.'*

Mars in aspect to Jupiter
Defending a vision or belief

I gave this as an example above: a person with a 'big picture' style. I have this one myself and, apart from the judgemental side that I wouldn't admit to on a CV, I experience this as a style that starts a session with a rough idea of where we are heading so that I can have a strategy. I always want the whole picture first before I get into detail. (The chapters for this book have been in my head for a long time.) It's like the archer who needs a target. Once I have that, I can get on with it. This aspect also produces people who like having adventures and taking risks. It might be a style that focuses on being outside in the open air or defending the environment. People with this aspect will need a certain amount of freedom. As with all these aspects, you have to merge the planets involved and consider the sign and house placements of Mars.

> *Astrologer idea – putting my money where my mouth is – from my site (Jupiter is about patterns): 'Faye aims to listen with what she calls an astrological ear, to hear patterns, and help put them in perspective and try to turn them into qualities which clients can use positively. Nothing in a horoscope is good or bad. The trick is to understand these patterns and use the potential seen in the chart in positive ways.'*

Mars in aspect to Saturn

Defending rules, plans or structures

A careful and measured style and, as with Mars in Capricorn, a deal is a deal. This is someone who should be good with deadlines and takes responsibility for their approach. An authoritative and goal-orientated style. Someone with a very structured way of doing things. There could also be a teaching/mentor element in the style. Someone with this aspect will not be happy in an organization where no one arrives on time to meetings or where there is no structure or defined goals.

> *Astrologer idea: 'My method is to first read the basic chart. After this you may ask any questions and I will then spend time on what to expect for the coming year.' (Or some such clear structure.)*

Mars in aspect to Uranus

Defending individuality and honesty

This aspect can produce a somewhat erratic style. You never know what to expect. This style is noticeable because it is unorthodox, surprising or unpredictable. Sometimes the element of surprise can work wonders. Someone with this aspect will be unhappy when they can't do things their own way. They need the freedom to attack a problem with their own strange (to some) methods. They may be rebellious but there are certain situations where this can be an asset. An understanding of an issue might be necessary before action. Directness is another quality of this aspect. Nike has this aspect, and their slogan is 'Just do it'. (The horoscope of the company, founded on 25 January 1964, that later became Nike, shows Mars is in Aquarius exactly quincunx Uranus.)

> *Astrologer idea: 'My unorthodox approach can help give you different ways of looking at a problem. It can awaken you to certain strengths you may have.'*

Mars in aspect to Neptune

Defending the underdog and fighting for a better world

Perhaps this would produce more of an intuitive aura-reader type than your everyday astrologer. Mars–Neptune people have a very intuitive style. They may be chaotic, but we don't want that in the profile. However, chaos does produce concepts and often great imagery. It is a non-concrete style, but the strength here is being able to stand in another's shoes. A caretaking, empathic approach. A compassionate and helpful style. It is similar to Mars in Pisces. As an aside, when I was doing my therapy training, seven out of fifteen of us had Mars in Pisces!

Astrologer idea: 'My intuitive approach to a chart means I will deal with what is important for you to know now. My aim is to help you with your spiritual growth.'

Mars in aspect to Pluto
Defending privacy

Mars with Pluto can produce a very dominant or even cruel style. But there is also a positive expression of this powerful combination that you will want to discover for the VP. This style belongs to someone who gets to the bottom of things. Someone who will not give up until the answer is found or the research is done. These people need to be passionate about work and need to be in control of how the work they do is approached. In the right job, this is someone who can move mountains. They really go for what they want and don't like to lose. They can keep a secret.

Astrologer idea: 'Finding answers to superficial questions is not really my strength but if you're looking for a safe, private and real discussion, I'm passionate about getting to the bottom of an issue with you.'

Another idea of style

David Hamblin, in his book *Harmonic Charts*,[1] writes that the 5th Harmonic represents style. Now, I don't want to get into harmonics, even though they are fascinating. If you are interested, I refer you to Hamblin's book, which is one of the best on the subject. However, the 5th Harmonic shows indications of 'fiveness'. So perhaps the quintile and bi-quintile aspects I use might also say something about style. Hamblin comes to the conclusion from his own research that 'fiveness is essentially the idea of making, arranging, building, constructing, structuring and forming'.[2] Because of this and other astrologers' views, I take the quintile series to represent talents, and I will cover them in Chapter 7. But do experiment with them yourself to see if they represent the style I am referring to here.

The elements

Many career advisors, as well as astrologers, use the elements to help define style. The exercise below uses our usual four elements. It's based on drawing a square.

The idea is to show how much of each element you feel you have. Clients can fill this in themselves, which gets them involved. This exercise, provided as a handout, includes a description of what the elements are. As an astrologer, you can provide your own material or you can give an explanation during a session and give

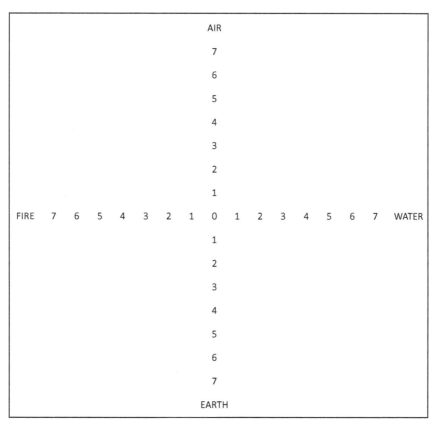

the exercise as homework. The goal is to create your own visual lopsided element-square, which can be helpful for some clients. This can be a starting point for a discussion, particularly if it doesn't match what you are seeing in the chart!

Myers-Briggs (MBTI)

A test commonly used in many organizations is the Myers-Briggs Type Indicator (MBTI is the registered trademark). I was subjected to it many years ago in one of my previous incarnations. You end up with a four-letter indicator that is supposed to sum up your personality. Actually, it's as good a test as any other used in companies.

The original developers of the test were Katharine Cook Briggs and her daughter, Isabel Briggs-Myers. It is based on Jung's psychological types: Thinking and Feeling, Sensing and Intuition. These are, of course, the elements that we astrologers use. Jung then added Extrovert and Introvert and Myers-Briggs added Judgement and Perception, so you end up with sixteen personality types of four letters. There was never much literature on the fact that this was based on something much older than Jung, but that has since been addressed. An interesting article by Garry Phillipson,[3] written with Peter Case, points out this fact. It appears in 'Culture and Cosmos' Vol. 5. No. 2 (2001) and also on the web.[4]

I mention the Myers-Briggs here because you may have clients who have done this test and so it can be a starting point for discussion. What did they think of it? How did they experience it? Does it work? But I've also added it because it gives astrology a little more 'street-cred'. If companies use tools based on something we have always used, it can help make an astrological profile seem more acceptable. There is a lot of information online about this test and you can find which questions are asked. See what you think of it.

Style for my client Jackie
To remind you, here are the notes that I made from the bio:

> My notes: Mars is in Pisces with a square to Neptune, so we can see this theme as a repeat of the Neptunian issues with her Sun. The way she approaches something (Mars) will have some overlap with her heart's desires (Sun), e.g. she likes taking care of people and reading people, and that will be seen in her approach to getting what she wants. I want to find out how aware she is of this. She is working to make the world better, perhaps – how might this happen? How does being 'of service' affect her in her work? She also has an aspect between Mars and Venus – I see this in her coordination roles on the CV. Her style might be one of discussion and needing feedback. Saturn and Pluto also aspect Mars: a trine from Saturn and a quincunx from Pluto. The Saturn comes across quite clearly in her bio. The way she operated had to be responsible, she also picked up a strong work ethic from her mother. She also 'waited to participate'. She 'hated disturbing people'. Pluto can be seen in the bullying, both by her as the bully when young and later being bullied herself.
>
> This needs a reframe, as reading her bio makes me think these aspects act more as blocks: being bullied and having to be so responsible. There are questions relating to how these aspects work. Is she jealous? Too compliant with others' rules in her approach to getting

things done? How does that work with a Mars–Uranus trine, which would suggest a style of wanting to do something her own way?

The results

After each session, Jackie was asked to write up her version of it. The exercise I gave her was to try to distil her style from the conversation we had. Like many people, she found this quite difficult because, for her, style is difficult to separate from who she is. You might need to have a few attempts at the beginning until you get a result that can be used in a CV, a letter or a website.

Below is Jackie's chart with aspects to her Mars, plus her summary. We spent the session investing a lot of time in Neptune. As mentioned above, she has Mars in Pisces in the 6th House making aspects to:

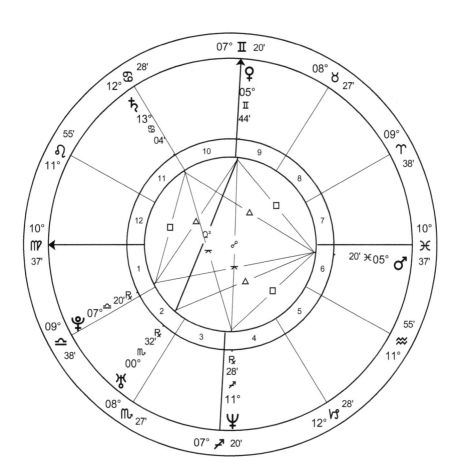

- **Venus, a square** Here we discussed her need for feedback and her role as a coordinator or sounding board.

- **Uranus, a trine** We discussed a style of independence, mental stubbornness, doing things her own way, and how much freedom she needs.

- **Saturn, a trine** This is a big block, which she recognized and is thoroughly sick of.

- **Pluto, a quincunx** Yes, she does like to get to the bottom of things. Here we discussed loyalty, passion and privacy. She said that she is slightly jealous and has a tendency towards 'what's mine is mine!' She can keep a secret and doesn't talk out of school.

So she recognized all of these themes. Most of the session was about the Mars square to Neptune (in effect, a double whammy with Mars in Pisces). Working with Neptune is always somewhat vague. Sessions take on a creative Neptunian flavour. I think this is also why Jackie's style is difficult to put into words. As I have mentioned in the examples above, she is someone whose approach is to look after people, to listen to people and to put herself in others' shoes. A feeling, compassionate style – in her case, it is at odds with her Aries planets. The following were mentioned: listening first, tuning in, being helpful, taking care of everything, getting lost in activities, daydreaming, creative imagination and 'painting pictures' with her writing. She recognized these but was having difficulty seeing how this aspect could be useful at work.

Here's her summary:

I can very readily exist in someone's shoes, sympathize with who she is and create a space for her to open up. I like listening to people's stories, my curiosity usually leads me to delve deeper. In written word, my imagination fuels my ability to describe with creative clarity and feeling. I put my off-kilter, quirky Jackie stamp on everything I write so you can easily tell authentic from adulterated. I find the truth so terribly seductive that I'm hungry for it in the people I interact with and activities I engage in.

I like to try to do things in a Neo state of mind. When Neo finally learns to dodge bullets in The Matrix, *when he's mastered some part of himself where everything gets slow and deliberate, he knows exactly how to move. When I'm on stage and my mind is a vacuum, no back-chatter, undermining second-guessing and there's nothing to do but do, I am Neo. When every action is the only action, when every word comes out exactly as I intended for maximum effect, when I write as if possessed by the part of me that never doubts what she wants to say, I am Neo. When the tingling in my body swarms as someone opens up an intimate part of herself to me, I am Neo. When I let the sweet music dictate the movement in my receptive body, when a child chuckles so heartily I am beholden to copy, when delicious dining gives way to scrumptious chatter, I am Neo. Nothing else matters when I'm doing these things.*

My body lets me know when I'm doing something I love. There's an electric lightness swirling in my chest, the good ole familiar tingling all over, excited anticipation in my limbs. I like listening to people's problems and giving advice. I get to a place where I'm presenting my point with such clarity it surprises me. I didn't know I felt so strongly and yet listen to me in such animated tones. There's a place where the one I'm talking to stops but-but-but-ing me, a point he's totally receptive and reading me loud and clear, where she knows, maybe somewhere deep, that she is hearing the truth, that's the place [my] body starts coming alive. I like seeing how my words have had effect, I can see it in their being. It's very powerful.

Acting can offer a stillness of mind I find hard to get anywhere else. I'm in a scene and, as Jackie, I have no past, no future; as the character, I have infinite possibilities to play with. The self-hatred has been vaporized and everything I do is exactly right. I am tall and mighty. Making people laugh is like playing with a whole bunch of puppies and kids. The energy in the room is crazy, palpable. It's as if I'm literally being electrified.

When I write, it is startling how easily I can script some of the most beautiful things, with little effort. It comes to a point where I'm so impressed by an experience that I feel compelled to give it voice in word lest I dishonour it. It is not a need, a

> *want, a must. It is what it is. I breathe. I write. I blink. I write. It flows through me. I feel correct, just right, when I write. I have tremendous fun on the way too. I get many compliments and blush at every single one. I am never as lucid and beautiful as when I write. When I read what I've written, I let myself be impressed because, yes, the same feelings come through even for the reader. I love taking the crazy things I've seen and done, playing with words to illustrate the events and create a world for the reader to visualize and participate in. I feel naturally connected when I write.*
>
> *When I have a problem, I must first get a quick overview of the situation before planning my attack. I need to have a general understanding of all the parts before deciding strategy.*

I very much enjoy the way she writes and this confirmed for me that she needs to be writing in her career. But getting back to style, it is definitely in there in a very Piscean way. She is talking about being lost in something, being in a creative space, so an employer who would allow her that would be great for her. I wanted a bit more clarity, though, to be able to connect it to style in a VP, so I added this exercise: please finish this sentence, 'My approach to solving a problem or starting something new at work is…'. She added the last paragraph (above), which I think highlights the Uranus (quick, understanding) as well as the Saturn, as I take her sentences to mean that she needs to know what the goal is.

Remember the VP is for the client to use. It has to be in their own language.

So, now take a look at exploring your image.

Books to use for this section (see the bibliography for further details):

The Mars Quartet: Four Seminars on the Astrology of the Red Planet, Lynn Bell, Darby Costello, Liz Greene and Melanie Reinhart
Earth and Air, Darby Costello
Water and Fire, Darby Costello
The Inner Planets, Liz Greene and Howard Sasportas
Horoscope Symbols, Robert Hand
The Contemporary Astrologer's Handbook, Sue Tompkins

1. *Harmonic Charts*, David Hamblin, The Aquarian Press, ed. 1987, pp. 47-63.
2. ibid., p. 48.
3. If you don't know Garry Phillipson, he has been an astrologer for many years and wrote *Astrology in the Year Zero* (Flare, 2000) and has a website with great material at www.astrozero.co.uk
4. There is one example at http://findarticles.com/p/articles/mi_hb4779/is_17/ai_n29091768/?tag=content;col1

Chapter 6

EXPRESSING AN AUTHENTIC IMAGE

... so don't be afraid to let them show, your true colors, true colors are beautiful, like a rainbow.
'True Colors' by Cyndi Lauper

In lectures and workshops I often talk about how to promote yourself. One of the simple exercises I do is to take the keywords for the signs of the Sun, the Ascendant and the MC in the chart and combine them to make a logo and/or a slogan. I find this works particularly well for companies, so I tried it out with personal horoscopes, and clients often found an instant recognition of what they were trying to achieve. Somehow it seems to capture the essence of someone's working profile.

Corporate branding is big business. One of my business clients works with big companies to help achieve their desired image in the market. This includes helping define all forms of outward communication, such as letterheads for stationery, corporate statements and press releases, interviews, any contacts with the press, annual reports, folders and brochures, how the telephone is answered, product branding and, of course, logos and websites. I have helped many business clients to brainstorm these using this simple astrological method. Clients seem to have an innate sense of the archetypes being discussed and the discussion that results is usually great fun. It works even better if a glass of wine is involved. Neptunian creativity!

Company image

You can study the websites of well known companies to see how they are 'branded'. As an example, KLM has Leo on the Ascendant, Aries on the MC and a Libra Sun.[1] The Leo rising is clear in their pricing, the fact they offer 'good quality' services and an image of quality; they are definitely not in the inexpensive part of the market. KLM is *Royal* Dutch Airlines and the logo features a crown. The swan used in the past is also not exactly a small bird. The blue sky as a background to the swan might show the beauty inherent in a Libra Sun.

When I did some work there, I couldn't miss the Aries MC. Much of the literature I studied showed 'firsts'. The first airline to carry animals, the first to carry mail long distances and, if I'm not mistaken, the first to fly long haul to Indonesia. This is a very competitive company – even though it always wanted a partner (Libra Sun), which it now finally has in Air France. The website has changed since I was there and has become more like other airlines, which I think is a pity. It doesn't highlight the three archetypes as well as it did, and to my mind the old site was better.

Incidentally, the chart I have for one of the UK's leading retailers, Marks and Spencer,[2] has the same three points. The Leo Ascendant shows their wish to provide quality food and clothing at competitive prices (Aries). Their site states: 'Our company values of **Quality, Value, Service, Innovation and Trust** are not new – they are the principles on which our business was founded.'[3] They have been very pioneering (Aries) and they aim to provide excellent customer service (Libra). If I were working with M&S I would first research whether this was the appropriate chart to work with (i.e. does it respond well to transits, progressions and Age Points) and, if so, I would probably suggest changing the colours in their logo! The green doesn't really work with this chart.

Your image

So why all this discussion about companies? Because promoting yourself, be it for a job, in a CV or in a personal website, is a similar process. One of the newer trends is called 'personal branding'.[4] The idea is that a brand or trademark labels you and sets you apart from others in your field. It identifies who you are and what you do. I'm not a big fan of the term but the idea is useful, and as astrologers we can employ the same process for individuals as we can for companies. Your horoscope is, after all, unique to you and reflects a very personal 'brand'.

Most clients don't know where to start with a website or a logo. Choosing a domain name is also really important for being found on the web. Even when writing a CV, this exercise is a good place to start. It definitely captures the main points.

The fact that this idea works is not surprising because it is a combination of where your heart lies and what you want (the Sun); how you put yourself across, your image and how others see you (the Ascendant); and where you are heading, your mission and reputation (the MC).

Let's try it

One of my clients has the Sun in Aquarius, Sagittarius rising and Scorpio on the MC. An example of a combination of keywords that fits her image could be: well researched (Scorpio) ideas (Aquarius) for international communication and marketing (Sagittarius). Her website is currently turquoise and blue, which is fine, and I suggested she add a bit of 'fire' to it.

Let's take another example of someone who is also a text writer. She does marketing and website work and is a Gemini Sun with Pisces rising and Sagittarius on the MC. Her homepage is image-based (Pisces), i.e. there is not a lot of text and it is very creative. It mentions copy (Gemini) and concept (Pisces). The website is in English, even though she works in the Netherlands, so the Sagittarius link is indirectly present. She also markets herself as a global brander and has many large international clients, so here the Sagittarius is clear, too.

And a last example: an astrologer and psychic reader with the Sun in Pisces, Libra rising and Cancer on the MC. One of the sentences he uses to explain what he does says, '…to mirror people on their way towards spiritual growth…' Certainly, Pisces shows the spiritual and Libra has 'mirror' qualities. Cancer can, of course, tune in well to people.

Using this technique can result in a summary of your personality, which I like to put on a CV. Here's part of one I helped make for someone looking for a new job. She has a Gemini Sun conjunct Venus (sometimes conjunctions need to be taken into account), with Aquarius rising and a Sagittarius MC. So here I suggested using these four archetypes, which are obvious in the following:

Objective

To express and further expand my talent for strategic web marketing and effective relationship development within a forward-looking, innovative organization. To identify and increase business opportunities on behalf of my employer.

Strengths and abilities

Good communicator, results-orientated problem-solver, fast learner. Team-builder. Functions well as relationship manager; efficient in liaison functions (internal and external groups). Strategic marketer, forward-looking and creative. Quick thinking, reliable and resourceful under stress.

I hope that the idea is clear and that you will try this out. All you have to do is compile a list of keywords for each sign and start putting them together. If you are looking to help with websites, then you might want to decide on which colours match which signs, images or text. The colours can be problematic as there are many views on this. However, together with the client you will usually arrive at something that suits. A Virgo site might need a lot of detailed information, whereas a Pisces one might need film or video. Libra might need art. Use your imagination, and combine the service that your client offers with the keywords and themes that belong to each sign.

It is good to look at what other companies and people have done with their websites, if you have their horoscopes. This will give you new ideas, as even though many sites are made without astrology, this technique often seems to fit, especially for companies. A service I offer is to improve CVs and websites for both companies and individuals, and this technique is definitely one I use to offer feedback. The philosophy behind this is that if you are putting out a message that is authentic to you, you will attract what you want to achieve in terms of work and reputation. And, in our case, clients.

My client's example

Jackie has Venus on the MC in Gemini, Virgo rising and the Sun in Aries. To remind you, here were my thoughts from the bio:

> Venus is prominently placed on the MC, which I see as representing goals and reputation. How does this work in Gemini? The writing is pretty obvious, but what has that given her in her career? When has she worked in a Gemini environment (10th house)? She mentions a couple of occasions in her bio. For me, Venus must be part of her reputation - but is it? How does she think she comes across? Can she see the Aries and how does she feel about that? For me, our image is a mix of Sun, Ascendant and MC. So can she see the Virgo part of herself? The service-orientated theme is again highlighted but how does she feel about that and how can we use it to promote her image?

Jackie has a lot of Neptunian energy and she is keen on making a website so I gave her the task of looking for images that might fit her. She loved this idea. Although she can write well, as you have seen, she is also very creative with images. It is good to identify the client's strengths and use them in this process. Each time you work with clients the VP will be made up of completely different things relevant to each person.

In this case we broke it up into what I called the Sun (her inside), the Ascendant (her front door) and somehow we ended up with her roof for the MC, to continue my house analogy, but she knew the MC represented goals, mission or reputation.

Here are her images:

I will be interested to see her website, as I think these images capture her quirkiness and humour and fit her well. I hope you can recognize the things I noted from the bio. Because she chose them they mean a lot to her, and to me they capture what is said in the horoscope. It was fun for both of us to work this way.

---

1. KLM started on 7 October 1919, in the Hague. I use midnight for company charts.
2. The data I have is 28 September 1894 in Manchester but there are several charts for M&S.
3. http://corporate.marksandspencer.com/aboutus/ourhistory November 2011.
4. http://en.wikipedia.org/wiki/Personal_branding   has   a   good description.

WHAT CAN I DO?

DISCOVERING TALENTS
AND WAYS TO MAKE MONEY
DEFINING COMMUNCATION SKILLS
WHAT CAN'T I DO? CLARIFYING BLOCKS

CHAPTER 7

DISCOVERING TALENTS
AND WAYS TO MAKE MONEY

*Hide not your talents. They for use were made. What's a
sundial in the shade?*

Benjamin Franklin

*One cannot consent to creep when one has an impulse to
soar.*

Helen Keller

It is my firm belief that if we truly love something, we will be good
at it. So this chapter adds to the strengths (which are also talents)
that you have already seen, as shown by the Sun in the chapter
on vocation. I am going to use Venus to define talents and ways
to make money. It can also operate as a stand-alone astrological
session, as long as you throw in a bit of Sun, too.

Why Venus?
I think Venus is a very underrated planet in this area. We use her, of
course, to look at relationships and I shall come back to her again
on the chapter about environment, when I'll be talking about ideal
colleagues. But here I want to take her as an indicator of what we
value, what we love and what we enjoy. Work should be *enjoyable*.
I often advise unhappy people or those in difficult situations to
go home and 'do more Venus'. I help them define what it is they
enjoy and attempt to persuade them to make an appointment with
themselves to do more of it.

So, if we could spend our time at work using Venus, instead of
having to fit her into our spare time, how happy would we be? We
are often talented in areas we enjoy, because if we allow ourselves
to indulge in these pleasures we will have had plenty of practice!
I like what Sue Tompkins says about Venus: 'When considering
your Venus, ask yourself what gives you pleasure, what makes you
excited and aroused, what makes it worth getting out of bed in

the morning?'[1] Wouldn't it be wonderful if the answer to this is your *work*? It would certainly be easier to get up! Well, maybe not aroused, although I love Barbara Marx Hubbard's term 'vocational arousal'. I think she is talking of the same principle – we get excited when we fall in love with our work.

So Venus' sign, house and aspects show our talents. We can use the same tables already set up for the signs and aspects, so I won't go through them all here. Simply change the word 'defending' in the headings in the Style chapter to 'enjoying': for Mars with Uranus I wrote *'defending* individuality', so here for Venus–Uranus it would be *'enjoying* individuality'. That's just a small example. Here are a few more real-life examples again to get you in the mood…

Examples of Venus as talents

A therapist doing bodywork with Venus conjunct Mercury in the 3rd House in Virgo trine the Moon.

She loves working with bodies. She is also curious about how people move, walk and carry themselves. Body language is one of her specialties and she enjoys analysing what posture may mean. It is a natural talent that she has – it's as if she can't help noticing how people use their bodies. The Moon shows through in her love of caring for people and making them feel comfortable. The downside of this is, of course, for herself (being too much of a caretaker), but on a CV or website, describing this quality has to be all positive!

An astrologer with Venus conjunct Mars in Aries in the 6th House in a T-square with Uranus and Chiron.

He loves astrology, of course (Uranus), and has a talent for defining the wounds that people might have (Chiron). He also enjoys taking the lead in groups and is a pioneer (Mars in Aries) in some of the astrological work he does (Aries, Mars and the 6th). He enjoys a good debate about his work (Aries, 6th), often taking the less conventional view (Uranus). Giving people insight (Uranus) is one of the things that brings him fulfilment.

A successful artist (mainly photography) with Venus in Aquarius in the 5th trine Saturn and Neptune, in sextile to Mercury and opposite Pluto.

It is often very easy to spot planetary aspects to Venus in someone's creations. Obviously, we are not going to spend time trying to create something we hate (hopefully not, anyway). In this case, the Neptune aspect shows her love of art, photography and images. Her art is very structural or often has only one subject on a black background – although it is not always obvious what the subject is. She loves the idea of nature as it decomposes and becomes very beautiful. So the Saturn and Neptune show their hands here. She has had many different relationships with men and women and, in her early creations, she has portrayed these people with herself in quite sexual photos. We see Pluto, Uranus and Aquarius at work here. She loves to hold soirées at her very eclectic house, mixing up buyers and artists, and she is very curious about life in general (Mercury).

I didn't have any handy examples of clients with Venus–Ceres but a good example is Jane Goodall (Venus quintile Ceres), who is considered to be the world's foremost expert on chimpanzees. In her life-long career in this area, she has worked tirelessly on animal welfare and conservation issues, receiving many honours for her environmental and humanitarian work.

Those are probably enough examples to get you thinking with your clients. Jupiter is missing from these examples but my client, Jackie, has this aspect, so you will see her example at the end of this chapter.

The quintile aspect

By now it is clear that I am a fan of aspects and, when it comes to talents, particularly the quintile (72°) and bi-quintile (144°). These aspects are linked to the number five. The circle divided by five gives 72°. If we mark these five points and join them, we get the five-pointed star or the pentagon. This has interesting symbolism, which I mentioned in the chapter on style. Some say the pentagon is visible in the well known Leonardo de Vinci drawing of Vitruvian Man, with head, arms and legs showing the 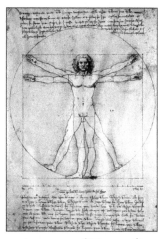 five points. Throughout the centuries, various qualities, often of a magical nature, have been attributed to the pentagon and the number five. Five has been associated with the apple (two pentagons when cut in half) – in itself a symbol of knowledge (Adam and Eve).

Because I use the Huber Age Point in my work, I have studied the number 72, which is the number of years Bruno Huber uses for one cycle of the horoscope.[2] In his view, this number is associated with the living universe, and I find this very intriguing. It may explain why I am attracted to quintiles. Huber also suggests, as do others, that it is the number of Man. In astrology, five is often thought to be assigned to Mercury (John Addey relates it to mind and to art, in the broadest sense of the word).[3] In the study of harmonics, in particular, five is attributed to 'the knowledge that gives us the power to shape and create our world'.[4] So you can see that it has a sort of human quality.

Personally, I am drawn to Robert Hand's summary: '...[these aspects] seem to grant the ability to turn creative inspiration into concrete end-products. They have long been noted as aspects of talent or even of genius, but more recent work suggests that these aspects do not in themselves grant the creative inspiration.'[5]

I believe that we can use quintiles and bi-quintiles to discuss talents with clients, bringing together the two planets in aspect. My own experience leads me to believe that, while these talents are definitely recognizable to clients, they don't appreciate them as being special. They might say 'Yes, I can do that', but they often think 'Can't everyone?' These seem to be innate abilities that we use automatically and that others can see in us more easily than we do ourselves.

Using quintiles and bi-quintiles

You can use these to start a discussion in the same way as you would with any other aspect, although you may have more convincing to do about whether to add these to the list of special talents that the client will compile. Sue Tompkins gives several examples in her book, *Aspects in Astrology*.[6] In books by other astrologers, there are two oft-quoted examples of well known people with several quintiles. One is Hitler, cited as a negative example, and the other is Mozart. With the orbs that I use, Hitler has three quintiles involving Neptune and two involving Saturn. Actually, these form a linked aspect pattern: Moon–Jupiter in Capricorn linked to Saturn in Leo and linked to Neptune–Pluto in Gemini. If you are using Chiron and Ceres, he has three more. A lot of quintiles! Hitler is a negative and dangerous figure in history, no argument there. But from his own point of view, and if I was making a CV for him, I would say that he must have been extremely talented to sway the masses in the way he did. That someone uses their talents to dire ends does not mean they are *not* talented. Imagine if he had used these gifts for beneficial ends.

Mozart was clearly very talented, too. We simply appreciate his end results more than we do Hitler's. He also has five quintiles between planets, and again another three with Chiron and Ceres. Having many quintiles seems to denote someone with numerous special talents. Many people have no quintiles at all. However, that doesn't mean they are untalented – it's a good job this is not the only way to find talent!

I find working with people, as opposed to simply looking at the charts of the famous, often gives a better idea of inner drives, so I offer you some examples I have come across in my practice.

A high-level management consultant with bi-quintiles to the Sun from Jupiter and Pluto

His work involves strategy and, often, some large change-management projects. He has a talent for seeing the big picture in management and dares to take control in very political organizations. He has transformed the way that many large organizations work, including government departments.

An astrologer with a Mercury–Uranus quintile

One of her talents, for which she is well known, is her excellent writing on many astrological subjects. She also collects and publishes articles from others, and is a tireless networker across the many astrological communities. She is a well known speaker.

One of my own examples

I have the Sun bi-quintile Saturn and I think this is one indication of what I am attempting with this book: to offer education about, and a structure for, astrological techniques. Astrology for me needs to be useful and lead to a result. In my teaching role, which I enjoy, I always try to offer concrete tools, which you can take away and apply.

I know many readers will not be using quintiles and may think, 'not more information!' But I urge you to investigate these interesting aspects with clients. I have found them extremely useful when working with vocation and, in particular, when helping clients with CVs or website text.

Venus, money and the 2nd House

When talking about money, I do in fact use one of the houses, which as you will have noticed has not, up until now, been my particular focus. The reason for this is that the 2nd House describes where we need to be secure. The sign on the cusp will describe the 'how' of security, and any planets in the 2nd House describe what makes us secure. Security for many people involves earning a crust somehow. The 2nd is an Earth house and associated with physical security, of which housing and food are often a part. Venus has always been associated with the 2nd House and the sign Taurus. I often need to explain the link between money and Venus (and relationships – but they are outside the scope of this book), as this is not immediately obvious to most people. Suffice it to say that a lot can be gleaned from looking at how we are with money and relating this to how we give and receive in relationships. But back to money... Money started as a convenient method of exchanging things. It became a common denominator. So if I want something from you that I *love* or *value*, I need to give you something that you value in return. There is an agreement between us.

This is the same in a job situation. You are offering something to your employer – you have something which is of value to him. He, on the other hand, must give you something in return, usually money. Venus is not always full of love and light. She was an excellent negotiator (showing perhaps her more Libran side) and was very grumpy if she didn't get what was promised! If we feel undervalued at work we may also act as Venus did when she felt crossed. So the 2nd House and its planets will show how we want to be recompensed. What is it that makes us feel secure? It isn't always money, of course. So although the 2nd House can represent other things, I use it in this context as an addition to talents (the 2nd can represent assets) but more to help answer the question: 'How can I make money or, perhaps, a living?' I have found it amazing how planets in the 2nd describe our work, so this is what I will focus on here. The signs on the cusp and within the house give good clues as to how money can be made, too.

Below is a list of examples of clients with planets in the 2nd House, aligned with jobs/talents. I have also noted the sign the planet is in. I have given a few general suggestions in italics, but there are many more ways that people can use these planets as talents. I am constantly in awe of how creative people can be with their charts. Of course, looking at charts of the famous can be useful, as what they do is hardly a secret. George W. Bush has Mars in the 2nd in Virgo – perhaps war was his talent... or how he made his money!

Table 6: Planets in the 2nd House

Planet in 2nd House	Job/Talents
Sun	Lecturer – Leo; politician – Capricorn; actress – Virgo *Earning by being in the spotlight or working with children*
Moon	Nurse – Pisces; author – Libra *Earning through caring, food, writing or by tuning in to needs*
Mercury	Writer for management strategy – Capricorn; career advisor – Libra; company owner who finds work for secretaries – Aries; author – Libra *Earning by communication, serving, assisting, networking*
Venus	Voice coach – Taurus; beautician – Cancer *Earning through art, voice, beauty, the earth or in relationship areas*
Mars	A fitness trainer for musicians – Taurus; mediation consultant – Scorpio *Earning through pioneering, encouraging, conflict, sport, defence*
Ceres	Doctor – Gemini; homeopath – Libra; ergonomics consultant – Sagittarius; architect – Virgo *My theory is that Ceres is connected with biology and cells, purity and also our physical environment, among other things*
Jupiter	Someone who works for Doctors without Borders (MSF) – Scorpio; drama teacher at an international school – Sagittarius (conjunct Neptune); politician – Sagittarius *Earning through politics, strategy, travels, cultures or discovering patterns*
Saturn	Teacher – Libra; ceramic artist – Virgo; several consultants – various *Earning through teaching, being an authority or expert, managing, making structures*
Uranus	Astrologer – Leo (a few astrologers but not as many as you might think!); management IT consultant – Leo *Earning through the weird, future-focused, freelance consultancy, technology or not yet invented*
Neptune	Film-maker, art historian – Libra; classical musician – Scorpio; Feng Shui consultant – Scorpio; hairdresser – Scorpio *Earning through the arts, design, creativity, concepts, the spiritual or healing*
Pluto	Therapist, the management consultant (above), researcher/speaker – all Leo; management coach – Libra *Earning through control, research, analysing, digging, psychology, secrets*

Talent session for my client Jackie

To remind you, here are the notes I made from her biography:

> My notes: What she loves is obvious to me from her bio. The question seems to be: why not at work? 'I get most of my stimulation outside of work.' I hear this a lot from clients. It is not that they don't know what they love. The problem is usually a block (or several!) that needs to be addressed in that session. But, in my experience, it is very important to confirm talents to clients. Venus, a major focus in this part of the VP, is right at the top of the chart, so this is an important planet for her. Some of the aspects to Venus repeat themes already covered (Venus square Mars, Venus opposite Neptune) and she has a Venus bi-quintile (which I see as a natural talent) with Uranus. However, she has two other Venus aspects as well, so I will address these in this session. Her 2nd House spans Libra and Scorpio, with Uranus featured again and in the sign of Scorpio. The two extra themes here are Venus trine Pluto, which I don't see at all in her working life, and Venus sextile Jupiter, which we could get more ideas about in this session to make the most of this theme.

On the opposite page is Jackie's chart again, showing Venus and her aspects, plus the 2nd House planets. Jackie also has a quintile between the Moon and Pluto (not depicted here), which we didn't cover in this session but would suggest a talent for intuitively knowing what lies underneath something. We covered this elsewhere. As is common in a horoscope, themes that are important are highlighted many times.

The session

Jackie recognized and was delighted by the strong Geminian theme. She could relate to the networking, the busy-ness, the writing and the storytelling that this can involve. She also saw how her siblings had played a strong role in this. In her work she deals with lots of pieces of information, which she enjoys. Considering the Pluto aspect, I suggested that she might like doing research using storytelling (narrative research, which I have used in my own research for my MA) and she loved the idea.

We discussed each aspect. Venus square Mars suggests Arian talents, which she has anyway due to her stellium in Aries. However,

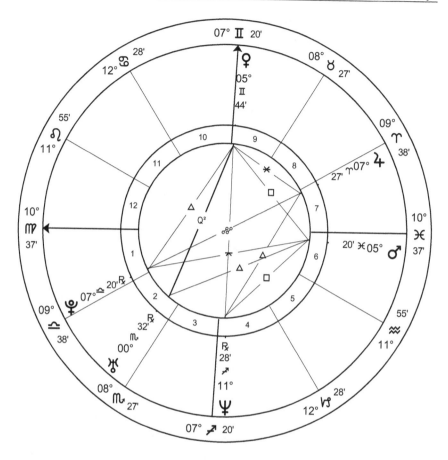

getting her to agree to these qualities being seen as talents was like pulling teeth. My aim when discussing talents in this way is to find something that can be illustrated on the CV using an example of work that has been done. In which jobs has she done pioneering work? Where did she have a challenge? Where has impatience been useful and moved things along? She recognized that she liked all these things but responded to my comment about 'being an initiator who never finishes things' (Mars) by saying, 'But where is that good?' Because I loved the astrological symbolism in the missile project, I asked about that. At the beginning she loved the challenge and the proto-typing phase – it was all 'cool and new. But it got boring.' Aries likes to start and then move on, I explained. So we discussed when that might have been a helpful quality in the past for projects and ideas. Her homework was to rewrite the experience in the missile project using Aries words. The idea behind this is that it emphasizes her strong Aries talents.

Because we had discussed Uranus already, and she has it strongly placed and in the 2nd House, I suggested that she use the work she had already done in the vocation session and add these ideas to her talents – emphasizing on her CV where she had demonstrated independence, technological knowledge or out-of-the-box thinking. Uranus in the 2nd House suggests she can earn money through Uranian pursuits, which she does at the moment, in information technology (IT). However, her real dream is to be much more quirky by having a one-woman show that wakes people up. I encouraged her to make a plan for this goal as, in my view, it really fits the chart. She loves change and anything new, and finally saw that when she feels at ease with her environment, she dares to let her impatience lead to action, which gets things going.

But Jackie has a huge block on all this creativity. This block concerns doing the right thing and being responsible. This theme, along with the fact that she separates fun from work, needs to be addressed in the blocks session. However, it doesn't mean that she doesn't possess these talents. When she is in her improvisation group, she can see all the things discussed so far working to her advantage. She can motivate and get people enthused. She can react quickly and be encouraging.

The new planets to her in this process were Jupiter and Pluto. Jupiter is visible in her bio: she has lived and worked in various countries. But I missed it in her CV. We spent quite some time discovering how the Venus–Jupiter talent manifests for her. She loves travel – yes, but so what? I suggested that it might make her comfortable in various company cultures and that she could adapt quickly. Was she good at strategy or vision? Discovering patterns or big-picture thinking? We had fun thinking up areas where she could use her skills. This session is often lots of fun – it is Venus, after all. More homework for her CV: to get some Jupiter words in there.

And last, but certainly not least, we tackled Pluto, which was noticeably absent from her bio and CV. Many people find Pluto qualities negative, and they can be. After all, who wants to be seen as bossy or manipulative? Are these talents? Well, yes, when you have worked on the negatives, they lead to a natural talent for leadership, for being in control. Venus–Pluto people have a talent for digging and delving, and are good detectives. We discovered that the combination of Venus and Pluto in her chart gives her the ability to analyse and read a situation (or people) very quickly. She can anticipate reactions and take appropriate action to achieve her goals. Although she doesn't like office politics, she is good at it. And she *loves* writing or doing stand-up comedy about taboo subjects. She revels in affecting and influencing people with her words (remember, Venus is in Gemini). And she loves to move people emotionally.

The talent session is great for working out which skills you have, and where you have used them and enjoyed them, both inside and outside work. You can use this as input for the list of what you have done on your CV, which is an area on which astrology can't really comment. However, by using appropriate words in each description, the real 'you' is highlighted.

So what did she make of it?

Her description

Talents

I am rooted in a long line of loud Kenyan matriarchs. These women love to spin a tale, argue with each other and gossip about everyone. They have bestowed these treats on me; curiosity and storytelling are in my DNA.

I am a human mainframe linking people with people, translating a culture's code to be understood by all, processing needs and providing solutions. I quickly pick up the essence of a situation or person, I have an immediate understanding of the big picture. This allows me to adapt easily to different environments and situations.

I often drill down to the heart of a problem. I will 'but why?' until I've struck gold. I mine for meaning until I'm satisfied. My senses are alert to what's really going on underneath. I am good at reading tone and playing detective on people's motives.

I jump into challenge and dig in, my enthusiasm propels me forward. I have a go-go-go spirit that stirs people up. My independence and initiative mean I can be trusted to spark my own fire and keep it burning. I am good at creation, at the beginning, at first light.

Communication is my life blood. I write lucidly, beautifully. I listen with deep intensity. I argue and entertain with imaginative creativity. I have a unique, funky, offbeat voice.

I've recently just declared: I will never have another standard office job, ever, again. Weird job descriptions have become more and more appealing to me. If I have to answer that question 'what do you do' over and over again, then I want to have a shocking unusual answer no one has heard of. Jobs with obscure titles make me run the other way. Jobs with frequent costume changes would make my day.

How to make money
Luckily for me, I can make money where my talents lie: communication, cultures and strategies. Writing seems to be the front-runner of the communications. My job title is funky, unique, individual, perhaps doesn't yet exist. Later on in life, my words may actually have the power to heal.

It is clear how this part of her profile gives a very good picture of what she loves to do and is good at – and it's all from an in-depth look at Venus, aspects to Venus and any 2nd House qualities.

Here are some books to use for this section (see the bibliography for further details):

The Inner Planets, Liz Greene and Howard Sasportas
Horoscope Symbols, Robert Hand
Money: How to Find it with Astrology, Lois Rodden
The Contemporary Astrologer's Handbook, Sue Tompkins

---

1. *The Contemporary Astrologer's Handbook*, Sue Tompkins, Flare Publications, 2006, p. 115.
2. For more information on this see *LifeClock*, Bruno and Louise Huber, HopeWell, 2006.
3. John Addey's *Harmonics in Astrology* (L N Fowler, 1976) is the main text you need if you are interested in harmonics.
4. *Working with Astrology: the Psychology of Harmonics, Mid-points and Astro*carto*graphy*, Mike Harding and Charles Harvey, Arkana, 1990, p. 184.
5. *Horoscope Symbols*, Robert Hand, Para Research, 1981, p. 133.
6. *Aspects in Astrology*, Sue Tompkins, Element Books, 1989, pp. 52–5.

CHAPTER 8
DEFINING COMMUNICATION SKILLS

There is nothing either good or bad but thinking makes it so.
William Shakespeare

Man can alter his life by altering his thinking.
William James, American psychologist
and philosopher

It will come as no surprise that in this chapter on communication skills I will be discussing Mercury and his aspects in the natal chart. The 3rd House is an area I will also touch on, just to keep you happy if you are a fan of houses!

However, first I want to discuss Mercury's function in general, as I consider it a vastly underrated planet in the horoscope. Yes, it's small; yes, it's near the Sun and sometimes gets overshadowed. But in times gone by, Mercury was given much more significance as a god than he gets nowadays. After all, 'In the beginning was the word.' I take this to mean that *thought creates*, hence the quotations at the beginning of this chapter. The current thinking in cutting-edge science, as I write, is going some way towards rectifying the theory of the importance of our thoughts. What is clear in many experiments, particularly in the quantum field, is that what we think has an effect on the outcome. I don't want to get too scientific, as the focus here is to define communication skills in terms of your working life. However, it is useful to realize that what we think, as well as what we believe (which will be covered in the chapter on norms and values), affects our professional lives. As well as indicating how we think, write and communicate (including listening), Mercury rules our opinions, which matter at work as well as everywhere else.

The whole point of this book is to help you and your clients to become more authentic – by first knowing who you are and what you could be capable of. Being able to communicate in a working environment is clearly vital if you want to achieve anything at all.

Hundreds of books and articles have provided suggestions about how to do this well. How to have influence, how to present, how to be 'naturally conversational'! I remember once on a sales course being taught to notice a picture on the wall of a sales prospect's office and make some comment about it – in order to get a conversation going about something that interests your potential client. Even at the time (many moons ago) I thought that was a bit far-fetched. And even having come across what initially appeared to be a good article online about authentic communication, it says that I must 'use short sentences, be honest and direct, be fun, tell personal stories and use I/me statements.' Another site presents a table to help us analyse which of the four types (a promising start, suggesting the four elements) we are dealing with and how to talk to them. But that article turned out to be a disappointment, too. And so it goes on. Good grief! What happened to being 'who you really are'? And I think we have all encountered the phenomenon of help desks or telesales workers and being asked scripted questions and offered 'learned behaviour' – it smacks of falseness.

Recently I communicated with someone who makes wonderful videos. If you are interested, have a look at Nic Askew's Soul Biographies online. I was taken by what he said – 'Authenticity is very seductive' – and he's right. Communicating in a way that is true to yourself and your nature is powerful. And everyone has authentic communication skills. We just have to dare to use them and/or analyse why we don't.

So what I will present here is how to analyse your ability to communicate, how that might have developed, and how you can make the most of it in order to benefit from your true skills. There are many ways to do this and, of course, I will be using dialogue again. I want to cover the following:

- Mercury and Sun signs
- Mercury retrograde
- Some ideas on the 3rd House
- Mercury aspects with reference to siblings

Mercury and Sun signs

As you will be aware, Mercury can only be in the same sign as the Sun, or in the sign before or after the Sun sign. We have looked at the Sun in terms of vocation, and it would seem easier to have Mercury in the same sign as the Sun if we wish to express what we want. Indeed, this is my experience. There is a dilemma if Mercury and the Sun are in different signs because, being one sign apart, it means that they reside in elements that aren't the best of friends: how you think is not in line with what you want. So the first thing to discuss with clients is how this works. Many people who have the Sun and Mercury in different signs find it helpful to know this, as they recognize the frustration it can cause. The one example that comes to mind is an Aries Sun with a Pisces Mercury. Here you have someone who really wants a challenge in life and wants to fight or defend, but can't always find the words to do so. How can they best communicate so they get what they want? Or consider the other side of this Mercury – Mercury in Pisces but with an Aquarius Sun. How can they get their fantastic, innovative ideas across? What they want is logical, but their communication skills don't work in this rational area. Or what of the deep and passionate Scorpio Sun that wants to transform the world but, with Mercury in Libra, has to communicate in a reasonable manner? How does this work for you or your client? There is a way to communicate but to my mind that means coming to terms with being able to express yourself in a manner that may feel alien to your Sun. Describing what this simple technique can mean to clients, and suggesting how they communicate in a way that fits Mercury's sign, is extremely helpful. The client often feels they have been 'given permission' to do this.

Mercury retrograde

In astrology books and on the web, much is made of the fact that communications go haywire whenever Mercury turns retrograde. There is often an underlying suggestion that retrograde Mercury (or any other retrograde planet) is difficult. I totally disagree with a negative view of this, as do many other astrologers. Robert Hand says, 'First, it is clear that in a natal chart, at least, retrogradation does not destroy a planet's influence or make it incapable of doing good… I also reject the idea that retrogradation weakens a planetary energy or makes it less capable of manifesting.'[1] The latest blog I read on the subject of Mercury being retrograde is one I particularly like. Dharmaruci: 'Mercury is the Mind, and when Mercury goes backwards, our attention collectively shifts inwards. For those three weeks we are not paying quite the full attention to the world out there that we usually do, so the world does not work quite so well, and my broadband slows down. It doesn't matter that I as an individual may be paying full attention, because the collective as a whole is not, it's a bit more reflective and inward than usual.'[2] I go along with this inward-focus theme, which is ideal for some things. And someone with Mercury retrograde in their natal chart has a different way of learning, thinking and communicating than someone who has it direct. How this works needs to be discussed with your client. However, the positive aspects of Mercury's sign, house and aspects will still be present when it is natally retrograde.

Some ideas on the 3rd House

The 3rd House has always been associated with communication, so it is definitely worth a look when defining communication skills. The way I look at it, planets in the 3rd will indicate the energies we want to express in the life areas of learning, writing, speaking and communication in general. You need to ascertain if these energies are being used positively or negatively. Howard Sasportas considers the 3rd House to describe the development phase of learning language and being able to name things, as well as being able to get around by crawling and learning to walk. Bruno Huber, on the other hand, relates it to the ages of 12–18 and puberty. To me, both observations are connected. We learn to talk, and later during puberty we learn what we think, what our opinions are and how to express them. You can learn a lot about communication styles by asking about the period of life between 12 and 18. Even if there are no planets in the 3rd House, you will get clues as to whether expressing things was easy or difficult, which sets patterns for your client's (working) life. If there is a planet in the 3rd, this will provide major clues as to how this planet is being used in the area of communication. Each planet in the 3rd House has the potential to become a specific type of *communication skill*. The 3rd House will also give information about siblings, which I will describe in the next section, so you can use the descriptions below for planets in the 3rd and ask appropriate questions about the clients' brothers and sisters.

I will first offer a couple of examples of planets in the 3rd House.

Someone with Mars in the 3rd may have experienced a lot of fighting, aggression or competition with siblings and/or later experienced peer pressure in puberty. This can result in a negative expression of Mars – someone who is a bully or an aggressive communicator. If you can uncover experiences during puberty that may explain why this is the case, you can turn the negative expression into a positive one: being brave and honest in speech, or pioneering when it comes to ideas and writing. These are skills that can be included on the CV.

Let's look at someone with Mercury in the 3rd, as I won't cover that with the aspects. How can Mercury be expressed in the area of learning, thinking, writing and communication? It may describe someone who is curious about learning and who brings that curiosity into later life. Perhaps it is someone who is witty. Taking the Virgo side of Mercury, it is someone who may be very precise about using the right term or getting the right spelling and punctuation, so that editing is a skill. Or someone who likes to have order – in their mind, at least. Taking Huber's idea, it would suggest that siblings are very important during puberty. So ask your client about that. Mercury is a networker, a linker and an agent. So in that role, a skill that people with Mercury in the 3rd may have learned early within the family is as a go-between for passing information – possibly between siblings. I know someone with this aspect who tries to convey her brother's viewpoint to their parents. This has developed into a skill of being able to understand both sides of an issue and to help in conveying facts to differing parties.

People with Mercury in the 3rd learn by reading the information available, or having the drive to find it, and even by being nosy. There is an aptitude here, too, for finding information and communicating it. They believe that expressing views is necessary and important. Generally, people with Mercury in the 3rd like to work in busy, communicative environments.

Mercury and aspects using siblings
Mercury also rules siblings, so discussing earlier relationships with brothers and sisters can provide clues to communication styles. It is my experience that, in general, people with Mercury and the Sun in the same sign have had easier relationships with siblings than those who have the planets in different signs. As Howard Sasportas writes of the 3rd House, 'Consultant astrologers will find it useful to question clients about early sibling relationships in the light of placements in the 3rd House... Patterns established with brothers and sisters early in life may repeat themselves with husbands, wives, **co-workers, bosses** and friends at a later stage of development.'[3] I agree, and I also include aspects to Mercury in my list of questions. Working on siblings has proved insightful and clarified many patterns for my clients, not only about communication.

Brian Clark's experience of Mercury retrograde, which he talks about in his excellent book, *The Sibling Constellation*, leads him to believe that a retrograde Mercury natally '...does correlate with an estrangement or loss of a relationship to a sibling, or simply an intense and powerful identification with a sib.'[4] My own experience is that these clients often feel that they don't belong in the family and so they withdraw from them. This sets a pattern for how they communicate with peers in later life. So one way to explore communication patterns and skills is to research Mercury's workings in terms of siblings. Brian's book also has some very useful material on birth order, which I don't want to cover here other than to mention one theory I have come across which seems to work. It concerns the roles taken in the family and suggests that Child 1 takes the role of hero or Sun archetype, Child 2 takes the outsider, black sheep, Uranus role (I have come across this one so often it is almost a rule!), and Child 3 takes on the lost child or Neptune role. You can glean information by asking your client about roles and birth order.

Not everyone has siblings, but some do have step-siblings and I include these in the discussion that follows, too. Even if we don't have siblings, we do seem to have an internal idea of what it is to have brothers or sisters. These relationships are interesting because they are really the only life-long relationship that we have. Siblings not only share our history but are also witness to it, which can be extremely important. The relationship we have is different from the one we have with our parents. We learn about gender and possibly sexuality from brothers and sisters, and about how to deal with our peers, including how to express our thoughts and opinions. Just like Hermes who was a guide for the dead – going from one world to another – older siblings often serve as guides for entering new life phases. It is strange, therefore, that so little is written about these relationships compared to patterns with parents. To me, they are just as important. You are probably familiar with the idea that girls marry their 'fathers' and boys their 'mothers'. Try asking whether your clients have married their siblings!

I have often given workshops on this theme and one exercise I give will serve well here. It will lead to ideas for communication skills that can be included in the VP. You can do this with your client and also for yourself.

The exercise
    1. Which aspects do I have that involve Mercury?
    2. Which brother or sister represents each aspect?
    3. How did/does this work positively and negatively? Then and now?
    4. How are these patterns repeated with my peers?
    5. What are my expectations concerning men and women (peers)?
    6. How can I express these qualities in a more positive way?

Step 1

This is clear – make a list of all the aspects involving Mercury. Also look at aspects which are 'out of sign' and, again, I urge you to try the aspects that I use (defined in Chapter 4) to see if they add anything.

Step 2

You will often find that each Mercury aspect you have will describe a sibling. This is a description of how you see them (or how you might if you had a sibling). It is interesting to note that a particular sibling will most likely have a set of different aspects to their own Mercury, which will show how they see you! I did some really deep work once with a brother and sister using only the fact that they had different Mercury aspects. They were gob-smacked – really, the only word I can use – to discover how they saw each other. Much healing resulted from these conversations, but that is somewhat off the subject here. Once, when I gave a lecture on this topic and asked the group who had planets in aspect to Mercury, an astrologer in the audience raised her hand for *all* of them. I assumed, since she is a good astrologer, that she could quickly see all of them applying in different combinations to different siblings, which can happen. But I had to ask. She had 13, if I remember rightly, and could place each of her Mercury aspects with a sibling! So before you embark on this exercise in a session with a client, it might pay to check on the number of siblings they have. You will, of course, need to help your clients to understand what a 'Uranian' brother or 'Neptunian' sister might be. It usually means listening to their answer when you ask 'What sort of relationship did you have with each sibling?' and finding the appropriate aspect.

Step 3

This involves discussing how the exercise worked. In the example above, the brother had Mercury–Pluto and saw his sister as bossy and dominating. He was also jealous of the attention she received from her father, whereas she, with her Mercury–Venus, saw the relationship with her brother as very fair, close and loving. OK, she had both Mercury and Venus in Pisces, too! The discussion needs to focus on how this relationship was while growing up and how it is now. Things can change. You are looking to find a description that fits each aspect. In this example, the Mercury–Pluto is described rather negatively, so you need to find out what the brother did about this. Did he keep quiet? Hide information?

Not tell her things? Or just quietly analyse what was going on? And how did Venus work for the sister? What did she learn? Did she share everything? Tell him everything? Try to get feedback? Be overly charming? Once you have an idea of each aspect, you can go on to the next step.

Step 4

This step sees if the patterns picked up in childhood are repeated today at work with peers. What happens unconsciously is that we draw conclusions about our peers based on our early experiences. The brother above is drawing conclusions about women of his age from his sister. His experience is that they may be controlling and dominant – as was his first wife! He didn't speak up with his sister and take control, feeling it was of little use, so he tended to repeat this pattern with women – his first wife among them. When there are no brothers, it is often easier to have better relationships with men, as that is a blank slate. And vice versa – it will often be easier for people with no sisters to have less complicated relationships with women. How does your client get on with men and women in the workplace? Is there a difference? The sister from my example above has harmonious relationships with both sexes.

Step 5 and Step 6

I will combine these, as I want to give examples to start you off on finding possible communication talents for each aspect. The descriptions are offered to help you discuss ideas with your clients.

Mercury in aspect to the Sun

One of my findings about people with this aspect is that a sibling can either act as a parent or authority figure, or just the opposite – as the child of a sibling. There can also be a very close relationship or an element of hero-worship. It can be a good and grown-up relationship but, as with Mercury and Apollo in mythology, there can also be competition for the limelight. The lesson learned here from a sibling is in getting attention for your own thoughts and opinions. The conclusion about communicating will depend on how well this worked. If your sibling was always in the limelight because of their thoughts and ideas, then what needs to be learned is to appreciate – and get attention for – your own opinions.

The potential skill here is to be a good presenter, or someone whose ideas are really seen and recognized.

Mercury in aspect to the Moon
In a similar way to the Sun, people with this aspect sometimes act as either a mother to a sibling, or as a child of a sibling. There is an emotional closeness and an expectation of either having to listen and look after peers, especially people of the same sex as the mother/child sibling, or an expectation of being heard on an emotional level. With this aspect, you will expect a closeness with peers and have probably learned how to talk about your emotions. The more negative side of this is that you have learned that you should always be careful about what you say as it might hurt someone, which can often lead to not expressing things.

The skill here is an ability to hear what is really going on. To read the emotion in a situation or a group – to express feeling. But first you have to learn to listen to your own feelings and express them, and to limit your caretaking of others.

Mercury in aspect to Venus
This sounds as if it should be a loving relationship with a sibling – and it often is. Siblings with this aspect often value their brother or sister. But this can also be a difficult aspect and I have seen it in incest cases where the brother or sister is a lover. This can be very confusing as it is seems to be easier to experience something as being wrong if it is unpleasant. With this aspect, you learn how to communicate charmingly, but this can be too sweet. It can be an experience of having a sister who never fights, leading to an expectation that women never stick up for themselves. The lesson learned is either that you should be nice all the time and everything in a discussion should be fair, or that everything requires negotiation. The downside seems to be that there is often some comparison with a sibling and, in the case of a Uranian person for example, this can prove very difficult. It can lead to a feeling of always being compared to others (and maybe not measuring up) in the workplace.

The skill here is someone who is good at negotiation, someone who can see both sides. Someone who can create peace, perhaps in a customer complaints department, or someone who can listen to all sides of an argument. Firstly, however, you need to learn to value your own thoughts and ideas.

Mercury in aspect to Mars
This one often shows up as competition with a sibling. If you always fought with your brother, then you will expect to have to argue with men at work. I have seen competition being created in

families over a sibling who has died – or even with an aborted or a miscarried child. The mother who always talks about a lost child can create a feeling of competition (and therefore anger) in her other children. This is very difficult. It is easier to be in competition with a living sibling – at least that way you can fight with them. The negative results of this aspect can be aggression or sexual problems. Sometimes you learn that the only way to communicate or to be heard is by shouting.

But on the positive side the potential is to be able to express pioneering ideas, to be enthusiastic and competitive in a good way with communication, having learned how to stick up for your ideas and views in your youth when arguing with a sibling. The expectation is that you might need to fight to be heard, but if you can see where the pattern came from, you can turn this into the skill of being an excellent debater or the defender of an idea or group of people – a fighter for a cause.

Mercury in aspect to Ceres

I haven't had many examples of this, as I have not been working with Ceres for very long. So the following are my ideas based on what I have seen in other areas. My suggestion is that you look at the areas I have already mentioned for Ceres, such as older women – so perhaps an older sister who was a member of the women's liberation movement or who fought for the environment; perhaps a sibling who loves the land; a sibling who helped you with rites of passage such as puberty or marriage; or a sibling who is interested in the cycle of life and death. I have this aspect and I do have a much older sister who is fascinated by the cycle of life and death and all the philosophy associated with these themes. I learned a lot about life from her, as she was so much older. When I was very young, I witnessed her becoming the mother of twins and all that this involved. She went on to have several more children, so I saw the mother–daughter relationships from a very close perspective. I also think that Ceres is connected with purity and I learned a lot about the purity of food from my sister, too. You need to explore this aspect for yourself if you are using Ceres, but hopefully this will get you started.

The skills with this aspect may be as an expert in the areas above, although Ceres does have a reputation for being very stubborn in her communication which, I hate to admit, I also recognize.

Mercury in aspect to Jupiter

Taking the general themes of Jupiter, we might expect to see sisters who have a vision or brothers who are philosophers. Siblings may have attended church services together or religion may have been important in other ways. Even as children we can experience these energies. But more often this aspect is experienced as a sibling who formed judgements about you. This aspect can make you judgemental yourself, too. If you had a brother who was great at strategies, you might expect men to lay out an approach to a project. If you had an enterprising sister, you might expect women to be entrepreneurs.

If you can own this aspect for yourself, then your communication skills can lie in these areas. You can understand and communicate the big picture. You can think up great strategies, or describe a new philosophy at work. You might be skilled at understanding the cultures of different countries or companies. This can give a natural teaching ability, but more in the style of a university lecturer where big ideas rather than information are presented, as long as you accept that others are no wiser than you. Jupiter siblings can tend to pontificate or play God, so the lesson is to embrace your own philosophy.

Mercury in aspect to Saturn

Saturn, as the ruler of time, often seems to produce much younger or much older siblings. In my experience, this is an aspect often seen where there are no siblings. The result of either of these scenarios is that you learn to communicate as an adult. So the expectation is that communication might need to be sensible and grown-up. There can be a serious side to this. This is the child who learns to be seen and not heard, to either speak seriously when asked, or not at all. There are rules about speaking. Naturally, there is a plus side to this: the skill of having the discipline to listen and read in a very focused way. Responsibility, another of Saturn's words, can also show up here as one sibling being responsible for another, which can lead to taking responsibility for peers. It depends what sort of conclusions the client came to about this early experience. Negatively, it can lead to being afraid to speak for fear of being overridden or of getting the blame for your opinions. Or believing that the way you think or talk is not good enough. Your accent might be wrong or you are just too slow. Or, on the other side of the coin, you can be too authoritative and harsh.

However, this aspect gives skills in planning and structuring. This can eventually lead you to becoming a communication expert or an authority on a particular subject – provided that your blocks are worked on. You need to take your ideas and opinions seriously, then you can structure them well in writing or speaking.

Mercury in aspect to Chiron
There can be a deep wound here associated with a sibling. I have seen it in those who have been exiled from the family, or subjected to rejection or name-calling by a sibling. I have also seen it in the case of adopted or step-children. There is often a feeling that 'I don't belong'. As with Neptune, I have also encountered this aspect in the case of someone who loved her handicapped sister but this sister got all the attention. It has an element of the Saturn 'I'm not good enough' quality to it.

The positive side is *healing with words*. This is someone who has insight into pain, who can help break through blocks and, maybe like Chiron, knows about what we would now call alternative or complementary forms of medicine.

Mercury in aspect to Uranus
Either you or a sibling is different in some way – the rebel in the family. There are often breaks with a sibling and usually the conclusion is that your ideas don't fit, or there is a crazy sibling somewhere in the family who had to leave. Conclusion = out-of-the-box thinking leads to being ousted. Or this can work in having a genius sibling that you can never measure up to, so you feel stupid. You may even have a sibling who has told you this. Either way, something made you detach from the family – the expectation might be that close contact with people is not possible. You are either too weird or too smart, and everyone else is boring. There can be a coldness in family communications.

However, if your unique and crazy ideas were supported early on, the gift here is one of independent thinking – someone who has innovative ideas. The example sister might be one who did her own thing, so you see that it is possible to be independent of the family. However, her independence may have meant you needed to stay at home – so there might be a dilemma here. The expectation is that no one will understand you but, if you can appreciate your own unique ideas, you can use your unusual and surprising communication skills to wake people up and create awareness.

Mercury in aspect to Neptune
In our society this aspect seems to be experienced as difficult. Maybe this is only true for the people that I attract but I think, like

all aspects, Mercury–Neptune produces skills. However, these are not often valued in a left-brained society. As far as siblings are concerned, I have seen various ways of it working. There can be a longing for a brother or sister and never getting one – so as a child you create an imaginary one. There can be disappointment, a loss of a sibling in some way. A death, a miscarriage or a medical problem. Somehow there can be guilt associated with this aspect, knowing that you should care for a sibling who is handicapped and not living up to expectations. The message is that either people let you down, which could come from being too idealistic, or that you need to listen to everyone and look after them. Your communication needs are 'unimportant', or you worship a sibling, or are deceived by one. There can also be addiction in the family, leading to the attention being drawn away from you. The strategy for much of this is to disappear into a fantasy world, so one skill here in later life is a vivid imagination. If you have had a brother who can't speak, you learn to communicate in non-verbal ways. Intuition can be very strong. But mostly this aspect results in communication that feels like no contact at all. There is a mismatch. So going inwards and not trying to communicate might feel easier. Or there can be an addiction to communicating, trying to make contact through writing or speaking too much, which can result in having no borders and boundaries as to what might be appropriate to tell. There could be a victim-like sense that 'no one appreciates my ideas', resulting in an inability to communicate.

However, the skills here are many, if they are appreciated: imagination, conceptual thinking, communicating with images, an artistic skill; someone who can communicate with people who can't speak, or with children or animals. The intuitive or spiritual thinker.

Mercury in aspect to Pluto
Bullying is not unheard of with this aspect. Either you or your sibling had the power. It can produce verbal abuse. I had one client who described this aspect as a sister who messed with her mind. So much so that she lost all trust in others, particularly women, and eventually in her own ideas. There is some form of behaviour where privacy is not respected, such as a sister who reads your diary. This makes you very wary and careful about sharing anything. You come to a conclusion that analysing everything that might happen gives at least some sort of control. There may be things you don't talk about, and I have seen this in the case of the death of a sibling, where the death and loss were never discussed. It is also possible to

be jealous of a dead sibling, as they are often held up to be perfect, which can give a feeling of utter powerlessness. What you learn is to keep things private or not to talk, so the skill here is that you can be trusted with a secret because you have learned how painful it is when a secret has been made public.

On the positive side, you have seen from a sibling how powerful ideas can be. The brother as a politician or someone who can sway the masses. These skills are yours for the taking. And being a natural analyst or psychologist is a skill, too. You can hear the underlying story in any situation, having had to be alert all your life. My example client described this aspect as 'don't tell tales out of school'. If you have had a very deep bond with a sibling, then you will be comfortable with a deep relationship later in life – but expecting this at work could cause problems. However, passion at work needs to be the order of the day. The skills are powerful communication, insightful analysis and the ability to convince if communication is done openly and not through manipulation.

Mercury unaspected

If you use all the aspects that I do, you will rarely encounter an unaspected planet. However, when I have seen an unaspected Mercury, it was in the case of someone who had no siblings. I'm unsure as to what skills this might produce. In this case, I would simply use the house and sign of Mercury, and the 3rd House, to define skills.

Jackie's example

Since we had already focused a lot on Mercury because of his position and importance in her horoscope, Jackie and I didn't have a separate session on communication skills. She has no planets in the 3rd House, but Gemini featured prominently in some sessions. We did talk about her brother and sister and looked at sibling patterns in the course of the whole process. This is a reminder that each client will need a tailor-made programme for this work when doing more than one session.

Curiosity, one of Mercury's themes, is very helpful in the creation of a VP. Defining how you communicate as an astrologer will give you ideas as to how you want to work with clients. After all, your main services will always involve talking or writing. So, these aspects may also define your services, such as offering conflict resolution if you have Mars in the 3rd House or Mercury–Mars, or offering insight if Uranus is involved. So I hope you now have enough examples to set you working on communication skills with your clients. You may stumble across blocks on the way, which should be noted, but remember the objective is to help your client to define their own communication strengths.

Here are some books to use for this section (see the bibliography for further details):

The Sibling Constellation, Brian Clark
The Inner Planets, Liz Greene and Howard Sasportas
Horoscope Symbols, Robert Hand
The Contemporary Astrologer's Handbook, Sue Tompkins

Non-astrology books:

Gods in Everyman – A New Psychology of Men's Lives and Loves, Jean Shinoda Bolen
Homecoming – Reclaiming and Championing Your Inner Child, John Bradshaw

---

1. *Horoscope Symbols*, Robert Hand, Para Research, 1981, p. 42.
2. *Blog Astrotabletalk*, Dharmaruci, 'Why things go wrong under Mercury Retrograde', 30 August 2011.
3. *The Twelve Houses*, Howard Sasportas, The Aquarian Press, 1985, p. 51 (my bold emphasis).
4. *The Sibling Constellation*, Brian Clark, Arkana, 1999, p. 45.

CHAPTER 9

WHAT CAN'T I DO? CLARIFYING BLOCKS

It takes courage to grow up and become who you really are.
e e cummings

Don't compromise yourself. You're all you've got.
Janis Joplin

I will start this section by repeating what I said earlier. The aim with a VP is to define blocks, *not to work on them*. Defining them means they are clear and can be addressed later by you (if you have the skills) or by a therapist, who ideally is someone you respect and can recommend. Stumbling blocks and heavier issues are usually very clear from the bio, as was the case for my client, Jackie. I also noted that we would not cover relationship issues in any depth here, as the goal of the sessions is to get to a vocational profile. The blocks are covered with regards to what is holding someone back at work, but of course there will be an overlap with any parental or relationship issues mentioned in the bio. This is the biggest chapter in the book, which I feel is warranted due to the fact that most people who visit astrologers about career concerns are really experiencing some kind of block.

The purpose of defining blocks in this process is to make the client aware of what might be holding them back. Many people think they can't do a job which would, in fact, suit them admirably and would make them very happy. They give excuses, such as 'I'm too old'; 'I haven't had the training'; 'I wouldn't be any good at it', 'How can you make money doing that?'; or 'My family thinks art isn't a real job,' etc. I like to make it clear that if a job suits someone (and usually they will like the idea of it if it does), they should work on the blocks so that they can pursue that path. My experience is that these issues stop most people following their true calling. And it isn't that they don't know what they would like to do. In many cases, it has just been 'persuaded' out of them! They have reached a conclusion that they can't do what they would really enjoy.

There are many ways we can look at the horoscope to see how blocks work. I offer you my tools and again encourage you to use your own. I also advise you to find a practitioner (or, better yet, several) that you have tried yourself, to whom you can refer clients for this part of the process, as you can open a whole 'can of worms' by working in this area. Astrologers doing this work should invest in some basic counselling training. Learning listening skills and becoming aware of body-language are vital skills for any astrologer, in particular when working with dialogue. Knowing how to react to different client reactions has made me feel more secure when doing these sessions.

So where to start?

My first tool is what I call 'too much of a good thing'. Career counsellors and many others use a great exercise for this and it works well in conjunction with astrology. Daniel Ofman's Core Quadrant® Theory was developed in Holland and he wrote a book[1] about it which is now used as a personnel development (Human Resources) tool in many companies worldwide. There is a lot of information about it on the web. However, I will describe it briefly here, as it fits well with my 'too much of a good thing' idea. Firstly, here's what Ofman says about core qualities in his book: 'Core qualities are attributes that form part of a person's essence (core); people are steeped in these qualities, which place all their – more or less striking – competences in a certain light. A person is "coloured" by his or her core qualities. It is their strong point, the characteristic that immediately comes to mind when we think of this person. Examples of core qualities are determination, consideration (for others), precision, courage, receptivity, orderliness, empathy, flexibility, etc.'[2]

While working on the vocation part of the VP, you will probably have come across these qualities already. Frequently, the block is the shadow side of a quality that is the client's strength.

Ofman, again – an example of the quadrant model:

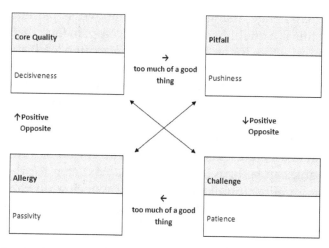

The idea is that you take a blank sheet showing the four quadrants and start by filling in one of them. Please note you can also use this model to find a core quality that you might want to include in a CV, as well as to define a block. This is an exercise that you can do with your client or give to them as homework.

Many find it easier to start with the 'Allergy' corner. So in this case you would ask your client, 'What annoys you the most about people at work?' In this example, your client may have said: people who don't act, ones who just sit there. This is an 'allergy' and you can already see how this might fit with a sign such as Aries, which is not keen on passivity (the answer given here). You then head to another quadrant by asking, 'But what would you get if people just took the initiative (i.e. acted) all the time?' This is the 'pitfall' of this core quality – in the case of Aries it might indeed be pushiness. Then we look for the good side of passivity to get the 'Challenge' quadrant. In this example the answer given is 'patience', which can be seen as passivity – if there is too much of it.

The idea of all this (and it works well in practice in getting the client to understand one of their core qualities) is to show that your allergy can also highlight a block (Pitfall) which is often the 'too much of a good thing' block. The four quadrants are linked. I hope you can see how to help your clients with defining possible blocks by knowing the zodiac signs. Almost anything they come up with, which can be matched to a sign (as either a core quality – i.e. what they think they are good at – or an allergy) can lead to a possible block. And approaching the model from any corner may help to define a talent.

My client Jackie does indeed have a lot of Aries energy. I didn't do this exercise with her but her example might have been similar to this. Her challenge, using the example above, is patience but I don't think this is a quality she needs to develop; in fact, that would be counterproductive for an Aries. Impatience often leads to action, which could have been a word used for an Aries in this model. The idea is to help the client come up with a few of these quadrants (one for each quality) in their own words because that enables you to define their blocks. Aries pitfalls or blocks might be pushiness, anger, impatience or aggression, etc. These qualities, if shown at work, can act as blocks, since they might not be helpful in the workplace and can be heavily judged. The next step for the client is to get the quality/pitfall in balance by working on the issues that cause them to be revealed. As astrologers we don't necessarily have the skills to do this but we can offer insight into patterns and possible causes. Astrology is a mental discipline that can provide understanding and insight, but to really work with blocks you may need to do therapeutic bodywork or emotional work. What you can do is help your client to define the block, and you may be able to give tips from the horoscope on types of therapy that might work too.

To make it slightly clearer here are a couple of examples of 'too much of a good thing' blocks:

An Aries/Mars block might be getting annoyed at everything. A Gemini/Mercury block might be talking too much. A Scorpio/Pluto block might result in being dominating or bossy. Sagittarius/Jupiter people might be too judgemental.

I'm sure you get the idea. You can spot it if your client sometimes goes too far with their qualities.

This is just an example of one factor – the sign or one planet – but of course that's often too simple in practice. I tend to use this idea more when I see a planetary aspect is working negatively, such as for my case-study client. Jackie's Sun–Uranus shows up as her sense of abandonment or of being painfully different. If she is too Uranian, she is not part of the group, so she blocks her Uranus and opts for being the good student. But her Uranus needs to be expressed. She could rebel in an over-the-top way – that would be a 'too much' block, which would cause problems. Instead, she doesn't express her quirkiness at all. This is where we can help her to see the potential in Sun–Uranus. She wants to be different and quirky but in a good way. In her life, this has been associated with pain. She had no role models in her youth to provide inspiration on how to do this. How can she be a bit crazy and still belong? The idea here is to give tips on how it may be possible, perhaps with therapy, to turn an aspect around and use it positively. All planets can cause blocks. However, in the next section, I will discuss those that are the main suspects.

My other tools for defining blocks

I will describe three here which I use regularly:

- Saturn and his aspects
- Chiron and his aspects
- The 12th House

There is a fourth tool that I use in conjunction with looking for blocks in order to find patterns and how they may have started. It is the Huber Age Point (or Life Clock) method. This one is not so cut and dried, but I will give you some examples in combination with Saturn, although I use the Age Point for all the planets. If you want to work with this method I refer you to the Hubers' book[3] and *The Cosmic Egg Timer*.[4] I am a huge fan of using this method for analysis, and plan to write more on it in the future. Using it and asking questions of my clients has taught me more about how each planet works for individuals than any other method.

Saturn and his aspects

Saturn is often said to be an indicator of profession. Personally, I have never found this to work very well. By sign and house, he does describe where our goals might lie, but more often I feel he represents fears that can cause stumbling blocks in life and, particularly, in our work. However, I do feel that whatever Saturn touches by aspect has the *potential for expertise*. Saturn gets very bad press from many astrologers, and I think we need to stop that! I am writing this as Pluto goes through Capricorn, Saturn's sign. To my mind, this means we are being offered an opportunity to raise the level of consciousness and transform it in at least one area of Saturn's domain: responsibility. To turn a Saturnian block around, we need to take responsibility for our Achilles heel, for our fears and our insecurities. These are all descriptions of his type of blocks. We prevent ourselves from reaching our potential by being afraid, by not feeling good enough about ourselves, or by not daring to try things. And we have that other Saturnian tool ready to provide an explanation: blame. It's our boss, or our parents, or our partner or 'the system' that has caused the problem and stops development. No, it isn't. It may well have been once, but it doesn't have to stay that way. However, that doesn't mean this situation is easy to fix. All of these external factors can cause pain and we dare not get out of some situations, fearing something worse. A Saturn block is caused by giving away our own authority; we fit in with others' rules and demands – and not without reason. At some point in life this has been a safer method than the alternative.

To deal with a Saturn block we need to develop and live by our own set of rules and goals. Let's face it – most of us need help to do this. It should be easier to produce a positive Saturn as we get older but that takes some work, particularly if there is heavy wounding in youth. Saturn problems in childhood will be such things as heavy discipline, strict regimes, too much emphasis on reaching a particular goal – such as in my client's case: 'You will be the engineer.' Parents, being afraid themselves, are often more authoritarian than they imagine. They want their children to do well and achieve 'the good job'. And this is all very understandable. But it can cause problems for their children later in life.

When I was doing the Inner Child Therapy training, the model used was as follows.

Something happens – an event. The next step is that you come to a conclusion about yourself (however young you may be – even in the womb), and so you then develop a strategy to deal with it, mostly to avoid feeling the physical or emotional pain. The reward system in childhood may even trigger a Saturn-flavoured complex: we don't do our homework, we get punished, we do it and we get an ice cream, movie, or are excused from doing the washing-up. The conclusion about this could be: *I get a reward when I do what I'm told. I get love if I am good.* The strategy might then be: *I'll do everything I am told.* The good child ends up being the good adult. This is killing for a Uranian child and for many others. It creates a block on having your *own* goals or rules. The Inner Child therapy model that I studied and use suggests that, although you can't change what happened to you, you can change both the conclusion about yourself and the strategy you developed – as long as you know what these are. As I mentioned already, astrology, being a mental discipline, can give insight by explaining why we have a certain pattern.

The astrology – Saturn's aspects

It is not necessarily the case that when Saturn aspects a planet in the horoscope it results in something negative. It depends on the consciousness of the individual and, also, Saturn has many good sides to him. As in the example above of 'too much of a good thing', Saturn can produce too much of a bad thing. Like every planet, he has two sides. What we aim to do when defining Saturn issues is to give clients hope and show them that Saturn also has another way of working. How could Saturn work positively? What are the opportunities in the chart for discipline, expertise, teaching, giving something form, etc.?

But first you need to gauge how Saturn is working. It can be vastly different for each client. Because this is an area that needs some explanation, I will go into it more deeply than the previous chapters. Blocks are one of the main reasons that clients come to astrologers, having got stuck in their careers or having arrived at some crossroads where they must make a decision. They often see it as a problem of not knowing what their passion is, but in my experience many people do know, they just don't know how to get there. I recommend you read about Saturn and get to know him thoroughly. An in-depth book I recommend is Liz Greene's *Saturn: A New Look at an Old Devil*.[5] However, there are many other good astrologers who have written on all the planets. As an astrologer, you need to have done you own work on your own Saturn so you are not being too authoritative or prescriptive with clients yourself.

I use the same aspects here as I have done previously. Sue Tompkins' book on aspects[6] is a good source of ideas for how these planetary combinations might work. Below are examples of possible themes that you need to discuss with your client to find out how each aspect works for them. Of course, Saturn's sign and house placement will also give clues as to where fears, insecurities, over-responsibilities and blocks might lie. I have not included Ceres, as I feel I haven't yet worked with her enough at an individual level to give good examples. I have tried to explain how and where an issue might have originated, as this often provides insight. I also give ideas for the potential of each theme; possibilities to turn an aspect that is working negatively into a positive expression. Being afraid of something and then spending time learning about it is a way of turning Saturn's impact around. In the process you may become an expert or even teach it.

So let's look at Saturn in aspect to each planet.

Saturn in aspect to the Sun

This can create a problem often 'caused' by a very authoritative parent, probably the father. A fear of going for what you want can manifest as indecisiveness about who you are. It may be safer not to have a goal than to have it taken away somehow. This is a child who has responsibility thrust upon them at an early age. So another issue resulting from this placement can be a very serious or overly responsible attitude. Or a perfectionist – being everything you think you should be. Not feeling good about yourself or feeling that you never have enough qualifications, but at the same time working very hard to gain them. Feeling inadequate about who you are, you become your own harshest critic. Whatever you do is never good enough. You may be generally insecure or fearful about life, having to do or be what authority figures dictate, and frightened to be who you really are or to accept any attention. When you have been in the spotlight in childhood, it might have resulted in punishment, so it may be better to stay out of the limelight. Better to work than to play – that way you can't be blamed. Having a fear of failure is common.

Sun–Saturn children are often not appreciated or even wanted by their father, so a child develops a strategy of pleasing him to gain love. Or they are too desired and have to be extensions of the father, following in his shoes. But Saturn as the ruler of time often doesn't allow the father to spend time with his child on the child's terms. This can manifest later as a grown up who is always trying to please the boss or an authority figure, but never feels that they deserve his time or attention.

Possible conclusions
It's my fault; I'll never amount to much; I'm no good; I have to work hard; I have to do everything the boss says; I always have to be on time; I should…

Potential of Sun–Saturn
This was covered in the Vocation chapter (starting page 49). If you can help your client turn this aspect around, there is the potential to be an expert on something. When a Sun–Saturn person steps into their *own* goals and takes responsibility for who they are, great things can be achieved. There is ambition here, and the goal-orientedness and the determination they possess can lead to success. Being a good teacher, offering structure, being a good manager, being disciplined and reaching a desired goal (slowly but surely) are all possible outcomes. I advise clients to take control of their own diaries and make appointments with themselves to do the things they want to do – to find time for themselves that, barring emergencies, is set in stone and cannot be changed. With this aspect, you have to give *yourself* time.

Saturn in aspect to the Moon
This can manifest as emotional coldness. It can be caused by experiencing a parent, probably the mother, as being cold or

distant – or by having a fearful parent who didn't know how to be a mother. On a material level, the mother has probably been dutiful; however, there is some block on expressing feelings. Often this comes from a pushy mother who imposes her goals on you, as in Jackie's case. For some reason you have been made to feel inadequate and over-responsible for the care of others. However, what can remain is a feeling of being unwanted or insecurity about being needed in a job. You might have been brought up with a lack of nurturing so are not used to being looked after at work. You might put up with a very harsh environment and not ask for what you need in order to feel comfortable. Any reward might have been given for being a disciplined child who didn't waste mother's time. The pat on the back, marginal as it might have been, was for hard work or good grades at school, or for something that the mother loved and wanted to do herself, but for which she was never given the opportunity.

There can be a sense of taking the blame for everything here, too. There is a need for structure and rules – that way you can't make a mistake for which you might be blamed or punished. Anxiety is a common experience. In her bio, my client Jackie puts this well – 'a lonely and quiet sadness' – and in other ways, which I have repeated below. She also had that common complaint: her mother had little time for the family, because of being a single parent, studying and working full-time.

Possible conclusions
If I work all the time I don't need to feel; it's my fault if others aren't feeling OK; I need to please everyone; I'll never get an interview – no one will want me; it's a hard cold world; I don't deserve a good job; other people are more important; there's no sentiment in business; I'm not good enough to land a comfortable position; I should…

Potential of Moon–Saturn
Turning this aspect into a positive factor, at home and at work, means you have to take responsibility for your own feelings – to own your anger, fear or happiness, and act accordingly to get your needs met. Working well, this aspect offers reliability, adult emotions and having a job where some responsibility is emotionally fulfilling. A management position can be fine, as you may have learned how to run things early on. Looking after children, the sick or the elderly can be very rewarding. This can be the signature of a very sensible and practical person who

gets the job done. The learning challenge is to not be too strict with others and particularly with yourself, and not to bury your feelings.

Saturn in aspect to Mercury

Not daring to speak up is a common block with this aspect. In Mercury's guise as ruler of siblings, this could be a result of experiencing difficult relationships with a particular brother or sister (or all of them). Older siblings sometimes don't listen to or take younger ones seriously. This can result in you not being able to communicate, not daring to, or talking too much. On the other hand, this can give an authoritarian personality, which may have come from having too much responsibility for your siblings. Perhaps the environment in which you were brought up meant there were rules about speaking. I have often seen this in people who have been made fun of as children, where their ideas were cause for hilarity or their mistakes in speech were the object of teasing or ridicule. You may either expect your word to be law – although underneath you may doubt if it is – or you may think your opinion is worthless so there is no point in communicating. It can also show someone who is very careful or shy about talking. In the 'too much of a bad thing' mode, a very cold, hard personality can be the result. The fear here is about feeling stupid at school or at work, or in not being understood, heard or listened to. You can also be sensitive about being teased for something you have said. The block here can be one of not daring to be curious or ask questions at work for fear of being seen as unintelligent. It is far safer to follow someone else's ideas than your own, as being wrong can be very painful.

Possible conclusions
Who am I to say anything? My opinions are worthless; being seen and not heard; 'I can't say that!'; I'm not interesting, I'm stupid; my accent is wrong; I can't make a mistake, so I need to know more.

Potential of Mercury–Saturn
As usual, the potential can only be achieved by taking responsibility, but this time it is for our ideas and opinions. To use the potential in this aspect you need to take your own thoughts seriously. Mercury–Saturn people can concentrate incredibly well and spend time on an idea. They are often happy studying because of this, and can end up being an expert on a chosen subject. At work, this can be very valuable. This is

someone who is good at giving structure to the written word or the PR campaign. Writing in a structured way comes naturally. Editing, teaching and mentoring are also areas that can be very rewarding. Sue Tompkins gives the example of thinking about structures in the same way as an architect or sculptor, and I have also seen it often where a plan at work is involved, such as in project management. Saturn gives form to speech or writing when our own ideas are taken seriously. That's the challenge in this aspect. Mercury–Saturn people have some very good, practical, problem-solving ideas that are very useful to the workforce.

Saturn in aspect to Venus

The issue here is one of self-worth. Venus shows what we value and enjoy, so something in the past has damaged the capacity for doing the things we love. Perhaps there have been rules about who can be a friend, so decisions about people are doubted, too; relationships have to be authorized by others. But that can lead to an expectation of rejection, as these are not the friends that one chooses, so these friendships or matches often don't work. Saturn makes us wait, so what can result from a system of reward for hard work is that you think you can only receive a gift – such as a pay rise or promotion – if you really deserve it or have been in a job for a long time. It is not about getting a reward for what you are good at and enjoy, even though we often have a talent for something we love. The presents (or lack of) for your birthday were given out of obligation and not out of joy. Love has to be earned and relationships are hard work. There is a block on that feminine quality of 'receiving' in men and women; both can find it hard to accept anything nice, such as a compliment, thanks or praise. 'Oh, it's nothing,' they say, feeling they haven't earned it. It is as if happiness is not allowed.

One way this aspect often seems to work is that there is a rule about how you can earn money. The image I have of this is the woman in a pin-striped suit, doing what she thinks is right to earn respect, giving up her own taste in the process. The childhood home often had very strict norms and values about what was acceptable, so it was clear what sort of job might be 'suitable' for the family, but often this is not work that might suit you. As compensation, what often happens is that Venus–Saturn people take on responsibility or blame for colleagues, seeing this as an 'adult' way to act at work.

Possible conclusions

I will never be happy, I don't deserve happiness; I'm no good in relationships; everyone hates me; I'm not good at anything; I'm unattractive; I'll never find a partner (or good colleagues); I'll always be poor; work is work, it's not supposed to be fun; only men get to the top.

Potential of Venus–Saturn

Using the same formula, taking responsibility for what we value, enjoy and love is what will help to get over this particular block. I try to persuade clients, after helping them to define what they enjoy (because some with this aspect have even lost that knowledge), to do more of it. Giving time to what you enjoy boosts self-worth. Taking your loves and talents seriously can mean actually going to that pottery class and finding you have a talent for it. It raises confidence. Venus–Saturn people are very good where money and relationships are involved. They can take on responsibilities in these areas, such as a manager of customer complaints. I have also seen this one in a voice coach (Venus – throat, Saturn – teacher) and in the charts of couples' counsellors. At work, Venus–Saturn will respect company norms and values and treat colleagues in an adult way. They may be mediators, feeling responsible for any peace-keeping needed. They can also take responsibility for budgets and for long-term commitments in any projects. As mentioned in the chapter on talents, people with this aspect can love and be good at Saturnian pursuits such as teaching, coaching and anything where structures are important – from accountancy to architecture. Saturn can also produce expertise in Venusian areas, such as the beauty industry or perhaps floristry.

Saturn in aspect to Mars

I know a lot of people, and see a lot of clients, with this combination. Perhaps this says something about me! But I suspect it has more to do with how society views Martian qualities, which are seldom highly valued, that makes this one a common block. It gives a fear of initiating, competing, acting (as opposed to doing nothing) or of going for goals. In particular, I see it at work in someone who is unable, or too frightened, to stick up for themselves or defend their 'territory'. Somewhere in youth the Mars–Saturn person has been inhibited in starting things, which can lead to giving up what they want to do. If you have had parents who are over-careful – 'Don't go down the slide'; 'Be careful not to go too high on the swings';

'We don't like angry children' (I actually heard this one once in a shop) – then what can happen is that the element of risk and fun is taken from us, as is the ability to learn to express our anger and indignation. What's the point of wanting something if you never get it? It creates a sense of impotence, so it's better to not even try to get what you want. Working negatively, it also strips a child of enthusiasm, which can lead to depression in later life. This can also be seen in families where working hard is the norm. It produces, as we saw in the style chapter, a disciplined and serious approach but often these rules have come from someone else's will: punishments might have been very harsh and disputes were not tolerated or given any attention. Having had Mars blocked for so long can, of course, create the opposite effect of over-compensation, leading to a very cruel and harsh individual, taking over that style from an authority figure for themselves. Mars–Saturn can also produce someone who will never break a contract or agreement, believing that once something is agreed it should not be broken, even when it is clearly damaging to allow it to continue. At work, this is the person who never leaves a horrible job or continues to go to work out of duty even when they are unwell; someone who never changes an appointment with the boss (because it is the boss), even though there is something personally more important to do.

Possible conclusions
I'll never have what I want; arguing is wrong; if you start something you have to finish it; do as you're told; I have no right to ask for what I want; it won't work anyway; never break an appointment or agreement.

Potential of Mars–Saturn
There is great strength and discipline here, which can be seen by the fact that sportspeople often have this contact. In fact as I write this, two great tennis players are battling it out. Roger Federer has this aspect and his opponent Rafael Nadal has something similar (Mars in Capricorn, along with Sun–Saturn and Moon–Saturn aspects). However, when Mars–Saturn is working negatively, what is needed is to take responsibility for your anger or frustrations, and for the way you want to do something. Your approach and style are just as valid as anyone else's. What needs to become conscious is that realization that your focused, disciplined and strict approach to getting things done at work is not necessarily shared, so there is little point in being angry or frustrated by it. However, that doesn't make

your style any less valuable. In fact, it gives you an advantage as you can obtain the goals you want to achieve. This can produce experts in any Martian area, such as sport, fire-fighting, surgery (my knee surgeon has it) and maybe even bull-fighting, although I can't say I have had a matador in my practice. The mix is one of *disciplined bravery*; taking a huge risk but with the knowledge and expertise to back it up. 'Nerve-holding' can come naturally to people with this contact as there is a certain measured coolness, which can be very valuable in some jobs. It is also lends itself to a somewhat scientific approach, which can also be extremely useful where the authority of knowledge or proof is needed, such as in an expert witness.

Saturn in aspect to Ceres

As stated earlier, I feel I haven't worked enough with Ceres at a personal level to give good examples of blocks. However someone with a Ceres–Saturn aspect would have the potential to be an expert in her areas, which are outlined in Appendix 1.

Saturn in aspect to Jupiter

Saturn can damage or hurt whichever planet it touches, and in this case it's your life's philosophy or belief system that has somehow been affected. This aspect is in line with a strict religious upbringing or one where there were strong norms in the family or strongly held political beliefs. The environment experienced in childhood could have been very judgemental. Somehow one's faith in life has been called into question. Saturn can also block other Jupiterian pursuits, such as travel or starting a business where a certain amount of faith, belief in yourself and entrepreneurship is needed. At work, it can be seen as a fear of risk-taking or a lack of vision: 'There should be no adventures and one should not be too optimistic' – what goes up must come down. It appears often in people with fundamentalist beliefs and that can include scientism, such as in the case of Richard Dawkins, author of *The God Delusion*, who has the conjunction in Taurus and is rigid in his atheist views. With this aspect, a fixed philosophy feels safer.

Possible conclusions
Life has no meaning; if I don't get the world on the right track, who will?; I couldn't start my own business; travelling is difficult and unpleasant; I'm afraid of flying; I'll believe it when I see it.

Potential of Jupiter–Saturn

If we take Saturn as representing the expert, then possibilities of a positive use of this aspect can lead to great politicians, lawyers, explorers, university teachers, philosophers and religious leaders. Richard Dawkins is a respected university professor; Margaret Thatcher was a lawyer before she was a Prime Minister. To reach our potential here, we need to define and own the life philosophy or belief system that actually fits us. The work is to really study what our faith or belief may be, and have the determination to live by it. The philosophy of the company we work for should fit in with ours. Used well, this aspect gives a great balance between taking risks and using our common sense, so it is a good one for an entrepreneur. A strategy department might be a good place to work, as would somewhere that involves giving form to vision or philosophy in other ways, perhaps politics, law-making or publishing.

Saturn in aspect to Uranus

My client Jackie is a typical example of how this aspect manifests in the workplace: fearing to be weird or fearing to stand out as being too different. There is often frustration about the stupidity of management and a rebelliousness about the rules, particularly at petty rules concerning being on time, thinking 'Well, if I get the job done what's the problem?' There can be a sort of arrogance associated with this aspect. However, it often results in a block on being your authentic self – on being able to express your quirkiness and individuality, as the fear of being alone is very strong. In my experience, Uranus working negatively comes from abandonment in youth, either physical or emotional. So you will do anything to fit in and not be the black sheep, because that has been painful in the past. If the block is an over-reaction, this can result in someone who rebels against any form of rules or authority at work. The Dutch have an expression 'Say yes, do no', which typifies this aspect – agreeing to a certain action and, in an underhand, rebellious way, not actually doing it. Or, more overtly, the strong trade unionist who never agrees with management, seeing this as sticking up for the rights of the workers.

Possible conclusions

If they really know me, they won't like me; I'd better fit in or I will be fired; the future is scary, who knows what can happen?; management think they know everything; I'm too weird; everyone else is stupid.

Potential of Saturn–Uranus

Uranian expertise can show itself in astrology, technology and future-orientated jobs. One of my clients, who is a very good trend-watcher and has her own company, has this aspect. It also shows up in people who are doing groundbreaking work in science, such as one of my heroes, Rupert Sheldrake, whose book *The Science Delusion* (Coronet, 2012) challenges the very basis of the current scientific view. Francis Crick, who is associated with the discovery of DNA, has a bi-quintile. It is good for changing the establishment and making the future fairer. At the time of writing, Barack Obama is attempting to put his aspect to good use but perhaps people with this aspect are ahead of their time – or in the wrong time in some other way. The healing in this aspect is to take responsibility for your own uniqueness, for your own weirdness or individuality – to dare to be yourself. Truly unique people can feel a sense of loneliness – being Uranian means there is no one like you, so it's important to learn to embrace your specialness and work on your fear of being alone. I often say to these clients that they need a job that has yet to be invented. Even if you do work for someone else, there are ways in which your special talents and ability to just 'know things' can be used in companies. With this aspect, you have ways of seeing things differently, but you must be authentic.

Saturn in aspect to Neptune

We are dealing with generational aspects as we move out to the outer planets, but these still work on a personal level. In my opinion, transpersonal planets are becoming more personal as the world's consciousness level rises. There may be more important aspects than this one in the chart but it will still be visible, both in a generation and individually. This combination can manifest as a lack of imagination at work. There can also be a fear of chaotic environments. The allergy that could be placed in Ofman's Quadrant model might be one of being annoyed by vague, creative people, or annoyed by people who take the victim role. I think this aspect produces guilt, so there might be a feeling that you should look after everyone and be compassionate, while underneath thinking 'Get over yourself'. The family background may have been one of denying anything that is invisible. It stamps out forms of spirituality, intuition or invisible friends; imagination is 'dangerous' in some way. This can lead to drug abuse as a way to escape reality, feeling that the world is a hard, concrete place. But it can also lead to a sort of authoritative caretaking of the 'I know what's best for you' variety. I have seen this referred to as the Woody Allen aspect and I think this fits – you can always imagine the worst. David Icke, of 'the global conspiracy' fame, has it. He can see a scenario of doom for the world, saying we are all hypnotized and need to wake up. His website sums it up: 'Exposing the Dreamworld we believe to be Real.' A great description of Saturn–Neptune! Interestingly, Icke had to give up a football career when rheumatoid arthritis spread throughout his body – another example of how Saturn–Neptune can manifest. He also became an expert in channelling. One way this can show up at work is in people who lose sight of their goals, either in daily life or as a focus for their career. There is a tendency to float through their working life, reconciled with the fact that anything is fine as long as it's work, and thereby escaping any responsibility for their actions.

Possible conclusions
I'll never decide what I want to do; whatever job I do is fine; my boss is wonderful; I can't go home until everything is finished; I could never be in a responsible position.

Potential of Saturn–Neptune
The life of actor Christopher Reeve (who had the conjunction) summed this up well. He played a hero who saves the world in *Superman* by rescuing victims, and he campaigned for real victims after his own accident left him a paraplegic. He demonstrated several ways in which this aspect can work: the actor who can make imagination come to life and in a sense be real; someone who takes concrete steps to make the world a better place; and a person who takes responsibility for the fact that he was a victim but used his position to do something useful. This can be an incredibly powerful combination for making dreams come true, but you need to *own* your dreams or imagination to do this. I have a client with this aspect who is setting up homes for old people with Alzheimer's, based on a totally new compassionate approach, where the patient really is at the centre of the model. Taking Saturn as the expert, we are looking at Neptunian pursuits such as nursing, the arts, the drugs or alcohol field or working with prisoners, to name a few. Dame Joan Sutherland, the famous Australian opera singer, has a tight square. Florence Nightingale, who made major contributions to nursing, has a wide square. It would also be good for teaching some kind of spirituality. The healing comes in taking responsibility for our imagination, sensitivity and also our own vulnerability.

Saturn in aspect to Pluto

This can be a dark aspect and, indeed, I have heard it referred to as the 'paranoia' signature. I seem to have many people around me born in 1956 who have this combination in square aspect, and I can recognize a 'they are all out to get me' type. The people I know are seen as quite bossy and dominating leaders at work, which probably comes from a fear of being out of control. This can, of course, also work the other way and result in a fear of being a leader. Going underground rather than taking any responsibility at work, some with this aspect can be quite manipulative. Many years ago I worked with one person with this aspect very strongly placed who was actually just plain nasty, not to mention dishonest. Many times I have seen it in action in companies, laying the blame on the people in control – the ones who have the power – which can be very subversive or can result in political power-plays. Pluto, in his role as survivor, seems to be capable of taking hard measures to gain authority too. The block here is either being too bossy, where there is over-compensation, or being powerless and letting yourself be manipulated. Passion can be stifled by this aspect, too, and I have often heard my friends say they don't know what their passion is, even though they are very successful and passionate in the eyes of others. I think this comes from a fear of exposing your true passion in case it is taken away.

Possible conclusions

I'm the boss, no one has the right to question me; I could never run anything; everyone is against me; I can't win; the boss is a bastard; I never have any influence; I need to work until I die.

Potential of Saturn–Pluto

This might work best where there is a death and rebirth in the career – an element of starting again and reinventing yourself every now and then. If we look at the expertise, it is of course in Pluto-type positions, ones with power but also those where there is depth and transformation. This could be anything from analytic work to scientific or other research. From archaeology to atomic energy. From psychology and therapy to mining. Saturn–Pluto people can handle very difficult situations. And they can take on major tasks. Emmeline Pankhurst, who fought for women to get the vote in the UK, has this aspect. There is strong willpower and a determination to win. Martina Navratilova, the former world number one tennis player, has it too. With Pluto going through Capricorn, reflecting this contact at the time of writing, it is clear that healing must come from taking responsibility for power. For an individual, it indicates the need to step into power and use it wisely. Otherwise the punishment will come, as is currently being seen (at the time of writing) in the so-called Arab Spring in which many despotic leaders are being challenged and brought to justice. This is also the case in the Catholic Church, where priests have been accused of sexual abuse. However, at its best, this is a combination that can move mountains.

General Saturn issues

I have given an idea of Saturn's effect on each planet. However, he has some general themes that come up in conversations which, when they arise, make me look at how Saturn is working. One of the things you need to learn to do when using dialogue in astrology sessions is to analyse the conversation and listen with what I call an 'astrological ear' for the planets involved. I then use the Huber method to investigate further. Some general themes that direct me onto Saturn's trail are:

Time

Any issues where you notice a pattern associated with time. For example, if you have a client who is always late or far too early. Perhaps there is always an excuse of never having time.

Blaming

If Saturn is causing problems, then blame often comes up in the conversation. It's the fault of someone or something else. It's the system or, as I often hear, the country. If you are in a situation, on some level there is agreement about being there, even by tacit agreement or by not taking steps to get out of it. Some would go so far as to say that there is agreement to choosing this life. If you hear any form of blame, take a look at how Saturn is working in the chart.

Not good enough

You can feel Saturn in a conversation when there is a sense of depression or feeling not good enough. 'Life has no point.' This is another reason to research Saturn issues with the client.

Caesarean birth

I have often come across Saturn themes with people born by Caesarean section. There is research done by (among others) Dr William Emerson, a pioneer in the field of pre- and peri-natal psychology, which indicates that children born by C-section suffer more often from a fear of failure than others. An abstract of one of his articles states, 'Twenty years of clinical and behavioural observation indicate that Caesarean births cause considerable trauma to babies. The physical and psychological effects are subtle and powerful, occurring at the unconscious level of the infant psyche. Negative impacts include excessive crying, feeding difficulties, sleeping difficulties, colic and tactile defensiveness. There also may be long-term psychological effects such as rescue complexes, inferiority complexes, poor self-esteem, and other dysfunctional behaviours and feelings.'[7]

To me, it's as if these children get messages that they have been born in the wrong way. There is often fear around the birth. But the child, experiencing himself as rightly being the centre of everything, picks up the fact that he is the cause of the problem. There is blame accepted from day one, leading to Saturn issues in later life. There are subtle messages that a child may pick up too – 'Lovely baby but pity it was a C-section, shame about the scar… It took that long?' According to some studies, the anaesthetic can cause sluggishness and lack of response, and if that continues there is now even a diagnosis known as baby depression. Of course, this doesn't always happen with a Caesarean birth, but if clients know they are born this way I discuss any possible Saturn themes, particularly if Saturn is near the Ascendant.

Being born early or late or altogether at the wrong time
This one is similar to the Caesarean, which is a birth at the *time of another's choice*. A child seems to sense that the timing is wrong, and it's their fault again. I have seen this often and it leads to issues with time later in life. Always being early or late can arise here, as do many other Saturn themes. A very long and difficult birth can also result in similar issues, with the child getting the message that he has caused his mother problems.

So once we see Saturn as the culprit, what then?
Once I have a found a planetary culprit I try to find out when a particular pattern might have been formed, or at least heavily triggered, and why. I use part of the Huber Life Clock, which is really simple and is easy to calculate from a horoscope, provided the Koch house system is used. The question I ask is: what happened when the planet was picked up by the Age Point by conjunction or opposition (or both, depending on the client's age)? The Age Point is like the hand of a clock. Starting at birth and the Ascendant,

it ticks around the horoscope and spends 6 years in each house, restarting at the Ascendant at age 72. The 1st House is from age 0 (birth) to the 6th birthday (the Aries phase of life), the 2nd House is from 6 to 12 (the Taurus phase), the 3rd House is from 12 to 18 (the Gemini phase), etc., until we get to the 12th House (age 66–72 and the Pisces phase). So by knowing which house Saturn is in, we can see at what age(s) a planet is activated. Taking the example of Saturn in the 2nd House, it will be picked up between the ages of 6 and 12 by conjunction, and then between 42 and 48 (the 8th House) by opposition. If Saturn is in the 8th House, the reverse will apply – i.e. it will be picked up by opposition between ages 6 and 12 and by conjunction between the ages of 42 and 48. The difference between the aspects doesn't really matter here; what you want to hear from the client are the themes to determine whether Saturn is working negatively or positively. There will always be a link between the events or experiences at these two ages (the conjunction and opposition). You can identify the specific ages by using software that calculates this (including astro.com), or simply by dividing the number of degrees in the house by 6 to show each year. The size of the house doesn't matter – a house will always cover 6 years, so one sixth of it will represent one year.

Some clients are not very good at remembering events or how a particular time in their life felt, but I have been amazed at how many clients tell anecdotes that could come straight out of astrology textbooks. Using their own examples is a way to clearly explain to them what caused a pattern to form (or at least what the pattern is), or how the planet is operating in their life.

Jackie's chart showing Saturn just in the 11th House

Because she has not yet reached this point (age around 60–61), I am interested in what happened to her at the opposite point – Age Point in Capricorn just at the beginning of the 5th House (age 24–25). Of course, patterns have been long formed by then, but this will give a clue as to how Saturn works in her life.

Jackie's Saturn story: age 24–25

> *I don't remember exactly but early 1999 I left my engineering job, initially to pursue a Master's degree in electrical engineering but instead studied film and video. Before starting school, I went to Rome, Cape Town, Nairobi, Arusha, visiting aunts and family. For a present, my friends gave me a black Labrador for the company. We had no idea how much work went into taking care of a dog.*

Often clients won't remember much at some of the Age Points, as is the case here. However, if you read Jackie's bio, you'll see that it was a huge step for her to leave the engineering field and to pursue a study she enjoyed. She is starting to turn Saturn around, which is a good sign – starting to have her own goals rather than her mother's goal for her. The Saturn area of responsibility shows up with the dog. This was probably a reality check on many levels, including what it might be like to have children.

A bit of Uranus as an aside

I spent more time on the Uranus Age Point, as this seemed more important in the blocks process. Because Uranus is in the 2nd House, Uranus was triggered in this system at age 9–10. Here's what Jackie wrote:

> **Age 9–10**
> *I was in the 4th grade then, which doesn't conjure any particular memories. At some point in elementary school, my mother sent my sister, brother and I to Tanzania for the first time. We went as unaccompanied minors... the plane trip was fun but it was very scary being in TZ without her. I can't be sure if the trip was during this time but it feels right somehow.*

This was an important trip for her. She hints at a sort of abandonment when she says it was scary without her mother. For some reason, being independent (from her mother) is not a good experience at this stage, which has set the stage for how she may be able to use Uranus later. Remember, she mentioned that her father was a really bad father, so we explored this further.

Chiron and blocks

The work and books you need to study when looking at Chiron are undoubtedly those of Melanie Reinhart.[8] I tend to see Chiron as a wound and I don't always use him when doing vocational work but, as I did in Jackie's case, I might mention him in passing. Where I see him working very clearly is in regression work. I learned how to work with regression during my Inner Child training and later with Hans ten Dam, whose book on reincarnation I wholeheartedly recommend.[9] Hans has a school in the Netherlands and is internationally well known in his field.

To past lives or not to past lives...

Who knows if past lives are true? During my study for the Master of Arts programme in Cultural Astronomy and Astrology, I wrote a paper researching what astrologers have said about the subject and I find reincarnation useful as a model for what we bring into this life. My idea of it is pretty much the same as the Inner Child model. I don't buy into the 'karma as punishment' idea, unlike many people. I think it works the same as it does in life. Something happens and we make a conclusion about it and form a strategy, in this case about this life. Although the planets have a focus on this life (having done many regression sessions with clients I can see the whole chart in the stories), I feel that Chiron, being immortal until he swapped places with Prometheus, does have a different impact. There are good astrologers who can interpret Chiron (and the other Centaurs which really, if you are using Chiron, you should use too) just by analysing his sign and house. Dick van der Mark, who is one of the best astrologers on the Centaurs and based in the Netherlands, suggests interpreting Chiron as if there is a Saturn–Uranus conjunction on the point where Chiron is in the chart. I found this to be very helpful. Chiron orbits between Saturn and Uranus and symbolically connects the two. (As an aside, you do something similar when interpreting the other Centaurs: Saturn–Neptune for Pholus, as Pholus orbits between Saturn and Neptune; and Saturn–Pluto for Nessus because Nessus connects Saturn and Pluto.) However, I get more out of the planetary aspects with Chiron.

Knowing a little about what shows up as a wound in regression can give a clue to a possibly painful block caused by something that can't be attributed to anything obvious in this life, such as upbringing, parents or early environment. It's nobody's fault, you could say, unlike Saturn – where the tendency to say that there is someone/something to blame is much greater!

I won't spend much time on this because you already have enough to be going on with for a VP. However, possible themes that have come up during regressions can offer tips about what might be a theme to explore. You can, of course, also use the Age Point method for this, too. Even though the Hubers didn't use Chiron, in my experience the Age Point works for Chiron and other heavenly bodies such as Ceres and the other Centaurs.

If you look at the aspects for Saturn (see pages 149–63), the themes for Chiron's aspects will be similar. For me, they are more deeply rooted patterns, though, as they started earlier. To get more depth, look to Melanie's work. Incidentally, I have found that the earlier a planet is triggered by the Age Point, the deeper the patterns – starting in the 1st House and the Ascendant. Any planets in the 12th House are the exception, which is what I shall look at now.

12th House planets and blocks

One of the things I have noticed is that 12th House planetary patterns seem to come to the surface early on during regression sessions. They appear to be easier to uncover than other patterns. Yes, they act as blocks in life and work but, when they are understood, they can be some of *our greatest gifts*. The often-cited 'weak house' is not what I have seen, as planets here are very influential and important and, I think, misunderstood in astrology to a large extent. The research done by Michel Gauquelin also suggests that planets here play a large role in our profession. They show patterns we come in with – both positive and negative – but, for some reason, when we try to put them to good use they get rejected. So we hide them away, perhaps to keep them safe. We put a 12th House planetary toe in the water, so to speak, and realize the temperature is not right. So the talent that we are born with goes underground until we work on the block. Dana Gerhardt writes: 'Ultimately, the 12th-House path is meant to transform us. Behind its darkness lies a brilliant light, but it takes time and faith to develop our spiritual eyes. If we insist on negotiating this world with our material values intact, we'll operate blind.'[10]

What I will do in this section is provide examples of what I have come across during regression sessions and offer a possible conclusion for each planetary placement that your clients may recognize. Even without doing regression work, clients seem to resonate with these life themes.

Back to the clock

The Huber Life Clock states that 12th House planets are triggered by opposition, a strong trigger point, during age 30–36. I began to notice something about these 12th House planets because I started asking questions about the situation during gestation (i.e. the time the client was in the womb). Because of this, I have come to the hypothesis that not only does the 12th House represent our time in the womb – as many astrologers believe – but also that the *sequence* of the planets is experienced in that order during our gestation. As an example using Koch houses, if you have Mars halfway through the 12th House, you may have registered a Mars-type event inside your mother's womb – and come to a conclusion about it – when she was about four and a half months pregnant. You will have a chance to heal that possible trauma at age 33 (midway through the 6th House). This means that age 30–36 is a major opportunity to heal wounds caused during your time in the womb.

Now, when I see planets in the 12th House, I always ask whether the client knows anything about their parents or the pre-birth situation. If they don't and can still ask parents or a relative, I suggest they do that. The stories are sometimes very helpful, as clients can then imagine what it may have been like for them in the womb. We *do* come to conclusions this early in our lives, and these form deep-seated patterns. If we can learn to express these planetary energies without fear, there are great gifts here for our working life and, of course, for our life generally.

My client, Jackie has no planets in the 12th House but I have many examples of clients who do. Here are a few to give you some ideas. Sometimes during regression you discover an experience in the womb, but more often it leads back to a chain of experiences in many different lives which are connected by the same planetary themes. The following examples are by no means intended as a complete cookbook of interpretations. They are ideas to give you possible themes to explore with your clients.

The Sun in the 12th House

The father is often a theme during pregnancy. A good example is a client who was born on 29 February, with the Sun just before the Ascendant in Pisces. A television crew had asked to film the newborn and were given permission from my client's father. He was very proud to be a new father, too, so was happy to do it. However, my client experienced this in the regression as receiving far too much attention. She just wanted to be quietly with her mother. And her father's wishes would become a very strong influence in her life.

I have seen this placement often where the input (or, more often, the lack of it) of the father results in a conclusion that 'who I am is unimportant' or 'I can't have what I want, someone else will direct my life'. (This placement can also suggest that God is that 'someone else'). It is found in the charts of those who have submitted to a higher authority in a previous life, perhaps as a monk or a nun. Letting yourself get attention for who you really are is a block.

The gift

Someone who has the gift of inner peace and the ability to connect with other sources. The actor who steps easily into others' shoes is one example. So, this can be a very intuitive placement for you, once intuition is seen as a positive trait and you are happy receiving attention for who you are. There are many world leaders with the Sun in the 12th House, so this is definitely not a position that indicates being shut away. The work needed here is to go for what *you* really want. But it does imply a career in being of service somehow, as many world leaders have been. I think there is a need to break away from the father, which is what often happens anyway before birth with the Sun in the 12th. Having done that, it is easier to follow your own heart and develop the gift of intuitive leadership.

The Moon in the 12th House

This is the caretaker. For some reason the child in the womb feels the need to take care of the mother. The mother is often unwell or delicate. One of my clients had a mother who didn't want to be fat while pregnant – to the mother, this would have been unattractive. My client was not nurtured in the womb and suffered a form of malnutrition. Unsurprisingly, this caused eating disorders later in life. The pattern that developed is one of 'my life depends on looking after others. If I don't take care of the other person I will die.' Although it might not seem likely, babies in the womb can do things to help their mothers. Decisions I have come across include 'if I keep still it will be better, I won't cause a fuss'. Many people with the Moon in the 12th recognize the fact that they take care of everyone, especially women, to the detriment of their own nurturing. Showing emotion carries some sort of block, and the feelings of others are more important. One past life regression of a male client showed a man who watched from afar as his wife and daughter were raped by soldiers. He was powerless to do anything about it. In this life, his pattern has been wanting to protect and look after women, especially if they have children.

The gift
Someone very compassionate, supportive and intuitive – once you can look after and nurture yourself. Someone who can read public opinion very easily. Many writers have 12th House Moons, as there is often an instinctive 'knowing' of what others feel. Work in caring professions may be healing and rewarding.

Mercury in the 12th House

The shy person. The block seems to be that it is dangerous to have an opinion. I have seen this in someone who always asks his partner what he should do. He is not shy in the usual way we would see this, but he never comes up with his own ideas. In regressions, clients with Mercury in the 12th House have been people who have not had a voice (sometimes literally) in previous lives – being unable to speak or sometimes being deaf. I think we are supposed to heal 12th House planets in this lifetime, which is why they are easier to access. They are near the surface as unfinished themes from past lives. Mercury in the 12th people enter this life with something they need to express. But the conclusion is often 'no one understands me, so why bother?' Or there is something dangerous about speaking out.

Sometimes, this placement suggests something going on with siblings during pregnancy. During one regression back to the womb, a client with the Moon in the 12th tightly aspecting Mercury saw an image of herself looking at her sister, who is not much older than she is. She saw herself as blue (she is a Pisces) but she had red hands and she already knew in the womb that her sister was very jealous and that she would have to fight her to get their mother's (Moon in 12th) attention. There was also a Moon–Mars aspect. As in this case, aspects to 12th House planets often show up in the clients' stories, too.

The gift
Being deaf or unable to speak gives other talents. A 12th House Mercury can intuitively pick up many levels in conversations. They are great listeners. Sound is important – my client above, who always consults his partner, is a very talented musician. Musicians are very good at distinguishing sounds. Perhaps this would be someone who has a gift for languages. Some research suggests that people who learn music early in life are better at learning other languages. There is an intuitive understanding and knowing what others are thinking. A job giving expression to intuitive ideas or imagination could be good.

Venus in the 12th House

This position can manifest as a self-worth problem, but it can more often highlight a vital need to take account of the other person, to consider everyone else. Whatever the 12th House person loves is irrelevant, and this can produce someone who, when asked what they want, asks 'but what do *you* want to do?' There can be real fears about being alone. Relationships are therefore a main focus. In my experience, a 12th House Venus can also produce someone who is 'too nice', the pleaser. One client of mine rarely does the things she wants – her husband's hobbies mostly take priority. Doing things together is a must for her. I can't find any past life examples for this placing, although there have probably been many. However, I do have a client whose father was in the military. She was born overseas, her mother following her father everywhere because 'that's what you did' – the dutiful wife who puts others' pursuits first. So you can see how this might lead to a lack of self-worth or a giving up, or even not being aware of what you love yourself. My client has taken over this pattern from her mother. There is sometimes a fear of expressing the feminine because the senses of taste, beauty and harmony have been called into question in childhood. I have seen relationship issues and money problems between the parents during the client's gestation in the womb.

The gift
Being able to see, or rather feel, things from differing viewpoints. The mediator. An intuitive sense of what others love. Working intuitively with art or beauty. The artist. This placement would suggest someone who might be good where money is involved, but I don't have an example of this. The intuitive negotiator.

Mars in the 12th House

I have had three clients with Mars in the 12th who virtually said the same thing during regressions: 'It wasn't my idea to come here [in this life]. I was pushed.' Or words to that effect. This suggests a giving up of will. The image I always have is of a teenager sitting grumpily in a corner at a party she's been told she has to go to. Not that people with a 12th House Mars are always grumpy, but there is a resignation about not having a choice of what to do: 'It doesn't matter what I want', 'No point in wanting anything – I'll have to do what they say.' So there is sometimes a block over knowing your direction in life. It may be easier not to say what you want and then go for it, than to express it and have it taken away.

I have also seen this placing when there was a lot of conflict during the gestation. The decision here is 'I won't fight; sticking up for yourself makes it worse'; 'Keeping still is safest'; 'Anger is dangerous.'

The gift
The Gauquelin research[11] showed that successful sportspeople (along with doctors and military people) often have Mars in what are now known as the Gauquelin Sectors, which include the 12th House. I suspect that the gift lies in having an intuitive knowledge of how to compete; to be fine-tuned to the will of your opponent. To have a feeling of how to direct the ball, for example, in tennis or football. In the case of doctors, I would expect to see it more in surgeons, although I have no idea if this is true, as the gift (once the 12th House person dares to go for what they want) is to be able to control the Mars in a way that is very focused, such as the way in which a surgeon uses a knife, perhaps intuitively knowing where to cut. I have also seen it in my clients who have a career in which defending the underdog forms part of their *raison d'être*. I think this comes from a possible past life where defending others or yourself has proved impossible.

Jupiter in the 12th House
One way a 12th House Jupiter often shows up is when there is a religious background. The child in the womb already seems to have a sense that his own faith will be overshadowed or put to the test. Your own belief system or philosophy is sacrificed. This is also someone who won't dare to take risks at work. Adventures can be threatening. Travel can be scary. There is an inner sense of wanting to find meaning and to have a vision, but these desires are initially blurred by the environment you are brought up in. I have witnessed past lives regressions with those who have Jupiter in the 12th where religion plays a role and particularly where there has been a judgement of some kind.

The gift
An intuitive sense of the big picture. Someone who is good at recognizing patterns, so a job in demographic research could be fulfilling. Political gifts or a feel for marketing a standpoint or an idea. Publishers could be helped by having this – a feel for what might sell well. The intuitive entrepreneur – one who just senses what the risks are. The gambler (in the positive sense).

Someone who has a vision. The lawyer or law-maker. Astronaut Buzz Aldrin has this – any career where Jupiter is put to good use in space, exploration, discovery, broadening of horizons and adventures! These are all fulfilling options for anyone with Jupiter in the 12th. The work is to discover your own faith in life and what your own philosophy is, and go for it. Jupiter is often referred to as the Guardian Angel, but I think any planet can have this effect if we use it correctly. Jupiter, when working well, just takes more opportunities and has the faith that the outcome will be beneficial – the optimism and belief lead to success. If you read Benjamin Disraeli's life story you can see the theme of Jupiter in the 12th running through his life and developing into success as he gets older.[12]

Saturn in the 12th House

Many people with Saturn in the 12th suffer because they seem to know already in the womb that their own goals will not be allowed. 'It's no use having ambition because what I want to do won't be acceptable.' This feeling can come from a strict background or one where angst reigns supreme. One strategy developed is to avoid having goals altogether – at work, this manifests as a lack of ambition. However, what has been experienced early in life is that someone else's authority and rules are more important than our own. We give up our own versions of these very early on. I know someone who really suffers from this signature. She is number five in a family of six girls. Perhaps in the womb she already knew she was not the preferred option. The decision is 'I am not good enough'. There is a real fear of not being taken seriously, but equally a fear of stepping into one's own mission. It is a painful placement. Past lives reveal events where the regressee has fallen short in some way. 'I am to blame for the death of my companion soldier, my wife, etc. I should have…' The strategy is to take responsibility for everyone else's orders – better to not have any responsibility in this life because of the failure to carry out one's duty during the last life – or to over-compensate.

I also have a client whose first son has Saturn in the 12th House. When she was pregnant she was quite unhappy, as the decision to have a child was her husband's. He really wanted a child and she didn't, but she went along with his wishes. She worked hard when she was pregnant and didn't really have time for a child. This is a common theme. You can see how this might have affected a growing baby and how a pattern of not having your own goals (i.e. doing something for someone else) could have been passed down. 'I am not worthy of having anyone spend time with me' is a common conclusion. The patterns mentioned above about Caesarean births are, of course, relevant with Saturn near the Ascendant.

The gift
Gauquelin suggests that this can indicate the scientist, but I must admit to not having found many examples of this. I can imagine, though, that there is a desire for clarity about what the rules are, so I would expect it more in scientists who are looking for concrete physical proof. Or in geologists, perhaps. Since Buzz Aldrin was mentioned, another astronaut is Harrison H Schmitt, a geologist on the Apollo 17 Lunar module and the twelfth man on the Moon. Funny how we all know the Jupiter-in-the-12th Buzz and not the Saturn-in-the-12th Harrison!

Saturn in the 12th House would fit with an instinctive knowing of how to structure an experiment or how to prove something. Science can be very Saturnian but there are also many Uranian and Neptunian scientists. Saturn in the 12th would give an aptitude for the Saturnian types. The lesson here is to learn to feel good enough to go for your own mission and goals in life. To appreciate that you can spend your time in the way you choose. The potential here is to become the intuitive teacher, planner, architect, or anyone who works with structures.

Uranus in the 12th House
'I was burned at the stake' is a common cry of the regressee with Uranus in the 12th. At some time during pregnancy there is a shock or a break point. The decision by the child, caused by a feeling of abandonment, is 'I can/will/have to do it by myself', which, in my experience, is a deep-seated feeling that Uranus in the 12th people strongly relate to. The fear of commitment is strong, as it is better to do things by yourself and in your own way than to feel the pain of being left again and being alone. There is forbidden knowledge here, hence the idea of being burned at the stake for what was known. But also a sense of the unfairness or hypocrisy of this. Uranus in the 12th people can 'download' knowledge, they just know something – but it is dangerous to show it. The desire, which is given up, is to be special and unique. In many regressions there have been accidents, sudden occurrences or shocks, which have given the person a need to understand things, to know the future. Many good astrologers have this Uranus. Long ago I heard this referred to as the 'street angel, house devil'. It's a pity I can't

remember who said that. When you are in a safe place you can show how rebellious and quirky you really are, but to the outside world you fit in perfectly. Uranus in the 12th House gives up authenticity.

One client's mother realized very late that she was pregnant, which was a complete shock, as she thought she was menopausal. She considered an abortion, fearing her husband would leave her again. She didn't want to be unattractive and fat, as her husband had just returned to her after a long affair. My client felt the rejection physically during the regression. It dawned upon her that she was unwanted and she developed a strategy to go it alone. Although she felt wanted later, particularly by her father, she always felt different and not part of any group when growing up. Both parents encouraged that, believing in her specialness in a positive sense. However, she was very lonely as a child.

The gift
Someone who has dared to be different can develop an intuitive sense of tuning in to hidden knowledge. I often refer to this as being able to 'download' information and knowing something to be true but not being able to explain why you know it. Using this talent can make someone extraordinary. This can be someone who can see the special qualities that others have and can accept them. Their gift can be to bring insight and understanding. Or to be agents of change, or even to see the future.

Neptune in the 12th House
I have encountered Neptune in the 12th when there has been some sort of loss or grieving by the mother during pregnancy. This results in the child feeling that there is no connection with the physical realm and, during the regressions I have done, the child often expresses a wish to stay attached to other realms. There is often a strong 'spiritual' connection and no desire to be born. There is a theme of sacrifice and a need to disappear. You might expect to see this in cases where the mother has an addiction, but I haven't any examples of this. However, the result that seems to be recognizable by clients is one of taking care of everyone. It is similar to the Moon in the 12th house, but emphasized. The belief is that to make the world a better place you need to help everyone and to sacrifice yourself. 'I'm not important in the scheme of things.' If a mother is grieving a loss, she may feel guilty about being happy about her new child. Or she may be unable to connect to the fact that she is pregnant and the child becomes a sort of victim of circumstance. Children often disappear into fantasy worlds and

dissociate from their bodies so as not to feel the pain this can cause. It is safer to disappear. Chains of past life situations can include being both victims and saviours, or those shut away in monasteries or nunneries. Any of the Neptunian themes can apply.

Interestingly, William Emerson, who I mentioned above, has written a book[13] about birth traumas caused by intervention. In an online book review[14] which gives a summary, it states: 'Dr Emerson has noticed that some anaesthetic babies [i.e. where the mother was anaesthetized] have difficulty bonding and later have problems with substance abuse.' To my mind, Neptune near the Ascendant would be a possible indicator of this problem.

The gift
A great imagination, huge amounts of compassion and a feeling of connectedness with the world. The ability to 'be' another person; to merge with others. The actor. The aura reader. This can be a helpful signature for people who work with animals or with children who can't communicate. Or it can be found in someone who can communicate with other realms.

Pluto in the 12th House
The control freak – and not for nothing. It is often mentioned in astrology books that Pluto near the Ascendant indicates a birth where the survival of either the mother or the baby is at stake, and I have seen this particularly where the umbilical cord has been wrapped around the baby's neck during birth. Pluto in the 12th House has a similar theme – there is a question of survival earlier on in pregnancy. The question is, 'Shall I stay or go?' And if you have a client in your practice with this, then obviously on some level they have decided to live. But the decision results in 'I have to be alert to everything, I have to watch out. Earth is a dangerous place.' The most dramatic example I have seen of this is a client whose mother felt unwell and was sent to have an examination. It was decided that she should have a D&C (dilation and curettage), an operation that clears out the uterus, which is usually done when infection or uterine bleeding or other female problems are encountered. In this case the surgeons were halfway through the operation when they realized that what they had taken out was a foetus. Unbeknown to everyone, she was pregnant but they realized this too late for the foetus. However, my client's mother was carrying twins. The surviving foetus was my client. He was born at full term and was fine, but you can imagine what he might have concluded during the operation: 'I need to hang on tight and

I need to control what is going to happen, otherwise I will die or lose those I love.' He has had a very difficult relationship with his mother. (He also has Mercury – siblings – in the 12th House!) He admits to being a control freak. His life changed dramatically when he became a father (after his wife had miscarried several times) and when he stood up to his mother and took his power back, between the ages of 30 and 36 (opposite the 12th House phase in the Huber Life Clock.)

Pluto in the 12th can also signify a death of some kind during pregnancy. I have often seen it in the charts of people born in the Netherlands during the Second World War when Holland was occupied by the Germans, particularly in clients born in the years known as the 'Honger Winter' (the Hunger Winter) of 1944–5. There were genuine fears of not only starving during the pregnancy, but also of death. What is given up is our power. We know we have no control over anything, although we still try.

In the review of Emerson's book mentioned earlier, one possible Pluto near the Ascendant manifestation might be suggested here: 'The administration of such drugs as Oxytocin and Pitocin (for inducing labour) have the effect of making the foetus feel as though it is being overpowered and controlled. Both classes of such drugs interfere with subsequent bonding and sometimes result in substance abuse in later life as well as [a] feeling of being interrupted and interfered with.' His suggestions on the use of instruments are also Plutonic in nature: 'They [people born by forceps or vacuum] have a tendency to recreate their trauma by manipulating others... They feel that they have been invaded and subjected to violence. Often they don't want to be touched and/or held. A result can be the avoidance of sex or only engaging in sex with minimum touch. Contrariwise, some subjected to this trauma may be attracted to masochistic or sadistic sexuality in order to re-live the trauma and resolve it.' This makes sense to me. The power we have in the birth process has been taken away. The conclusion can be either to want to control everything or to feel powerless about life.

The gift
Being able to step into and take power, this placement gives someone who can transform the world. One of my clients has finally worked through some old issues of abortions and other powerless situations in her life and is coming into her own power. She is a powerful presence, her work is important and she is well known in her field. Not only does she have Pluto in the 12th but also Uranus and Mars conjunct that Pluto. Her

life has reflected this struggle, but the gift is that she has made, and will continue to make, a huge difference in her field. Pluto's gift is one of intuitively being able to research and get to the real truth of an issue. She has a quiet power because of this and exposes things that need to be revealed in society. Her subject actually concerns life and death situations. A regression I did with her shows her dilemma with this conjunction. She saw a past life where she had to choose for herself (Uranus) to either flee, leaving her family in a burning building (Mars), or to rescue them and die in the process (Pluto). She recognized the dilemma of choosing for herself or for her family in this lifetime, both with her parents and with her own children. The Mars in the 12th shows her ability to campaign for the underdog, which she often does. Uranus reveals her sense of wanting equality for all.

Summary blocks

So that's a run-through of the way I work with blocks. I trust you now have enough material to select some themes to discuss with your clients and to examine them for yourself. To close this chapter I will return to my client and offer you a final exercise that is fun to do after all that heavy stuff.

My example client

To remind you, here are the notes I made from the bio in preparation for this session on blocks.

Mommy, to name an obvious one. As well as the Uranus issue and aspect with the Sun mentioned above, and the fact that her father 'was really, really bad at being a father', the Moon also picks up Uranus, so the aloneness/abandonment issues will have to be discussed again in this session. We need to add the Moon–Saturn conjunction, as this is mentioned several times in the bio. Actually this conjunction is a bit wider than I would normally use but I can't help thinking it works here, so I let the chart–client combination speak. 'Mother dished out orders.' 'She wanted us kids to be a lawyer, doctor and engineer' (assigned engineer). 'I was someone my mother could count on, responsible enough to handle household duties early on.' 'Insecure kid.' 'Social angst of the cafeteria' (what about eating problems?) 'My mother's hard stance on education paid off' (!) 'I couldn't go against my mother's wishes.' 'Lonely and quiet sadness.'

These comments all point to someone who will have trouble setting their own goals and feeling authoritative. The pattern is probably to wait for orders and be given instructions. A real dilemma for an Aries. The Moon is in Cancer, so the need to belong will be strong, which goes completely against the desire to stand out. In Jackie's case, this is probably a very deep and painful part of the chart. The block here will probably be fear of 'going for it' for fear of being totally alone. The pattern might be: have fun and do what you love at movies, etc. when you are allowed time off, but otherwise 'you do as you're told'.

In these block sessions, I listen with an astrological ear to ascertain which aspects are being expressed negatively. The ones I chose to work with for Jackie were:

- The T-square: Uranus opposite the stellium in Aries (Sun, Mercury and Ceres) and squaring the Moon. Chiron is in there, too, so there's also a deep wound.

- Saturn and his aspects: Saturn is in Cancer in the 11th House and picks up the Moon (a wide orb, but clearly present in her story), Mars, Jupiter, Neptune and Pluto.

The session
I sometimes work using Voice Dialogue – a technique that gives a voice to different parts of the chart. Because Jackie is an actor, I thought this would be fun to do with her and that it would work well. She recognized that the part represented by the Moon–Saturn was the strongest and got the most airtime in her life. She saw that she had taken over her mother's drive to be well educated and that she came from a long line of black women who wanted to prosper – and for her female line, that meant being well educated and working hard. This was blocking the other part of her: the Aries–Mercury–Uranus part. Some of her conclusions were:

- You can be silly but work comes first.
- If I stand out I'll be bullied; if I am different I will be teased.

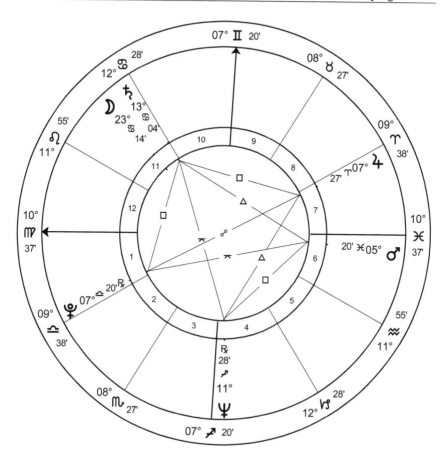

- It's normal that kids don't have an opinion.
- I need to see everything because the future might be dangerous; there will be trouble.

I suggested that she write a letter to the different parts of herself. One part was very scared to be seen and, as she says, needed a hug. Another part needed, as she puts it, to be encouraged to 'jump around' more. She has written up her blocks using some of the parts of her that we identified. The blocks in her chart are easily recognizable. Here's what she wrote:

> **Block 1:** *There is a part of me that is banished to the corner. In this corner, fear reigns. Most seemingly tame situations can appear dangerous to the girl in the corner. She doesn't like to have responsibility, prefers to escape. She suffers from lack of*

development. This part of me is fairly sensitive to situations but is often ignored by the other, more dominant voices. She is in desperate need of a hug, some positive attention, a secure space to mature.

Ms 'Who Says?' runs the show. She's the warden. She makes sure this ship runs smoothly (according to her). She is over-developed, too strong, too strict. She has the final say, judging any suggestions/opinions that may come her way. She is the biggest voice to me, most likely influenced by my mother. Ms 'Who Says?' overpowers all others but is tired from having to maintain this power.

'Jump Around' loves to move, be excited and have fun. Only, she hasn't been given much opportunity to do so, Ms 'Who Says?' keeps her in line. This is starting to frustrate 'Jump Around' terribly but she too has not been allowed to grow and finds her 'childish' wishes dismissed.

'In the Corner' and 'Jump Around' need to take Ms 'Who Says?' on to restore balance. This conflict prevents me from fully trusting my intuition, from being free to play, from taking action.

Block 2: *School bullying and teasing taught me to act as normal as possible so as to avoid being a target. If I didn't speak up, stand out, if I smiled and nodded my head, I would be safe. My quirkiness was never appreciated so I learned to hide it away.*

A memory from a past life experience made me come into this life believing I will literally be killed for daring to be different. I learned I am not allowed to have what I want because this will lead to my destruction.

Block 3: *When I spoke up for my unique self as a young girl, teachers, parents, adults pointed the finger back at me. I shouldn't bother to stick up for myself because it was all my fault anyway, my opinions didn't matter. I learned to focus on everyone else's needs and to be good in a 'normal' way so I wouldn't have any ideas that needed defending.*

Although I am a therapist myself I sometimes work with a close friend whom I also value as a good therapist. Jackie came to me through her, so in this case she could continue her therapy work on these issues with her trusted therapist. Having people to refer clients to works this way as well. The other advantage of having a network means you get referrals, which are always useful!

A final fun exercise

There are two ways you can look at blocks. Career counsellors in the Netherlands often use one called 'Disastrous Conclusions'.[15] The other is the 'Alien Warning'.

Disastrous conclusions

The first part of this exercise is to get you started. You are given a few negative statements and you have to fill in their positive equivalents. Here are some examples – and you could also take some of the conclusions from the blocks above.

- If you're over 40, you'll never get a job. This could become: *If you're over 40 you have a world of experience.*
- Life isn't supposed to be fun. This could become: *Life is full of fun opportunities.*
- Let's keep it real. This could become: …
- Work is a necessary evil. This could become: …
- Anger is dangerous. This could become: …

There are many of these to practise with. The second step is to take your own conclusions and write them down. Then work out for yourself what they could become. As with the blocks sessions you can help clients to define their conclusions. This is very helpful, as in order to change a belief you first have to recognize it. Many of the things we take for granted are just plain wrong! You may be able to encourage your clients to see this.

Alien warning

This one is simple. Just get a group together and ask them this question. If you met an alien who had never been here before and you wanted to give him some advice, what would you warn him about here on Earth?

This often shows our fears and can lead to a fun discussion about our blocks.

Now we have done the most challenging part of the VP and we can get back to finding our direction in life.

Here are some astrology books to use for this section (see the bibliography for further details):

Saturn: A New Look at an Old Devil, Liz Greene
The Twelfth House, Karen Hamaker-Zondag
LifeClock, Bruno and Louise Huber
Your Secret Self, Tracy Marks
Chiron and the Healing Journey, Melanie Reinhart
Aspects in Astrology, Sue Tompkins

1. *Core Qualities: A Gateway to Human Resources*, Daniel Ofman, Scriptum Publishers, 2002.
2. www.mijnkernkwaliteiten.nl/corequalities/whatarecorequalities.html
3. *LifeClock: The Huber Method of Timing in the Horoscope*, Bruno and Louise Huber, HopeWell, 2006.
4. *The Cosmic Egg Timer*, Joyce Hopewell and Richard Llewellyn, HopeWell, 2004.
5. *Saturn: A New Look at an Old Devil*, Liz Greene, The Aquarian Press, 1983.
6. *Aspects in Astrology*, Sue Tompkins, Element Books, 1989.
7. http://birthpsychology.com/journal-article/treating-cesarean-birth-trauma-during-infancy-and-childhood
8. *Chiron and the Healing Journey*, Melanie Reinhart, Starwalker Press, 2009.
9. *Exploring Reincarnation: The Classic Guide to the Evidence for Past-Life Experiences*, Hans ten Dam, Rider Books, 2003.
10. From a wonderful article from a 12-part series that started in the October 1994 issue of *The Mountain Astrologer*.
11. There is a lot of information on the web now on this controversial research. If you are unfamiliar with it, it would be wise to study it, as it is often quoted in arguments both for and against astrology.
12. See the Rodden database at www.astrodatabank.com for his chart and a short synopsis of his life.
13. *Birth Trauma: The Psychological Effects of Obstetrical Interventions* by William R Emerson, Emerson Training Seminars.
14. www.primal-page.com/emer1.htm
15. From Adriaan Hoogendijk.

WHAT DO I WANT?

DETERMINING GOALS
DEFINING NORMS AND VALUES
FINDING THE IDEAL ENVIRONMENT

CHAPTER 10
DETERMINING GOALS

*There is nothing so useless as doing efficiently that which
should not be done at all.*
Peter Drucker, writer and management consultant

Often, when discussing vocation, I ask clients, 'What do you want
on your gravestone?' My example client in this book really didn't
like this question. She found it a bit morbid. But I think it makes
clear what I mean by goals. At the end of your life, what do you
want to have achieved? What reputation would you like to have?
Or, in other words, how do you want others to see you now, and
also remember you after you have gone?

These questions have a way of focusing the mind on what you
find important in your life generally, and they also apply to your
working life. For many people reputation is tied up with career,
which to my mind can be paid or unpaid. The word 'career' actually
means a path, a course or progress through life. Being a parent can
also form part of your career (interesting perhaps that the root of
the word 'career' means 'race'!), as can doing voluntary work. I
say this because we are, of course, going to look at a horoscope to
define goals, and the point we will look at in the chart – the MC –
represents how we can feel useful in society. So, it is very helpful to
consider both paid and unpaid work when addressing this issue.
I have often found that there are ways of making money by using
skills learned in unpaid jobs. Not only that, but the results of these
activities can and do become incorporated into our reputation.
Career counsellors find life goals very important – and we should,
too.

The MC (or Medium Coeli), also known as the Midheaven
Of course, what I have already covered with the Sun ties in with
what we want to do in life. Here, however, I will look at the MC
for defining goals in the VP, as there is a subtle difference between
goals (MC) and what our heart desires (the Sun). In my years of

studying astrology, I have heard many definitions of this physical point in the sky. No matter which house system you use, there is no argument about the fact that this is an important point in the horoscope. Note that it is not the same as the 10th House, although in many house systems it is the cusp of this house.

However, as with many areas in astrology, the interpretation and use of this point varies from astrologer to astrologer. I have seen it described as destiny, whatever that means. But whatever astrologers might mean by this, I don't agree that the MC represents destiny. Definitions I do like include:

> Howard Sasportas: 'What stands out in us, how we behave publicly.'[1]

> Sue Tompkins: 'The way we go about getting where we want to be, our aims and ambitions, what we aspire to.'[2]

These are just two examples among many. Robert Hand's *Horoscope Symbols* is a book I would also recommend for more descriptions (see the bibliography).

The MC is defined by many as denoting vocation, but I really disagree with this. Some astrologers looking at my chart have suggested all sorts of good jobs for me. As I have Taurus at this highest part of the chart, Taurean pursuits have been suggested, such as working with nature, gardening and farming, to name a few. Now maybe I am a late developer, as it is only last year that I decided to grow vegetables on my roof, but if I had to make a living as a farmer or work outside while hefting heavy farm equipment, I would probably take to drink! However, I *do* think I have a bit of a *reputation* for enjoying food (one of my friends gave me the nickname 'Faye two-dinners Cossar' after a particular evening's dining), and for being stubborn. In my opinion, my vocation is definitely represented more by the Sun and its aspects. However, I would like to be known for offering something Taurean to the astrology world. My aim is to be practical, offering ideas that can be applied to actual situations. I hope this book is doing this and is adding to my reputation as having a type of down-to-earth, common sense approach. I hope that Taurus energy forms part of my image and reputation.

The MC/IC axis describes our orientation at a certain place. It shows which signs are 'above and below' us at our place of birth. (As an aside, it is interesting to look at this axis, in terms of reputation and goals, if we relocate to a different city or country.) In my early days of studying astrology, the picture I was often given for this axis, and found very helpful, is of the IC being the roots of a tree – suggesting where we come from, our past – and the MC being the leaves or fruit reaching for the sky. The axes work together. Our home environment (the IC as the cusp of the 4th House in quadrant house systems) affects our working environment (the MC as the cusp of the 10th house), and vice versa. So, how might we draw from our roots and family background to attain our aspirations? How can Scorpio (the sign on my IC) help me to be more practical? I also find it illuminating to see that we mostly show the MC, including in software such as Solar Fire, with an arrow, implying direction and movement. It describes where we are 'heading', as a compass might.

MC and Capricorn

Although the MC is not necessarily connected to the 10th House and can describe something different, there is a Capricorn connection. You can see that the words used when describing the MC are very goat-like: ambition, goal, reputation, achievement, aspiration, aims, and perhaps a bit of planning, too. Capricorn is about something concrete. Results. It has a sense of authority or expertise. You might say that the sign on the MC suggests where we want to gain expertise. Hopefully the link to reputation is now clear.

Aspects to the MC

I want to return to a point I made earlier in this book about the sign on the cusp of any house. The sign on the MC shows the 'how', not the 'what'. Aspects to this MC/IC axis will flavour the way we pursue our goals, especially if we have a planet at either of these points. Any planet on the MC or IC will be a very big influence generally in our life and particularly in the working environment. You will have seen by now that I am a big fan of aspects, but somehow I seem to use aspects to the MC less than others. This may be because I don't like putting them in the chart, the reasons for which I have already described in Chapter 4. It's not that I think they don't work or are unimportant, but the MC moves approximately one degree every four minutes so the birth time needs to be accurate. These aspects are different from planet-to-planet aspects, though, and need to be interpreted differently – something that many astrologers don't always do. Planets in aspect to the MC will add meaning to the question of how we make our reputation and the kind of goals we set to get there.

Questions to use when getting to grips with goals for the VP
I offer you some questions that you can use to start a dialogue with
your clients, but be creative. My client here used images for the
MC, as she is very 'visual', so let your clients be creative too.

- What do you want as an epitaph?
- What would you like people to say about you?
- Do you have a goal that you are working towards?
- What reputation do you think you have?

You can suggest that clients ask other people they know to comment
on their reputation. This is sometimes very helpful, not to mention
revealing.

Client exercise: SMART
One of the exercises I occasionally give to clients is an 'oldie but
a goodie'. It has been used for goal setting in various ways in
business for a long time and is called SMART. It stands for Specific,
Measurable, Attainable, Realistic and Timely. It may be a bit old-
fashioned now, but I still think getting clients (or yourself) to sit
down with a pen and paper and have a think about this is a good
exercise, especially when it comes to our life goals.

If you have helped your client to get an idea of where they are
heading, this exercise can take them a step further. I let my example
client off this one, and it can be quite confronting for some clients.
There is a lot of information on the web about SMART but, in
brief, taking the example of an astrologer setting up a practice and
defining some goals, it might look like this:

1. Specific Make it very specific. *I want to build an astrology
practice offering career advice to clients over the age of twenty-nine. I
aim to have ten clients a month.*

2. Measurable You have to be able to see if you reached your
aim and make it a little harder than you think you can manage!
*The first year my aim is to start with two clients a month as an
average. At the end of each year I will add two to my target, reaching
an average of ten a month after five years.*

3. Attainable You need to really believe you can commit to
doing this. Do you have the experience, the material, the
website, the contacts? What do you need to attain this? More
training? Don't make it so hard that you give up – this should
motivate you, not put you off.

4. Realistic Is your family on your side? Do you have enough free time to commit to this goal? Do you have the money to pay for any training? Do you need/have help?

5. Timely You need to have a time frame or a deadline. In this example we have a monthly ambition but you might want to add sub-goals. For instance, *I will mail two people per week and ask them to send out information to their friends about my services.* It needs to be concrete, otherwise you'll never start.

Getting clients to do this is a way of getting them committed and involved in their own life goals. You can even play the role of an 'encourager' if they come to you regularly, by acting as their conscience! Even if your client doesn't complete the exercise, the resulting discussion can be very fruitful.

My example client's goal

Jackie has the MC in Gemini with Venus conjunct it. Other planets make aspects to it too, but we didn't have time to go into all of these. However, we discussed Venus in Gemini at some length, using my suggestions as a starting point for what this might mean and how it might be relevant to her reputation or her goals in life. Here's what she wrote:

> *Captain Communicator to the rescue! Able to connect and relate to the world one chat at a time! I want to introduce myself to everyone and then introduce everyone to everyone else. I need to talk to people, listen to them, write movingly for them, be heard by them, understand and be understood. I want to broker in people, their norms and oddities and then share my wealth with all; learning and teaching, discovering and enlightening, an endless loop of exchange.*

To me this is a very good description of what she would like to do. The symbolism of Venus in Gemini is clear in her goals. She would love to have a reputation as a connector of people through stories.

Your mission may now be clearer than it was. This is a developing process that gets refined with age. You need to discover which environment would support you in gaining this reputation, but first let's have a look at belief systems.

Books

There are not many books specifically on the MC, but of course many of the books I recommend cover it. However, there is a very old book I would like to mention which I see is still available at the time of writing. It's a small but handy text called *Aspects to Horoscope Angles* by Vivia Jayne. Knowing Frank Clifford's work on the Midheaven, I would also recommend his book *The Midheaven: Spotlight on Success*.

1. *The Twelve Houses*, Howard Sasportas, Flare Publications, 2007, p. 69.
2. *Aspects in Astrology*, Sue Tompkins, Element Books, 1989, p. 246. See also her *The Contemporary Astrologer's Handbook*, Flare Publications, 2006, p 280.

CHAPTER 11

DEFINING NORMS AND VALUES

The world is full of people that have stopped listening to themselves or have listened only to their neighbours to learn what they ought to do, how they ought to behave, and what the values are they should be living for.
Joseph Campbell, American mythologist and writer

Why bother with this?
If you Google 'values and career', you will see how many people and companies believe that being able to define values is particularly important when it comes to having a happy working life. On the web, you can find tests to do and lists of values you can use to make cards and checklists. You might want to use some of these or give them to your clients. According to most career advisors, discussing values is well worth doing, which is why it forms part of a VP. Most people don't think much about what they value at work. However, I agree that it is important. We will never be happy if our value system isn't satisfied.

In a way, we have already covered this topic astrologically when we looked at talents. I use Venus in the horoscope for defining values. As I wrote in the Talents section (see pages 117–28), Venus describes what we love and enjoy and therefore what we value. But perhaps a list of words from career counsellors is useful for creating discussion. Words such as commitment, justice, fairness, equality, integrity, love, caring, unity, diversity, openness, communication, independence, freedom, challenge, variety, contribution, making a difference, listening, attention to detail, punctuality, professionalism, safety, ethics, teamwork, prestige and reputation are all used to define values that might be important to you. Some of the exercises suggest that you rate values in order of their importance to you, so you have a checklist to compare with the values in any company where you might be employed. If you have a talent for making things, you could design cards with a value on each one (add your own, perhaps astrologically-based, values) and get your clients to put them in order of importance, going along with my mantra of getting clients involved in the process.

To define values using the horoscope, you can just reframe what you did in the Talents section. However, I offer a fun exercise here that you can do when working with clients (or for yourself) to help define what you really care about. I have done this often in groups and the results have sometimes been quite surprising and always enlightening. The exercise is simply to ask your student or client to bring something to the class (or to you) that they really love. (Not children or pets! Hopefully that's a given, but a photo of a loved one is fine.) The questions then are: Why this item? What does it represent to you? Why is it important to you? It is also interesting to investigate its history or how you acquired it. If it is a photo of a person or pet, why this particular photo? Often a favourite item shows many things that we value. You can then discuss how this might relate to work. Every time I have done this in a group, apart from the fact that much hilarity usually ensued, the symbolism of Venus in the owner's chart was clearly present.

The example of this that sticks in my mind is of a relatively quiet student who was in an astrology group I ran many years ago. He was the lone male in a group of women (what's new?) and came across, as his Pisces rising suggested, as being a bit chaotic and interested in strange things. He was a Sagittarius Sun, so was searching for meaning. Imagine our surprise when he carefully and lovingly unwrapped a large object that was swathed in many protective layers and placed a ceremonial sabre on the table. It was a beautifully crafted object with inlaid stones, and I imagine it was quite a costly item. The explanation of how he came by it escapes me now, but the story was distinctly sexual, and symbolic of deeper meaning and passions. He had Venus conjunct Neptune in Scorpio in the 8th House. He valued (and, with that Neptune, perhaps dreamed of) the strength and power that the sabre represented. It was a side that we had, understandably, never seen from him. It actually made him seem somewhat threatening. If I remember rightly, he kept the sabre under his bed... He had done research on this sabre and could tell us everything about it, showing his love of depth and finding information. This energy was also present in his current work, which was in line with what he valued.

Norms

I think 'norms' is a funny word. I don't really know why – maybe it conjures up old-fashioned ideals for me, or perhaps it goes against my Aquarian nature. But it is used in companies, mostly in the same sentence as 'values', and therefore in the VP. Here are a few shortened definitions from web dictionaries:

> A standard of achievement or behaviour that is required, desired or designated as normal; an established standard of behaviour shared by members of a social group to which each member is expected to conform; the rules of behaviour that are part of the ideology of the group.

> Norms tend to reflect the values of the group and specify those actions that are proper and those that are inappropriate, as well as rewards for adherence and the punishment for non-conformity.

So 'norms' is a word normally applied to groups, and in companies I would refer to it as the 'company culture'. It describes a set of beliefs which are not really about rules (so we don't want to consider Saturn) and it is different from values, as it also includes behaviours. And indeed there is a judgement and perhaps even (subtle) punishment associated with not adhering to the ruling culture. It is linked to belief systems. The reason yours are important is contained within this simple question: do they fit the company culture? If your beliefs are not in line with the company culture, then this might be a recipe for some moral torment, or at least some difficult dilemmas.

I have many clients who are working in a country other than their homeland, so there are culture clashes in this area, too. You need to take ethnic background into account when working with vocation and this can be tricky, especially when there are cultural similarities, such as speaking the same language, as in the case of New Zealand and the UK. It is all too easy to make assumptions about how something works at both country and company level. It is sometimes easier when the difference is very great, as then it is obvious that there are major divergences in cultural behaviours.

This was made very clear to me once when I attended a fun evening for a women's group. There were several tables set up where you took your place, but you were not allowed to sit with someone you knew. On each table were the printed rules of the card game we were playing. After several games the winner and loser moved to different tables. After a few rounds there were lively and heated debates and even stronger arguments. Why? Because, unbeknown to us, the rules of the game were different at each table and after the first round the written rules had been removed from all the tables! It was an eye-opener about the way we make assumptions. This type of mistake is often made when we move company or country. We assume that companies have similar cultures. And we do this with countries, too, especially if they have the same language as ours. So taking time to discuss norms and culture is worthwhile.

Belief systems, judgement, assumptions, cultures – we are, of course, talking Jupiter. He is the planet I use in an individual chart to look at belief systems. Jupiter by house, by sign and particularly by aspect, shows where our faith lies and our philosophy of life. True, Jupiter also shows how we grow and where we are optimistic, expansive and generous – where we need room to manoeuvre and where we are prepared to take risks. It shows how we solve our human need to find meaning. How we can broaden our horizons, perhaps by travelling, perhaps by reading philosophy. I must say I am often annoyed by the positive press that Jupiter often gets as the 'greater benefic'. Yes, he can be, but no planet is positive or negative. Jupiter has his dark side. A very strong belief in something can create problems at work as well as in private. Fundamentalism belongs to Jupiter's realm. This god of thunder was a judge, which can be good or bad. And it is all very well having a rigid belief, such as thinking we should be able to wear whatever we like to an interview, but it may well be counterproductive in a strongly conservative organization, perhaps one where Saturn and Jupiter are in aspect, which could result in a culture of strict traditional rules.

So, Jupiter represents our vision of life and our set of beliefs, which can also mean our assumptions. Spiritual teachers often advise us to examine these. There is a saying used in the title of a book by Wayne W Dyer – *You'll see it when you believe it* – that sums up what many are teaching: what we believe and think affects what is manifested.

But back to the matter at hand. Here, I want to use Jupiter to look at our own set of beliefs. If we have a horoscope set up for the founding of a company (the company chart is a wonderful tool), we can interpret Jupiter to describe the company culture, too. Does it match us? Can we live with it?

Jupiter and aspects

Taking Jupiter himself first in this context, here is something from the *Encyclopaedia Britannica*: 'Jupiter… worship embodied a distinct moral conception. He is especially concerned with oaths, treaties, and leagues…. This connection with the conscience, with the sense of obligation and right dealing, was never quite lost throughout Roman history.' Another example: when speaking of Jupiter, the question for Ariel Guttman and Kenneth Johnson is: 'What kind of attitude do we bring to the achievement of our goals?'[1] The question you need to answer in this part of the VP is: what do you see as 'right dealing', what is the attitude you bring to your work? What are your 'laws'?

One way to discover how aspects might work is to imagine the gods that correspond to the planets meeting each other. In other words, in this case, visualize how Jupiter in his law-making, moral, conscience, right-dealing function might be influenced by Mars, the god of war. And which laws would he make together with Neptune or Venus? If you are more visually orientated, this idea may work well for you. Using this imagery is a great way to discover meaning during meditation or even while you're in the bath! Picture the gods interacting with each other.

Instead of going through lists, I shall give you my ideas for this using this technique. I will only give the interaction of the gods (the planet combinations), but of course each has a connection with Jupiter in a particular sign (e.g. Jupiter in aspect to Mars has the same themes as Jupiter in Aries). And I am only looking at how all the gods will affect Jupiter in his beliefs and law-making capacity, not how Jupiter will affect the other gods. The result will give you ideas for discovering deep-seated belief systems that your client (or you) might have, which can of course operate positively or negatively.

Jupiter meets the Sun

When I was three, I wanted to be four. When I was four, I wanted to be Prime Minister – Jeffrey Archer, British politician and author (Sun conjunct Jupiter)

The two chiefs together. The Sun has been associated with different gods (and sometimes goddesses) throughout history, but the solar principle has always had a high status because of its obvious importance in the sky. In modern western astrology, kingship is usually a quality of the Sun. This Sun 'king' will want Jupiter to believe in the 'self'. He will suggest having a positive approach, one that perhaps gains recognition or attention. A sort of law that says 'I am important. I deserve attention.' But, as all planets revolve around the Sun, the Sun could want Jupiter to make a law that everything should revolve around him, which could lead to arrogance: 'It's all about me.' The belief is that life has purpose and anything can be achieved. 'I am the boss of my own life, my attitude to life helps me to go for my vocation.' This can result in a strong self-belief.

Jupiter meets the Moon

The search for human freedom can never be complete without freedom for women – Betty Ford (Moon square Jupiter), founder of The Betty Ford Center and wife of US President Gerald Ford

The Moon also has more than one god or goddess associated with her. However, we now tend to think of her as indeed a feminine, receptive principle – one that reflects the light of the Sun. I can't imagine that Jupiter and a female Moon/Cancerian goddess have much common ground. If she were dictating laws to Jupiter they might change frequently depending on her mood. However, she would want the family protected – and, of course, the children (or pets). Her beliefs might be: 'Home and country first – you must be patriotic and protective. However, you also need to look after others and feed them if they arrive at your door.' Emotion is important. How people feel is important. Looking after women and children is vital, as is taking care of the sick and needy. Ancestors must be honoured and the family line should be continued. Women's rights might be important to her, too. Or she might be anti-abortion so as to protect children. History is another important area for the Moon, so laws regarding antiquities, historical buildings or objects and traditions might be part of her remit.

The Moon has always been seen as a protector of the Earth, so her law may be to protect the Earth, plants, trees and animals and not have them plundered or destroyed. (Ceres also plays a role here.)

Jupiter meets Mercury

There is no more terrible fate for a comedian than to be taken seriously – Barry Humphries, Australian comedian, better known as Dame Edna Everage (Mercury quintile Jupiter)

A little sincerity is a dangerous thing, and a great deal of it is absolutely fatal – Oscar Wilde, Irish writer and poet (Mercury sextile Jupiter)

Mercury is a god with several functions. He is a messenger, so he will want a law that makes communication and information important. Everyone should talk, everyone should be curious. You should listen to me. He does what Jupiter says, but Jupiter would be lost without his information. Mercury's forerunner (Nabu) was a scribe who actually recorded Marduk's (Jupiter's) laws. Mercury's role as Hermes means that life must be witty and entertaining, as he is easily bored. He favours the intellect but he is also a thief. And Jupiter is not averse to a little mischief, so these two work well together. Life should be fun.

Mercury's connection to healing shouldn't be forgotten – in mythology he carries the caduceus. So, this might suggest he would also create beliefs about everyone needing to be fit and healthy, everyone having a routine and taking care of their body. This is, of course, more the Virgo side of Mercury, whereas the above quotes highlight the more Geminian beliefs.

Jupiter meets Venus

There is no virtue whatsoever in creating clothing or accessories that are not practical – Giorgio Armani, Italian fashion designer (Venus trine Jupiter)

It's all about good taste – Giorgio Armani

As with Jupiter, I feel Venus often gets too good a press. She can be tricky. She can persuade Jupiter to make laws that are fair (Libra) but then she gets very annoyed, as she often did, when they don't work for her. She can probably wind Jupiter around her little finger. She might tell him to make laws that are money-orientated, as long as she gets a good deal. In her Taurean guise, she will persuade him to be practical or earthy ('if you can't see it or prove it, it's rubbish') or she can suggest that being safe and secure is the essential philosophy of life. Practicality, nature, harmony or beauty may form the basis of beliefs. But so can greed ('it's all mine'). Building up a fortune might be an ideal to aspire to. Life should be enjoyed but this can, of course, lead to hedonism.

On the Libran side, she will want laws protecting marriage or other relationships, because having a partner is a very important issue for her. And she might want Jupiter to believe in dialogue and the weighing up of different viewpoints: 'Everyone should have their say'; 'Balancing everything you hear and taking all ideas and opinions into consideration is what everyone should do'; 'Be reasonable! Peace and no conflicts.' If this goes too far it can result in someone who always compromises or gives in for the sake of peace, i.e. harmony at all costs.

Jupiter meets Mars

The only time an aircraft has too much fuel on board is when it is on fire – Sir Charles Kingsford Smith, Australian aviator (Mars square Jupiter)

These two can create a bit of a macho philosophy. These are the tough guys getting on well together. Mars, being the god of war, will tend to suggest a law that says everyone must 'get on with it' and initiate things; that everyone must be able to defend themselves, their property or their country. 'Action is the only way to go'; 'No waiting around – if there is a conflict then let's deal with it'; 'You need to stick up for yourself, defend yourself.' Perhaps Mars makes Jupiter more opportunistic or selfish. 'Let's get started' might be the catchphrase. 'Life should be a challenge or even a bit dangerous.' 'It's all about now.' Working in a negative way, this can result in a belief that violence or aggression is the only way to solve problems.

Jupiter meets Ceres

I want to speak up for mothers who are fighting for good schools, safe neighborhoods, clean air and clean airwaves; for older women, some of them widows, who have raised their families and now find that their skills and life experiences are not valued in the workplace; for women who are working all night as nurses, hotel clerks, and fast food cooks so that they can be at home during the day with their kids; and for women everywhere who simply don't have time to do everything they are called upon to do each day – Hillary Rodham Clinton (Jupiter quincunx Ceres)

In the current astrological literature Ceres is often seen as a sort of earth mother – a strong protector of her child, which she is. But she is also a good match for Zeus or Jupiter in myth and is definitely up to the challenge of getting her point of view across to him. She is on an equal footing and, in this mode, will dictate laws to Jupiter that are pretty strong. I envisage her as a pretty tough cookie, quite like a female Saturn in fact.

Her laws will be about protecting rites of passage, the cycle of life and death and particularly nature, the Earth and the environment. The Moon, of course, will want to protect the Earth, but Ceres is more practical than emotional about it. Ceres goes for purity. I think she's against any messing about with nature. So, her philosophy will not allow genetic engineering or any other form of DNA manipulation. She might be an animal rights activist or a campaigner who wants to do something about climate change. After all, it was she who first created the seasons and she probably wants them to stay as they are. I think she will want an equal rights law too – not only for women, although that is very important, but for all. She values the wisdom of older women and may want to promote this group in some way.

Jupiter meets Saturn

Life is full of misery, loneliness, and suffering – and it's all over much too soon – Woody Allen, US film-maker and actor (Jupiter square Saturn)

Faith is the great cop-out, the great excuse to evade the need to think and evaluate evidence. Faith is belief in spite of, even perhaps because of, the lack of evidence – Richard Dawkins, British evolutionary biologist and author (Jupiter conjunct Saturn)

I imagine these two have been at odds forever, although they will probably end up with a good balance of laws, since Saturn is quite happy to dictate his wisdom. It should be remembered that Saturn was dethroned and banished by Jupiter, so this is probably a businesslike meeting, rather than one between friends. Saturn in a suit will want everyone to be responsible and work hard. That's how life rewards you: by having a goal and not straying from your path. Saturn has a philosophy that says 'there is a time for every purpose' and time itself should be revered. 'One shouldn't waste time or be too early or, especially, too late.' 'A deal is a deal and don't break appointments.' He can also contribute to creating a very traditional view on life or a sober, even depressing outlook (the type for which Woody Allen became famous). 'Life isn't meant to be fun.' Scientists often have a Saturnian philosophy, too – only things that can be proven are 'true'. The discipline required in science is compulsory in life.

Jupiter meets Uranus

I'm a catalyst for change. You can't be an outsider and be successful over 30 years without leaving a certain amount of scar tissue around the place – Rupert Murdoch, Australian–US media baron (Jupiter square Uranus)

Nowadays we tend to associate the god Prometheus with the astrological Uranus. His name means 'foresight'. Having stolen fire (enlightenment) from the gods, Prometheus gave it to humans and defended them against the gods. So although this will be a pretty explosive meeting, Jupiter will get lots of creative new ideas from Uranus. It is probably more like a brainstorming session. Uranus wants laws about independence and freedom, all have a right to free speech and everyone should be honest. There should be the opportunity for everyone to be unique and authentic, but people need to be independent and to take care of their own needs. Everyone should do their own thing. Giving the outsider or rebel a chance will be something Uranus might insist on, knowing he's right. 'We must look to the future and break down barriers.' 'Technology and innovation must be allowed in all areas as we must push our knowledge as far as we can, even with controversial topics.' Human rights activist Ludwig Minelli, the founder of Dignitas, an organization in Switzerland that offers dignity in death through euthanasia, has this aspect. He believes that everyone who is capable of free choice has the right to kill themselves.

Jupiter meets Neptune

Imagination is more important than knowledge – Albert Einstein, German theoretical physicist (Jupiter quintile Neptune)

The god of thunder meeting the god of the sea suggests a stormy, tumultuous event. In myth, Jupiter gave Neptune the oceans to look after, so we might expect them to agree on looking after the waters. The ocean represents the collective unconscious which, since Lynne McTaggart's book was published,[2] we might now call the 'field' – something that encompasses all mankind, animals and the planet that we live on. 'We are all connected, so we must help each other to help ourselves.' 'Compassion is a must.' Neptune's laws suggest we must dream. We must use our intuition and imagination and lose ourselves in fantasy. He might want laws that honour artistic creativity as opposed to the more mentally-orientated laws that Uranus concerns himself with. We must dance and sing and listen to music, and be able to escape from reality somehow. And a glass of wine now and then doesn't hurt either. Working negatively, this can make you believe you are a victim of life or that life always means loss and sadness.

Jupiter meets Pluto

It is the role of good journalism to take on powerful abuses – Julian Assange, Australian Wiki-leaks founder (Jupiter sextile Pluto, Jupiter trine Mercury)

Jupiter gave Hades, or Pluto, the underworld to look after and, as with Neptune, the gods are brothers and both very powerful. But I think Pluto, being sneakier, might get everything he wants. His laws involve his being in control, deciding his own fate, being the one in charge. 'Everyone should be passionate and emotionally involved in their work.' He is not above using office politics to get his way. 'If you are going to do something, you do it.' To quote Yoda talking to Luke in *Star Wars*: 'No! Try not. Do, or do not. There is no try.' He also believes in researching issues deeply, that nothing should be superficial. As ruler of the underworld, Pluto wants to know what is happening in hidden places. The fundamental belief in life is that there will always be crises and you will have to start your life again. But there is a belief that from death comes life; that we must always transform, and root out any 'rubbish'. 'You can only stay in control by being alert and knowing secrets.' Expressed negatively this could result in a very cruel philosophy – 'if it doesn't suit me, get rid of it'. Or even sexual, or other types of, abuse. Operating in another way, when feeling powerless, it could result in becoming someone with a philosophy that includes sabotage, manipulation or subterfuge.

All of the above are offered to get you started on a discussion so that, as usual, your client can write up what it is they believe in and what is really important to them in their lives. This shouldn't be too compromised in their working life. Here's my client's example.

Jackie's norms and values session
As a reminder, here's what I wrote about the bio:

> This will probably be a repeat of themes already mentioned – Jupiter (her beliefs) is in Aries and Venus (values) is in Gemini, which resonates with the Sun–Mercury conjunction. This will just be a discussion about her norms and values.

The session covered many themes we had already touched on. Over the page is the chart with the relevant planets and aspects highlighted.

We talked mainly about the aspects with Neptune and Pluto as they pick up both Jupiter and Venus, so it was hard to differentiate between norms and values. We didn't really talk about Saturn again, but it is obvious from other parts of the VP that sticking to deals, appointments and agreements forms part of Jackie's belief system. Respect for others was something she mentioned, too, which has a lot to do with Saturn.

The rest of the session was spent discussing how her ideas, which follow, would operate in a working environment:

- Everyone should be allowed to have opinions and should be heard.
- You should talk to me.
- Banter is fun.

- I need to hear the 'why' and then I'm OK.
- Valuing the curious.
- Action and things happening are good – I hate it when it's quiet.
- There was a big drive from my grandmother for the women in the family to learn and be bright. To get an education.
- I love intelligent women.
- There is a family pattern of learning.

These ideas are all related to Venus in Gemini.

And regarding Neptune, we uncovered a love and appreciation of the creative and also of what she called 'consideration'. 'You should be able to feel what I need.' Perhaps an organization with consideration and empathy for the staff would be the ideal workplace.

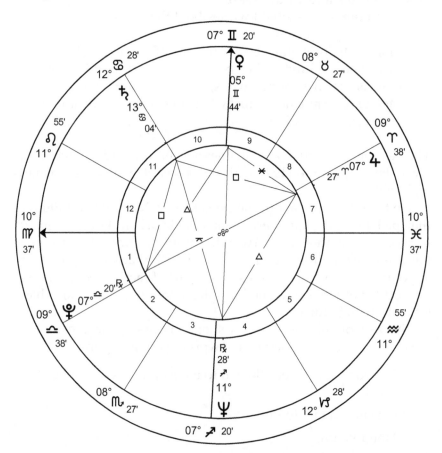

The Pluto is obvious in what she wrote about her norms and values below. In this session, the principles we discussed range from 'what's mine is mine' to issues of privacy and loyalty. We ended up with trust and 'keep your mouth shut', 'don't go behind my back', and 'don't tell tales out of school'. Here's what she wrote for her VP.

Norms and values

> Without a doubt, I have immense respect for other's feelings and opinions. I expect no less in return. I love exchanging thoughts and ideas in excited conversation with like-minded people, preferably over a good meal. Depth in discussion allows me to connect and understand. When I hit gold and discover an intimate part of a person, he can trust I will never betray his disclosure. Be true to me and I will stay true to you. Questioning people are my brethren; curiosity never kills this cat. A wondering mind can find delight in the simplest of things.

Books to use for this section (see the bibliography for further details):

Exploring Jupiter, Stephen Arroyo
The Inner Planets, Liz Greene and Howard Sasportas

1. *Mythic Astrology: Archetypal Powers in the Horoscope*, Ariel Guttman and Kenneth Johnson, Llewellyn Publications, 1993, p. 124.
2. *The Field*, Lynne McTaggart, Harper Paperbacks, 2003.

CHAPTER 12

FINDING THE IDEAL ENVIRONMENT

Don't blame the boss. He has enough problems.
Donald Rumsfeld, Secretary of Defence under
President George W Bush

Whether you work for yourself or someone else, the environment in which you work will have a great deal to do with how happy you are in your working life. The word 'environment' has many shades of meaning. The one I mean encompasses some of the following definitions taken randomly from the web:

The totality of the surrounding conditions

The area in which one lives or exists (or, in this case, works)

The working 'habitat'

And, from the ecological viewpoint, the external surroundings in which a plant or animal lives, which tend to influence its development and behaviour

The UK Health and Safety pages[1] define various things as being important for a working environment. These include noise, ventilation, temperature, lighting and stress. All important factors, but I'm not sure we can have much to say about these by using a horoscope. However, in a more general sense, we can investigate preferences for physical surroundings, such as the need for a light and airy office (as a general example, in my experience Air signs need light and Fire signs like a reasonable amount of space). Or we can investigate the location of the office, such as a particular town or country, or a cityscape or home. It can also mean such things as whether we need a desk in a fixed spot. Clearly, I am using a wide definition when referring to the physical environment.

When we use the definition 'things that influence our development and behaviour', one thing this could mean is food in the widest sense. What is nurturing for us? Now, this might mean in the literal sense, such as whether the company restaurant serves decent food. However, it could also refer to adequate or appropriate pay and employment conditions. And the people around us have a huge influence: who we work with and how we are treated and valued will affect us greatly.

The Moon as environment
The way I look at environment is to first take the Moon and her sign and aspects. Among other things, the Moon provides information on what is nurturing for us. What is it that feeds or nourishes us? What kind of working 'home' suits us best?

Venus for colleagues
Venus in a chart highlights how we feel valued and this is, of course, in relationship to other people. We feel best in an environment where we can relate to our colleagues in a way that is natural for us. Venus and her aspects show what makes us feel valued by others, and therefore she offers clues to the best types of colleagues for us.

The Sun is the boss
We have looked at the Sun and its aspects already, using it to discover what makes our heart sing and what we really want to do in our lives. However, as with many things in a horoscope, we can interpret it in another way. The Sun also represents how we get on with authority figures in our lives. The Sun represents the masculine, in particular the father, and finding out about that parental relationship will give clues as to how we are likely to perceive authority in both men and women. As an example, someone who has had a very strict father and has always been told what to study and which job to go for will likely opt for one of two ways when working for another: they might never want to take any initiative and will wait to be told what to do, or they might rebel and harbour great resentment towards their boss. From a horoscope, it is usually clear whether someone will eventually want to be self-employed. However, this is sometimes a long process. So my advice to someone who is not ready to take that step (and my advice in general) is to go for a job that doesn't take them off their chosen path. Many of my clients know that they would like to become self-employed. If this is an authentic and achievable wish, then what is usually stopping them taking this step is a fear, a block. I discussed blocks in Chapter 9. The idea here is to define what kind of authority figure your client wants, expects or can cope with.

Ceres as an environmental factor

Since she became a dwarf planet in 2006 and thus on the same level as Pluto, I have been studying Ceres and watching her in different ways, such as following global events, asking questions about aspects in natal horoscopes, and seeing when she is triggered in all sorts of charts. I have come to the conclusion that, on a personal level, she has a lot to do with *putting you in the right place at the right time.* In the mythology, later in her life Ceres taught the art of cultivation. She knew where to plant seeds, how to feed them and propagate them, and she had the power of producing abundance (or famine, in one of her fouler moods). I think looking at Ceres in the chart (and if we use Pluto, why wouldn't we use Ceres too?) can give us clues as to where and how we might be 'abundant', particularly referring to our physical (working) environment. Being in an environment that helps us flourish is clearly useful, not to mention fulfilling.

The total picture

So by looking at all of these things, we can get a pretty good description of what our ideal working environment would be. It sounds like a lot of effort to be able to describe something you think you know intuitively, but I have been amazed by how useful this process can be for clients. Like a lot of good astrological counselling, it seems to give insight and also permission to want and, in this case to ask for, a personally nurturing working environment. A lot of assumptions are made about good working space – we tend to think that everyone needs the same things. Naturally, there are some basic needs, but thinking that everyone needs good pay, a desk, a good rewards system or decent evaluations are indeed major presumptions. The way we work today has changed enormously. Developments in social media have blurred the boundaries between our working and private lives and hot-desking (getting or sharing a desk wherever we are) is very common in big organizations these days. The café has become an office. Clearly some people will have more trouble with this than others. If you have a lot of Taurus energy, where do you keep your stuff? If you are hopeless with computers, how are you going to get the information you need? Because our physical working environment is changing so much, we may need to redesign our homes to cater for these changes. How we get looked after for who we essentially are will become even more of an issue in the future. And these developments mean that the people around us become even more important. So I urge you to discuss this with clients. Helping them to define what would be good for them, and discussing the ways in which their current situation is problematic, can be of great assistance to them. Can you help them take steps to improve it?

Putting it into practice

The best way to understand this is again by using examples, so I will take the astrological groupings: the Moon, Venus and Ceres. The sign on the 6th House cusp will describe the 'how' of our daily rituals and therefore give a clue as to the way we organize our daily life and our approach to earning a crust. The 10th House cusp is more about our social status, and of course it says something about our career environment. The 2nd House cusp is also used by a lot of astrologers in terms of work, but I covered that in Chapter 7 on talents and making money. Again, my favourite tools here are the planets and their aspects but that doesn't mean there aren't others. The result you are aiming for is to get to a definition of your client's preferred working environment. How you get there doesn't matter to the client. Getting there *does*. Use your own tools to obtain the information needed from your client. I offer mine here, along with my questions for starting a discussion, to get you going. I have done three summaries combining the sign and the aspect. Although the sign and corresponding aspect are not the same, there are similarities and these tables are here to provide enough ideas to get you started on the themes to be covered. There is a table for the areas of environment, colleagues and 'abundance'. The 'boss' can be extrapolated from other Sun tables. You can add anything you think might be relevant by using the house placement and rulers as well.

Questions

Here are some good questions in general:

1. What was your favourite job?
2. What did you like about the environment?
3. Who was your best boss ever?
4. What did you like about him/her?
5. Who were your favourite colleagues?
6. What did you like about them?
7. What was the worst environment you have ever been in at work?
8. What made it so terrible?
9. Have you ever worked in a building or other working space that made you want to go to work?

Table 7: The Moon as environment – some examples

Sign, or planet in aspect to the Moon	You need... (these are my suggestions – add your own to create your own table)
Aries, or Moon aspecting Mars	A culture of going for it where risks can be taken – where there is action and a lot happening. New challenges are offered. A place where it is acceptable to argue. Room to move, not tied to a desk. Maybe a sports facility. Everyone looks after themselves.
Taurus*, or Moon aspecting Venus	A stable environment with good pay. Long-term or fixed position i.e. not a short-term contract. Comfortable and probably fixed (own space) environment physically. Humour is important. A good canteen.
Gemini*, or Moon aspecting Mercury	A busy environment with interruptions and communication or even gossip. Freedom of expression. Lots of different things happening. People coming and going. Happy without a fixed spot. A coffee bar! Intellectual stimulation and wit important.
Cancer	A home from home. Being part of a team or part of a 'family' in some way. A sense of belonging. A protective and safe environment in terms of people. Having a 'nest'. Being able to care for others.
Leo, or Moon aspecting the Sun	A culture where the staff get recognition for who they are. Perhaps a position that puts you in the spotlight or (more often) where you are recognized for what you are good at. An environment that notices you and gives you attention. A place to play and be creative. The best space, one to be proud of.
Virgo*, or Moon aspecting Mercury	An environment where you can be helpful and of service. A culture of providing information (as opposed to communication). A space that has a sense of order or practicality.
Libra*, or Moon aspecting Venus	A culture of discussion. Doing things together. An environment where feedback is possible. Being able to have a 'mate' at work. Sharing and doing things for each other. Sharing a space. A beautiful office. Harmony among the staff is important. A code of decency. Flowers on your desk.
Scorpio, or Moon aspecting Pluto	A political environment. A research environment or one where privacy is respected. Being able to go deeply into issues, so not somewhere that has a superficial attitude to the staff. Loyalty is very important. An environment where you can get stuck into something with a passion. A personal and private space.

Sagittarius, or Moon aspecting Jupiter	Room to move and expand, even a space outside or one on the move. Maybe where travel is expected. Where exploration is important. A shared vision for the staff. Few rules and regulations. A place to grow and take risks. Opportunities for adventure.
Capricorn, or Moon aspecting Saturn	A company with clear goals. A place where ambition is rewarded. A structured hierarchy with clear reporting. A sense of responsibility at all levels. Professional culture. Where expertise can be gained, for example through training. A set of rules is fine. A defined space.
Aquarius, or Moon aspecting Uranus	A place where independence is possible. A place to do things your own way. Working together but on your own thing. An environment where ideas are valued, exchanged and rewarded. A future focus. Respect for what you know. An intelligent organization. Good technology. No stupid rules. An honest environment – no hidden agendas. Your own laptop and mobile phone?
Pisces, or Moon aspecting Neptune	A place with compassion. A place to daydream and be creative, where concepts are the order of the day. Consideration for the staff. An environment that aims to make the world better. A creative, artistic, chaotic space, maybe with music. An area where you can 'meditate'. An organization with a dream.
Aspecting Ceres	An ergonomically and ecologically good environment. An organization that values women (or feminine values), particularly older women. A company that values the Earth.

* Whether an aspecting Venus is Libran or Taurean in nature can only really be discerned by checking with the client. It may be both. This also applies to whether an aspecting Mercury is Virgoan or Geminian in character.

Table 8: Venus for colleagues – some examples

Sign, or planet in aspect to Venus	Possible themes (similar to the above but applied to colleagues)
Aries, or Venus aspecting Mars	Colleagues who can handle heated debates. Enthusiastic colleagues. Working with pioneers or people who initiate new things. Doing sport together.
Taurus	Colleagues with common sense. Having solid, reliable, practical people to work with. Colleagues with a sense of humour. Going to lunch.

Gemini, or Venus aspecting Mercury	Working with dynamic, ideas people who are curious and love to share information or gossip. Going to the pub.
Cancer, or Venus aspecting the Moon	Colleagues who understand your needs as a parent. Working with people who care about how you feel. Colleagues who like being part of a family and make you feel you belong. Doing things as a team.
Leo, or Venus aspecting the Sun	Colleagues who are creative and enjoy playing and having fun. People who create a bit of drama from time to time. Colleagues who recognize you for what you are good at and tell you so. Going to the theatre.
Virgo, or Venus aspecting Mercury	Practical and helpful workmates, who give you the information you need to do the job. Going to the gym.
Libra	Colleagues who discuss and give you feedback. Workmates with a sense of decency and calm who create little or no conflict. A colleague who is a 'mate' to share things with. Doing things with a partner.
Scorpio, or Venus aspecting Pluto	Colleagues who are not too superficial. Ones who get the job done and have done any necessary research work. Workmates who understand political vibes. Passionate, trustworthy colleagues. Doing things alone.
Sagittarius, or Venus aspecting Jupiter	Fun colleagues who don't take themselves too seriously. Ones with a sense of vision and adventure. Enterprising workmates who enjoy some risk. Travelling or outdoor team-building together.
Capricorn, or Venus aspecting Saturn	Responsible colleagues who stick to a set of rules. Workmates who are on time for meetings and who answer messages. Achieving goals together.
Aquarius, or Venus aspecting Uranus	Future-orientated, idea-generating colleagues. Sociable ones who want to know what is happening. Workmates who can work independently. Brainstorming.
Pisces, or Venus aspecting Neptune	Compassionate colleagues. Creative visually-orientated colleagues. Workmates who look after you emotionally. Going to the pub together (for a different reason to Gemini!).
Aspecting Ceres	Colleagues who value the Earth. Ones who help you get into the right environment. Older women who support you. Discussing environmental needs together.

Table 9: Ceres for abundance? – some examples

Sign, or planet in aspect to Ceres	Possible themes Creating abundance in your life by...
Aries, or Ceres aspecting Mars	Sticking up for someone or fighting for something. Being a pioneer or initiating things. Defending. Abundance through a cause.
Taurus, or Ceres aspecting Venus	Being in a practical, problem-solving job. Abundance through the voice or an area that creates security.
Gemini, or Ceres aspecting Mercury	Expressing your thoughts or ideas. Being an agent. Abundance through networking, writing, curiosity or communication, including listening.
Cancer, or Ceres aspecting the Moon	Looking after your contacts. Creating a safe space. Nurturing in some way. Abundance through your circle of friends and family.
Leo, or Ceres aspecting the Sun	Being in the spotlight or on the stage. Performing, working with children. Working with celebrities or people at the top. Abundance through speculation or through being creative or playful.
Virgo, or Ceres aspecting Mercury	Giving information. Offering 'order' for someone else. Abundance through service, perhaps in health or the body-mind connection.
Libra, or Ceres aspecting Venus	Working together and cooperating. Offering dialogue. Acting as mediator. Working with fashion or beauty. Abundance through a relationship focus such as in PR or with client contact.
Scorpio, or Ceres aspecting Pluto	Research or analysis. Digging literally or figuratively. Abundance through loyalty, which has rewards.
Sagittarius, or Ceres aspecting Jupiter	Travelling or by being in politics or connected with international issues. Being an entrepreneur or taking risks. Abundance through being a visionary involved in the big picture.
Capricorn, or Ceres aspecting Saturn	Being a mentor or teacher. Offering a structure. Abundance through offering your expertise.
Aquarius, or Ceres aspecting Uranus	Offering a wake-up call or insight. Being an astrologer, the consultant, or the unique off-the-wall person who initiates change. Abundance through ideas.
Pisces, or Ceres aspecting Neptune	Through dreams, design or concepts. Being the artist. Abundance through using intuition or compassion.

I suspect that Ceres also describes an actual physical environment, such as a department at work. Below are a few real examples of environments and work areas of successful people from my practice (with their Ceres signs and planet aspects to Ceres).

Aries/Mars – Ministry of Defence, fire service

Taurus/Venus – Bank, orchestra, kitchen

Gemini/Mercury – GP practice, palm-reader (not really an environment but the two I know both have this!)

Cancer/Moon – Antique shop, boat and house builder, supermarket, B&B, real estate

Leo/Sun – Chic department store, management development

Virgo/Mercury – An organization that promotes working in NZ, Amsterdam archives (provides information), information management

Libra/Venus – Citizens' Advice, art world, fashion shop

Scorpio/Pluto – Founder of an organization that helps prostitutes, bank (stocks and shares area)

Sagittarius/Jupiter – International speaker, travel industry, KLM (airline)

Capricorn/Saturn – University, accountancy department, government

Aquarius/Uranus - IT department, technology

Pisces/Neptune – Hospital and care home, theatre

Client exercise – newspapers

One exercise that career counsellors sometimes give their clients is to suggest they look through the Situations Vacant columns and decide which jobs they might like. This exercise is normally used in the last phase of making a VP, as most career advisors can go further than us in terms of helping clients find a job. We stop at the definition and CV stage, whereas career advisors have the skills to help with getting interviews and can provide the next steps leading to getting a (new) job. However, I offer this as an exercise here to get the client involved in thinking about why they might be drawn to a particular company or position. This is useful for other parts of the VP, too.

Here I extend this exercise by getting them to do some research on one of the companies they have chosen. Information is easy to come by these days and, by doing some digging, clients start to recognize particular aspects they might need to consider, not to mention taking some responsibility for what they want to achieve. A company website speaks volumes. The look and feel of it give an idea of the type of values a company has. There is often a mission statement or information about achievements in company documents or on websites. For astrologers, there is sometimes even the history of the company, with a start date. Your clients can also ask for what are often free brochures or annual reports, which contain clues as to the type of company it is. Does the company match the environment the client is seeking? An excellent example of information about an organization is the Bristol University site. They were on *The Scientist*'s list called Best Places to Work in Academia in 2009. At the time of writing they have a page dedicated to a 'Positive Working Environment'.[2] The areas they cover might be interesting to discuss with clients such as 'work and life balance' or 'supporting you at work'. You can't find out everything this way, of course, but you can help to provide your clients with a list of questions they might want to ask at an interview and to help them be well prepared.

Environment for my client Jackie
A reminder from the bio:

> This session is to determine where and with whom she feels comfortable, and it includes environment, bosses and colleagues. Some of the environments Jackie likes can be inferred from the bio but I want to explore this more. Here's a start. Places with stories: 'Earl the photographer ... feel the merriment ... coolest thing was top-secret clearance ... genuine fun studying film ... excitable times with everything new ... interesting characters with dynamic stories ... time with Londoners ... meeting new people ... I sizzle when I am kept active ... I need human interaction.' Her preferences for bosses and colleagues need exploration.

These sessions on environment are often easier and less confronting than earlier ones, as the discussion mostly relates to other people. Discussions around the Moon and whether the client has been valued can bring up painful issues, but in general these sessions will be experienced as quite affirming and encouraging.

Back to Jackie's chart

The Moon is in Cancer in the 11th House. It is in a T-square with Uranus in Libra and the stellium of Sun, Mercury, Chiron and Ceres in Aries.

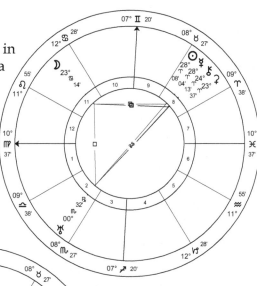

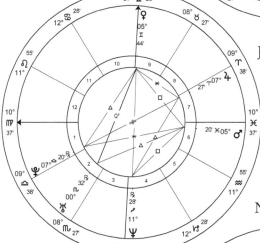

Jackie's Venus is right at the top of the chart on the MC in Gemini. Venus picks up several other planets by aspect, making a complicated picture in terms of colleagues. It aspects Mars, Jupiter, Uranus, Neptune and Pluto.

The Sun's aspects have been mentioned before but now we are using them to describe a suitable boss. The Sun is conjunct Mercury, Ceres and Chiron in Aries in the 8th House, all opposite Uranus and square the Moon. The Sun sesquiquadrates Neptune. There are dilemmas here.

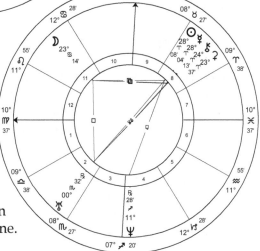

We had a long and interesting discussion about working environments. Jackie had never thought much about this aspect of her work but realized that, as she had moved through different jobs, people were very important to her (the Moon in Cancer and in aspect to the Sun). She likes the position in the room that she has in her present job – in a corner so it has a sense of overview and protectiveness. Her comment was 'I like to be hugged' (environmentally speaking) – I love this description for the Moon in Cancer.

One of the topics we discussed is whether it is acceptable to ask about potential colleagues or other people at an interview. My view on this is that it shows you are interested if you ask about the structure of the company.

- Who reports to whom?
- What is the purpose of the team? (important for Jackie with the Moon widely conjunct Saturn)
- How many in the team?
- What is the mission of the company?

These are questions that are perfectly reasonable to ask, and the answers will give some idea of the environment. In higher functions you can also ask to meet important people before deciding. This often happens anyway. In Jackie's case, I suggested that she should trust her intuition, as her ability to read people is very strong.

Here's her final description which, as you can see, covers a lot of the astrological aspects mentioned above.

Environment
The place where I work feels comfortable and creatively stimulating. Colour, natural light and materials are in abundance. The office is nestled in the bustle of a vibrant city. It is a busy environment that continues to pique my interests. My personal space feels protected and secure. I want to be able to show off my lush, fun, inviting workplace to friends and family. Being at work doesn't feel like being at work at all.

Colleagues
I like workmates that produce that family feel. I like to belong. I need considerate and sensitive people with whom I can form an emotional bond. We need a space that is nurturing which

gives us freedom to feel safe enough to express ourselves freely.

Colleagues are loyal to each other without personal agendas. They earn my respect by getting the job done, by being intelligent and on top of their game. We are considerate of each other's time; we are on time to meetings and return emails as soon as we can. We understand the basic decency that exists between professional individuals.

We are an international mix of fun characters that love to banter and make each other laugh. We also like to go deep and learn from each other's different perspectives.

I am a part of a team that knows what its function is in the grand scheme of things. We have a purpose governed by a broad set of rules but not necessarily bound by them. The clarity of vision keeps my signals from getting crossed so I can attend to the matter at hand. A very hierarchical structure does not allow much space for my team to flourish.

Boss
If I must have a boss, he needs to be communicative, understanding, witty and considerate. She doesn't have secrets, is logical, reasonable and sensitive. He treats me like an equal and is worthy enough to demand my respect. She offers structure and support but gives me the freedom to fly.

Bearing in mind Jackie's Ceres, which has aspects to Sun, Moon, Mercury and Uranus (wide for Ceres, but it picks up a stellium), let's look at her current job. This is from her original CV:

Produce storyboard and functional specification for interactive applications such as TV Guide and TV Search. Create customer-facing text and manage affiliate translations.

Her work is in the IT section (Uranus) of an Internet and broadband supplier (Mercury–Uranus), where she does client liaison (Moon) and provides specifications (Mercury) for new applications to be used by the public (Moon). She manages (Sun) this group. It's not her ideal job but somehow Ceres seems to put people in a place that fits. It pays the bills but, by working with her using astrology, we can offer suggestions for a much more fun way of making use of this energy.

Books to use for this section (see the bibliography for further details):

Moon Signs, Donna Cunningham
The Luminaries, Liz Greene and Howard Sasportas

And a book that is on my list to read: Steven Forrest's *The Book of the Moon* (Seven Paws Press, 2010). It sounds like a wonderful book but I'm not sure how useful it is for a VP, although anything that deepens knowledge of a planet is of course helpful for this process.

1. www.healthandsafety.co.uk/envi.htm
2. www.bris.ac.uk/pwe/

NOW WHAT?

THE RESULT
WHAT NEXT?

CHAPTER 13
THE RESULT

The supreme accomplishment is to blur the line between work and play.

Arnold Toynbee, British historian

The result of all these sessions should be a summary of all the parts of the Vocational Profile. The last step the client needs to take is to condense each write-up and create a single reference document. This is the final product – the VP – the reward for all the work. If it is done well, it will act as a guide for any future decision-making on vocation, career, work, job – whatever you wish to call it.

The VP should act as a quick reference guide to you/your client, and can be used as input for all manner of things, such as:

- Deciding if a job fits

- Helping to stay on an authentic path

- Asking questions at interviews

- Choosing between different options for work

- Writing a great CV or briefing someone to write one for you

- Distilling important words for a CV or a website

- Designing a website or briefing someone to help you with it

- Writing a brochure about yourself or one of your services

- Asking your employer for specific types of training (knowing what suits your path)

- Asking for what you are worth in terms of money and other available benefits

- Getting out of unsuitable environments

- Defining your stumbling blocks and being able to explain them to someone who can help

- **Knowing who you are, what you can do, what you want... and then going for it!**

These are just a few of the benefits this document can offer. The final VP will always be for the client and written in their own words. Here's Jackie's:

Firstly the checklist – this one has current job options but you can always match future positions with the column on the left.

Table 10: Jackie's Checklist

	Interactive TV Production	Acting	Writing	Improvisation
ARIES				
Fiery, enthusiastic, ARGGHH!!!		✓	✓	✓
Initiative	✓	✓	✓	✓
Challenge	✓	✓	✓	✓
Competitive, going for it		✓		✓
Acting quickly				✓
Direct			✓	✓
Jumping in, throwing myself at it		✓		✓
Real deep experience (8th House)		✓	✓	✓
MERCURY				
Communication, talking, writing	✓	✓	✓	✓
Observant, curious	✓	✓	✓	✓
NEPTUNE				
Getting lost	✓	✓	✓	✓
Creative, imaginative	✓	✓	✓	✓
URANUS				
Rebellious		✓	✓	✓
Unique		✓	✓	✓
Innovative	✓	✓	✓	✓

MOON				
Feeling of belonging	✓	✓		✓
Working with emotions and feelings		✓	✓	✓
Stars – Parans				
CAPELLA	✓	✓		✓
SIRIUS			✓	
SUALOCIN		✓	✓	✓

And the rest of the write-up:

Style
I can very readily exist in someone's shoes, sympathize with who she is and create a space for her to open up. I like listening to people's stories, my curiosity usually leads me to delve deeper. In written word, my imagination fuels my ability to describe with creative clarity and feeling. I put my off-kilter, quirky Jackie stamp on everything I write so you can easily tell authentic from adulterated. I find the truth so terribly seductive that I'm hungry for it in the people I interact with and activities I engage in.

Goals
Captain Communicator to the rescue! I want to broker in people, their norms and oddities and then share my wealth with all; learning and teaching, discovering and enlightening, an endless loop of exchange.

Norms and values
I love exchanging thoughts and ideas in excited conversation with like-minded people. Depth in discussion allows me to connect and understand. I appreciate people who take action and who value independence while still understanding their responsibility to others.

Talents
I am rooted in a long line of loud Kenyan matriarchs; curiosity and storytelling are in my DNA. I am a human mainframe

linking people with people, translating a culture's code to be understood by all, processing needs and providing solutions. I often drill down to the heart of a problem. I will 'but why?' until I've struck gold. I am good at reading tone and playing detective on people's motives. I jump into challenge and dig in, my enthusiasm propels me forward. Communication is my lifeblood. I write lucidly, beautifully. I listen with deep intensity.

How to make money
Luckily for me, I can make money where my talents lie: communication, cultures and strategies. Writing seems to be the front-runner of the communications.

Environment
The place where I work feels comfortable and creatively stimulating. I need to work with considerate and sensitive people with whom I can form an emotional bond.

If I must have a boss, he needs to be communicative, understanding, witty and considerate. She offers structure and support but gives me the freedom to fly.

Blocks
There is a part of me that is banished to the corner. In this corner, fear reigns. Ms 'Who says?' runs the show. She's the warden. She makes sure this ship runs smoothly (according to her). 'Jump Around' loves to move, be excited and have fun. Only, she hasn't been given much opportunity to do so, Ms 'Who says?' keeps her in line.

School bullying and teasing taught me to act as normal as possible so as to avoid being a target.

When I spoke up for my unique self as a young girl, teachers, parents, adults pointed the finger back at me. I shouldn't bother to stick up for myself because it was all my fault anyway, my opinions didn't matter.

These are the things that are important to her – things that she should consider when contemplating any new venture. Of course this is not fixed in stone, the VP is a living document. We learn as we go along, and a particularly interesting transit or progression might awaken us to new possibilities and challenges. As we work on our blocks, other opportunities open up. But it's a basis taken from our blueprint, the horoscope. I might have worded Jackie's profile differently but that's not the point. How she writes it – and uses it – is up to her now.

I wanted to include what she thought about the process. As astrologers, I think we don't ask for enough feedback on what we do. We can learn so much if we do this. Here's what she said:

The process
For one, the 'after' picture of my CV far outshines the 'before' picture. My CV now reads more like who I am. The old CV only had a hint of me. It had been a while since I updated my CV so the makeover was much needed. Quite quickly and clearly it details what I have done and what I have to offer.

Maybe the biggest impact has to do with getting clear about how I came to be, who I am and what next is in store. Some of the write-ups were taxing. It was agony writing my bio, dredging up the past. But I learned by getting this on paper, by laying all the cards on the table I could better see what I'm working with, where I'm holding myself back where my natural forces are pulling me to. The write-ups make it dead easy to whip out cover letters and tailor my CV's profile depending on the job I'm applying for. I don't have to start from scratch, which can deter me from starting at all.

A lot of times the astrology angle helped to validate a lot of feelings/notions I had swirling inside. It served as the confirmation I needed to anchor myself so I could take action. It is reassuring to know I share the same ideas as the stars and the planets. At other times, I didn't identify so much with what astrology told me. My tendency was to accept everything because most of it sounded kick ass. The bits about the past life or my future life didn't land with me so much, I had no frame of reference for these things.

And because she mentioned it, here's what she did with her CV. If you compare the before and after I think you will see how the new one much better defines who she actually is. My belief is that she will attract much more interest from employers who offer work in line with what she wants and loves to do.

PROFILE

I can very readily exist in someone's shoes, sympathize with who she is and create a space for her to open up. In written word, my imagination fuels my ability to describe with creative clarity and feeling. I put my off-kilter, quirky 'Jackie'-stamp on everything I write so you can easily tell authentic from adulterated. I drill down to the heart of a problem and 'but why?' until I'm satisfied. I find the truth so terribly seductive that I'm hungry for it in the people I interact with and activities I engage in. I chase challenge around every corner, inciting followers along the way.

EXPERIENCE

Interactive TV Production, UPC Broadband (Jul 2008 – present)

- Successfully and speedily adapted to managing the TV Guide and TV Search projects across the UPC European footprint.

- Coordinate between product managers, engineers and international affiliates to deliver the next-generation TV Guide to the digital TV platform

- Conceptualize storyboard and flowcharts to initiate interactive projects. Research comparable applications on different platforms for insights and ideas. Write functional documentation to facilitate engineering build.

- 'Jackie picks up new projects really well and is very proactive and fast in understanding a project and making it her own. She is very cooperative, a team player, a good listener and open to comments. She is continuously learning.' (Quote from Head of TV Production)

Interactive TV Operations, Chello Interactive (Mar 2007 – Jun 2008)

- Regularly revelled in on the fly, in the moment problem-solving inherent in delivering interactive applications to live television.
- Quickly grasped the overview of a situation to connect people and resources to problems and solutions.
- 'Jackie is much appreciated by her co-workers. She doesn't have her own agenda and is able to gather all feedback to a cohesive and consistent result.' (Quote from Head of TV Operations)

Self-employed, engagemedia (Jun 2006 – present)

- A business established to exploit talents in production, post-production, improvisational acting and writing. A business dedicated to engaging communication.
- easylaughs Improvisation – cast member (Jan 2007 - present)
- Mob. Handers Radio Pilot – cast member (Nov 2009)
- *Fate By Numbers* – 'Rosie Denton' (February 2007)
- Six Sigma Business CD-ROM – VO (February 2007)
- *Fascinatio* – VO (November 2006)
- Walki Talki Tours – VO (September 2006)

Post-Production Coordinator, Leopard Films USA (Oct 2003 – Mar 2004)

- Worked with British production company to produce *Cha Ching! Money Makers* (Discovery Channel) under hectic timetables and strained budget.
- Communicated and coordinated between production team, editors and contracted post house to produce 14 episodes.
- Relayed daily progression of each episode to the executive production team.

Post-Production Coordinator, Roland House (Nov 2002 – Oct 2003)

- Planned sessions in audio, narration and online/ offline edit suites. Managed elements and deliverables and resolved or dispatched any issue that arose.

- Anticipated client needs to ensure work was concluded on time and to satisfaction. Clients included Time Life Music, Discovery and National Geographic.

Production/Post-Production, Engine Pictures (Mar 2000 – Oct 2002)

- Always alert when assisting the camera, production and art departments on film shoots. Remained sensitive to what was missing to quickly remedy the situation.

- Researched film vendors, locations, cast and crew; loaded and edited location scout and casting tapes; organized and distributed director reels.

Missile Systems Engineer, Raytheon Systems (Sep 1997 – Jan 1999)

- Conducted computer analysis on a pioneering advance in missile systems. Upgraded and integrated simulation code for missile model functions. Secret clearance held.

EDUCATION/SKILLS

Ira Seidenstein Clown Workshop, 26–27 Jun 2010
Paris, France

User Centered Design Course, 20–21 Nov 2008
System Concepts, London, UK

The Art of Revision Workshop, 14–15 Jun 2008
Lisa Friedman, Amsterdam Writing, Amsterdam, NL

Master of Arts, Film and Video, March 2005
Awarded distinction in Comprehensive Exam (writing)
American University, Washington, DC, USA

Bachelor of Science, Electrical Engineering, Aug 1997
University of Southern California, Los Angeles, CA, USA

Multimedia:
 AVID, Final Cut Pro, Photoshop, After Effects

Word Processing:
 Microsoft Office Suite, Final Draft

Operating Systems:
 Macintosh, Windows

Languages:
 English (native), Dutch (conversational)

To my delight, after this process Jackie was brave enough to leave her job and is currently loving the volunteer work she is doing while planning her next move. And best of all she is getting gigs as a stand up comedian!

Update from Jackie, 2017
"It's funny, recently I've been thinking about how much our sessions influenced the way life is today, and for the good!

"As you know, I left my job in September 2011. I applied for many different 'dream' jobs — things that sparked my interest in fields new to me — but all were full-time jobs working in offices. I didn't have any luck in that arena but now I see it was for the best.

"I got a permit to stay in the Netherlands based on self-employment. I've been doing acting gigs (web video, interactive game), improv acting for corporations and high schools, teaching improv workshops, stand-up comedy, hosting travellers via AirBnB, holiday cover for my friend's touring company, babysitting, oh, and I've just picked up a one-day-a-week, work-at-home gig with my old employer.

"I'm not rolling in the dough but I am super happy with my days. I've got my fingers in different pots to satisfy my varied interests. There's a lot of movement, I don't feel stuck to any one thing. I realized I don't want an office job ever again. I probably knew that already but this year has given me the proof that I can actually do it.

"I'm much more upfront and outspoken. My first improv group recently underwent a refocusing of sorts and I took a big role in helping define that. Here's our mission statement:

> We perform high-quality improv shows in our home theater. The home show is the diva we lovingly cater to. We do this for the love of improv, not for profit. The home shows are high energy, dynamic well-rehearsed formats that entertain and excite regular and changing audiences alike. We offer courses and workshops to help cultivate our audience.

> We relish the privilege of performing weekly and bring our enthusiasm, joy and commitment to every performance. We get 'paid' in stage time, experience and development, creative stimulation, ridiculous fun, groupies and beer.

> We are a band of merry improvisers that operate with professionalism and respect. We are social, good-timers but when there is work to be done, it's business time.

> We are aware that personal lives happen and offer an open, welcoming atmosphere to tackle issues that may affect our camaraderie and commitment to produce quality shows. We understand that it is each member's responsibility, duty, to voice any grievances to ensure smooth operation. Silence, internalizing, gossiping, factioning etc. are detrimental (harmful) to the honest, effective communication we strive for. Each member values any advice/criticism given and assumes the honorable intentions of his fellow improvisers.

"Sounds A LOT like our session on work environment and colleagues!"

Jackie's updated C.V. profile 2017 has morphed into this version because of her new focus:

> I am a human mainframe linking people with people, processing needs and providing solutions. I drill down to the heart of a problem and 'but why?' until I'm satisfied. My independence and initiative mean I can be trusted to spark my own fire and keep it burning. I chase challenge around every corner, inciting followers along the way. Communication is my lifeblood. Curiosity is in my DNA.

CHAPTER 14

WHAT NEXT?

The first step to getting the things you want out of life is this: decide what you want.

Ben Stein, American lawyer, author
and presidential speech writer

I would rather regret the things that I have done than the things that I have not.

Lucille Ball

Having described your working life in one document, you now have the basic answers to the initial questions 'Who am I?', 'What do I want?' and 'What can I do?' So, now you have arrived here with your VP, what can you do next?

In the last chapter I mentioned a few ways that the VP summary document could be used. In this chapter I want to discuss possible next steps that you or your client can take in your work and also how you can go further with the process as an astrologer working with clients.

If your client (or you) has embarked on this endeavour, then they are probably looking for some kind of change in their working life. So they will need to decide the next move and this document will greatly help to fill in the details of any steps they choose to take. There are several scenarios and I will highlight a few to give examples of how you or your client can make use of a VP.

- Looking for a new job
- Improving your current work
- Going out on your own
- Improving your own company

Looking for a new job

There can be many reasons why a search for a new job is relevant, and this can involve a change in direction or a whole new career, starting work again after a break or starting out after your education is completed. Whatever the reason, probably the first thing you or your client will need is a new CV. The VP, if done well, has all the right words in it to use as input for this purpose. As an astrologer you cannot really help with this process unless you are good with text. But you can offer to read the result to see if it matches the VP/horoscope. I do this often, and I offer suggestions for where I feel something is missing or has an overemphasis. I sometimes work together with a text-writer and, with my shorthand, which she is now used to, she can quickly provide a professional CV for clients. Most people find it really difficult to write about themselves. So having a VP makes it much easier and speeds up the process.

The next thing you will probably need to do is write a covering letter. My client referred to this (and the CV) in her comments on the process. 'The write-ups make it dead easy to whip out cover letters and tailor my CV's profile depending on the job I'm applying for. I don't have to start from scratch, which can deter me from starting at all.'

In my experience most people find it very helpful to have done the write-ups. As an astrologer, you can't be of much assistance here, other than in giving feedback which in itself is very valuable.

The next thing you will need to do, if you are short-listed for a job, is prepare for an interview. Astrology cannot help directly with this activity but the VP can be used as a checklist for the job to see if it suits and for preparing any questions. However, as an astrologer, you can help your client prepare by looking at any company charts if you have their founding date and if you have the skills to interpret a company chart. Failing this, you can suggest a colleague astrologer for this task.

The rest of the process is up to the client but as an astrologer it is helpful to have good people in your network who you feel comfortable with. These might include career counsellors, who can take the process to the 'getting a job' stage, employment agencies, head-hunters or anyone else you know working with job vacancies. If the VP is satisfactory, then the time spent on these last steps will be much shorter than normal. Most of the defining work has been done, so it makes the process very efficient. The job-finder has a lot less work, so the cost is significantly less than it would be without a VP.

It is also helpful to have a list of websites with useful information, such as those offering help with writing CVs, employment benefits or schemes or anything else that is employment-related. Occasionally it has been useful to have someone in my network who knows about employment law, too. If you are going to specialize in vocational profiling you need a broad knowledge of the subject to be credible.

Improving your current work
There can be many reasons for wanting to do this – after all, why wouldn't you want to? Tackling this issue will depend on the presenting problem. If your client is in the wrong work area then you may want to discuss whether a new job is relevant. Many clients are happy with their profession and may even be happy with their employer. But often they have questions about their direction. Their questions may also be about decision-making: Should I move to another job I have been offered? In another department? In another country? I'm worried about a new boss. Should I do this new training? This new university course?

The VP process should have helped with most of these questions but, as an astrologer, you are able to offer a sounding board to help clients with their decision process. However, more and more, clients are taking responsibility for their own 'stuckness' and they want help in working on blocks. Just defining these, in the 'Blocks' session, is hugely helpful but, as I mentioned in that chapter, you'll need to be able to refer clients on if you don't have the skills to take this further.

Going out on your own
For you or your client, going through the process of making a VP helps focus the mind on what you really want if you are planning to set up a business. The areas of your enterprise should now be clear and usually clients already know which market area they want to be in. There are several ways you can help clients at this stage by using the VP. The first is similar to the CV but it involves extending the information to make publicity material, such as brochures or a website. I have covered this in various sections. A useful service is to give feedback on any design for websites or brochures, as well as having defined the basic information needed for these. Another service I offer clients in this process is to help choose a start date or an opening date for a business. The way I do this is a process in itself – it is almost the reverse of defining the VP. I ask questions such as 'what is your mission?', after I have ascertained a time frame. A full

description of electional astrology is beyond the scope of this book, but it is a useful service to add to your collection of tools.

Many who come for vocational reasons often want to start their own enterprise. I use quite a simple method, as most of the decisions need to come from the client. First, we decide which Sun sign might be relevant to the overall company business. This is often relatively simple, as there is usually a span of a few signs and clients choose very quickly. Choosing the Moon is often the next thing to do and it is clearly better if this fits well with your client's personal chart. Discussing such questions as 'What do you want to do with the company?', 'What are the products?', and 'What is your mission?', can help clients with the process of starting up and what they need to do.

There are obviously other astrological tools that might be relevant here, if you have them in your toolkit. Forecasting techniques help with the question of 'when'. And we can cover the ' where', too. Locational astrology (Jim Lewis' Astro*carto*graphy™) is something I use often, as I have a lot of international clients. This helps to discuss location for all manner of questions.

Improving your own company

I have many self-employed clients who often need help with direction. Making a VP (or at least part of it) is still a relevant process for them. I offer a 'check service' for clients – to check their horoscope with their website or other publicity material. Does it fit what you see in the chart? There may be a company chart but for one-(wo)man companies there should be a close match between the publicity material and the personal chart, so I check this too. As an astrologer you are a good independent sounding board for timing any future plans, new strategies and services, or for being able to discuss whether the company is still the right choice for your client. Is it indeed the right vocation?

As a last comment, working with clients in this way, offering more than one session, means that you build up a relationship with them. Having done this, it is much easier for the client to come back to you. It is far easier to get work from existing clients than to find new ones, so look after them!

I hope you enjoy working in this way and I would welcome any comments or suggestions for items that you might like to see included in this work in the future.

FINAL THOUGHT: AGE MATTERS

There is still no cure for the common birthday.
John Glenn, astronaut

In the previous chapters, I have talked about all the planets but have singled out planets no further away than Saturn. The Sun was addressed in 'Vocation', Saturn in 'Blocks', Mars in 'Style', and so forth. However, I did not single out Uranus, Neptune and Pluto for any special treatment. This is not because they don't deserve it. It has more to do with the fact that they are generational planets, i.e. people of around the same age will have them in the same signs. So looking at them on their own will say something about a generation, not necessarily about an individual.

We do, however, need to take this into account when looking at vocational sessions. Naturally, a person's age will determine how we work with them. Someone who has not yet started their working life is a very different proposition to someone who's about to retire. A Vocational Profile, or at least parts of it, is relevant even at retirement age. We still want to be fulfilled in our lives until the end of our days. While addressing issues with a client, we must take into account their age, generation and background.

I want to discuss the outer planets here and I also want to touch on different critical points used in the Huber Age Point system. Knowing where your client stands with the generational planets and the Life Clock will add useful background information to what has been covered already.

Your generation
An astrological model of life implies that we share archetypal patterns at a generational level. Astrologers refer to the three planets furthest away from the Earth – Uranus, Neptune and Pluto – as collective or generational planets. Uranus spends about 7 years in each sign, a bit short in terms of the length of a generation. Nonetheless, Uranus will define a group. I have often lectured

about the planet Neptune, which has a cycle of about 165 years. I have spoken about him in terms of addiction and dreams. He spends roughly 14 years in each zodiac sign. Pluto has a rather eccentric cycle, spending more time in some signs than others because of the tilt of his orbit. However, his total cycle is around 248 years. The combination of Uranus, Neptune and Pluto varies with each individual. By looking at what they represent, we can gain insight into specific age groups. Of course, when these planets form important aspects between each other, such as the Uranus–Pluto conjunction in Virgo in the 1960s, interesting subsections of a generation will be created.

My group is unique

Uranus is important in your working life, since where he is placed in the horoscope highlights where and how we try to be authentic and be ourselves, which is really what makes us happy in our working life. Uranus' sign will show how we are prepared to be rebellious, independent or different. The house will show the areas where we will dare to do this, if we are prepared to stand up and be unique or unconventional, which can often mean doing things alone. If Uranus aspects any personal planets, this will be even more important as a theme. It is as if we must carry the archetype and somehow use it for our group.

Jackie is an example of the Uranus in Scorpio generation. She is strongly Uranian anyway, but the Uranus in Scorpio will add an extra flavour, as will the fact that it is in her 2nd House. She is inclined to be rebellious about sex (Scorpio). She is prepared to use a different and deep way of waking people up. In the 2nd House of money and security, although she isn't yet there, she would like to earn money in a unique way and have lots of different ways of gaining an income. But all of these ways involve having some sort of influence (Scorpio). The possessions she will want to acquire (2nd House) are unusual or possibly surprising items that highlight her individuality. It may not apply to the whole Uranus in Scorpio group, but Uranus here would suggest a group that has very unconventional views on the deeper side of life. Sex, death, taboo subjects – all of these could be dealt with honestly. Uranus breaks through Scorpio issues, so this group could be the awakeners in this area. Uranus is also innovative with Hades themes. How might this be used to effect at work? Use the same rules of house and sign to look at other Uranus placements.

Follow your dream
What are these fourteen-year generations? Neptune suggests that each group will have a different dream, a different longing or even a different addiction. Each group will have an ideal to aspire to, even though this vision may seem unobtainable. Neptune is clearly visible in art and film, the themes of which follow the signs. We love to escape into art and the cinema. Neptune shows which 'drugs' we like, how we like to escape, and where to. Clearly our ideals will have an influence on the type of work we wish to do.

Here's a list of Neptune through the signs (1928–present – showing the precise years although not the precise dates, because Neptune can retrograde back into its previous sign one or more times):

- 1928/9–1942/3 Virgo
- 1942/3–1955/6/7 Libra
- 1955/6/7–1970 Scorpio
- 1970–1984 Sagittarius
- 1984–1998 Capricorn
- 1998–2011/2 Aquarius
- 2011/2–2025/6 Pisces

Here are two examples. At the time of writing, Neptune has just entered his own sign of Pisces. It will be interesting to see how his themes unfold as he progresses through Pisces. I would expect this transit to herald a group with a deep longing for a compassionate world – one that is connected on a global level.

The previous generation with Neptune in Aquarius has dreams of technology – are even addicted to it. Of course, we are all swept up in these themes anyway by having lived in this era, and children with this signature were born into a world when technology has come on in leaps and bounds. It feels as if it has been a time of no borders and boundaries in this area. This group may have technology as an ideal, as part of their 'DNA'. This is one example, as technology is only one of Aquarius's domains. This group has dreams of being unique and different. A film that illustrates Neptune in Aquarius is *Avatar*, which used computer-generated images. Many directors have used these techniques before but we are now heading for virtual reality with the 3D effect being used in many films, and also the sale of 3D televisions.

The Libra group yearn for the ideal relationship. The Scorpio generation have dreams of (and are perhaps addicted to) depth, therapy, sex, some kind of passion and deep commitment. They have dreams of being in control. Keeping things under control or having influence might be an ideal to aim for, too. For the Sagittarius group, freedom and starting your own enterprise might be the dream, or being able to travel. And the Capricorns will long for structure and responsibility. But in all these examples, somehow we often end up feeling disappointed in all these dreams. That seems to be the nature of Neptune: we may imagine and long for something which is too idealistic and unrealistic, and disappointment ensues.

And then there is Pluto!

Pluto is further out in the cosmos, so spends longer in some signs, with some long overlaps at the changes because of his weird orbit:

- 1912/3/4–1937/8/9 Cancer
- 1937/8/9–1956/7/8 Leo
- 1956/7/8–1971/2 Virgo
- 1971/2–1983/4 Libra
- 1983/4 to 1995 Scorpio
- 1995–2008 Sagittarius

His entry into Capricorn in 2008 saw the beginning of a period where his influence should result in responsible use of power (or suffer the repercussions). This can be seen at the time of writing with the phone-hacking case against several of Rupert Murdoch's companies, and the Catholic Church being brought to task for covering up the abuse of young children. Pluto will remain in Capricorn until 2023/4. Up until that time, he will be cleaning out all things Capricorn.

Pluto transforms the areas governed by the sign he is in, but what does that mean for each generation? Again, each of these generations is different in terms of how they seek to gain power and control. In each, there will be a different obsession. There is a fundamental belief system in each Pluto generation that operates very deeply in the psyche. The Pluto in Leo group has often been labelled as the 'me' generation. There is a deep belief in self-transformation and power at an individual level. This may be a reaction to the previous 'family as power' Cancer generation, where a small closed group holds power, and by belonging to this clan a group member also has influence.

Virgo believes in service and functionality. Health and medical issues are the areas where this group want control and influence. As US President, Barack Obama's first attempt at transformation was in the health area. One obsession here could be a drive to exercise or keep fit. Perhaps this describes a generation who want to have influence in how animals (Virgo) are treated, too. And for whom order is power.

For Libra, dialogue is power. The relationship rules. For Scorpio – well, power is power - but so is sex! Could it be an obsession for Pluto in Scorpio? We certainly learned a lot about death, another of Pluto's favourites, in this period through the rise of AIDS. There is a belief that researching and having an understanding of psychology or of the hidden world will give influence. Knowing secrets gives power. The belief is one of needing to be in control to survive. How out of control and powerless we were when confronted by AIDS. Pluto's fear is powerlessness, which often comes before the process of transformation. We sometimes need to go to the bottom of the well in therapy before we can take back our power.

For the Sagittarius generation, there is an underlying belief that anyone can be an entrepreneur. Power and influence are achieved by risk-taking and having a vision. Before Pluto left Sagittarius in 2008, people were rewarded for having the belief to start their own businesses. Now, as we settle into the Pluto in Capricorn period, the world has changed and the game is different. It is not enough to have guts – you must have the expertise or training if you want to gain power. Capricorn understands that influence can be achieved by having a clear goal and taking responsibility for it. Accountability. A belief in standing up and being counted. This is very different from the previous Pluto groups. The house and sign of Pluto will indicate where we are prepared to take our power and use our influence, which naturally affects our working life.

Your age

The Huber method of timing is explained well in Bruno and Louise Huber's book *LifeClock*. As I have already mentioned, I have been a big fan of this technique for many years. Without even a horoscope but by simply knowing a person's age, I have found Age Points extremely useful when it comes to knowing which phase someone is in. Having a horoscope gives even more information that can be used with this method. But here, I want to discuss the phases and the possible background reasons why someone may come to you at specific ages.

There are twelve phases in this system, each consisting of six years. It is simple – you start at birth. So from 0–6 is the Aries phase, 6–12 is Taurus, 12–18 Gemini and so on until you reach 66–72, the Pisces phase, after which you start again at 72–78 with Aries. Simply knowing this means you already have background information. But the Hubers do something else in each phase, too. They define a low point or a critical point which they call the 'LP'. This is based on the Golden Mean and is always a fixed amount of time after the entry into each phase. I have found these points to be remarkably useful for describing exactly what clients are experiencing.

The ages of these crises or turning points are as follows:

Aries 3–4, Taurus 9–10, Gemini 15–16,

Cancer 21–22, Leo 27–28, Virgo 33–34,

Libra 39–40, Scorpio 45–46, Sagittarius 51–52,

Capricorn 57–58, Aquarius 63–64, Pisces 69–70

The crises carry the nature of the sign, e.g. age 39–40 will bring a relationship or another Libra theme to a critical point. Remember, a crisis is not necessarily negative, it just means something coming to a head.

Why is this relevant to vocation?

As I mentioned above, you need to take account of the age of your client. I have been amazed by the number of people who come for job guidance at age 33. By being familiar with this model it is easy to see that this is a Virgo-type crisis. Many come at age 45 – for the Hubers, this is *the* life crisis – which is Scorpionic by nature. This is a very different question. The 33ers are struggling with a daily regime and how they want to earn their daily bread. Are they happy in the service they are performing? The 45ers are asking much deeper questions: What am I doing with my life? Why am I on earth at all? In this period all Scorpio themes can be relevant, including being affected by death. You will, of course, get clients from other age groups, but these two ages are far and away the most common for vocational questions. I refer you to the Hubers' book for more information, but I will give a table here so you can start noticing what kind of background question your client may have. It is interesting to note that there are many books written which give advice on the development phases of humans up to the age of 18. After that, writers seem to leave us alone – we are left to

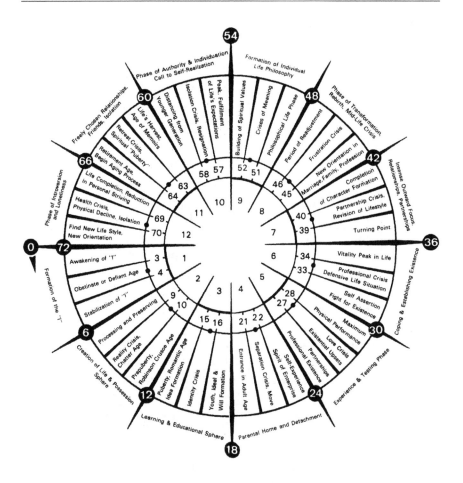

our own devices until we reach the mid-life crisis, where we are offered a few tomes. The Hubers' system offers advice about what we should be doing at any age, so is useful for that purpose alone.

The Hubers' diagram[1] (above) explains the phases. The houses are linked to the life phases or ages, as indicated by the large numbers around the edge of the circle. The focus of our life changes every six years in this system. In each house there is a crisis that has the nature of the house. To take the same example as above: House 6 is the phase between ages 30 and 36. The Hubers describe this as the 'coping and establishing existence' phase. The crisis, shown as the point between age 33 and 34, is called 'professional crisis'.

Table 11: The Hubers' descriptions of each house, taken from their book *LifeClock*

Age	House	Sign	Development
1–6	1st	Aries	Formation of the 'I'
6–12	2nd	Taurus	Creation of Life and Possessions Sphere
12–18	3rd	Gemini	Learning and Educational Sphere
18–24	4th	Cancer	Parental Home and Detachment
24–30	5th	Leo	Experience and Testing Phase
30–36	6th	Virgo	Coping and Establishing Existence and Livelihood
36–42	7th	Libra	Intense Outward Focus, Relationships, Partnerships
42–48	8th	Scorpio	Phase of Transformation, Rebirth, Mid-life Crisis
48–54	9th	Sagittarius	Formation of Individual Life Philosophy
54–60	10th	Capricorn	Phase of Authority, Individuation, Call to Self-Realization
60–66	11th	Aquarius	Freely Chosen Relationships, Friends, Isolation
66–72	12th	Pisces	Phase of Introversion and Loneliness

Over the years of using this system, it is clear to me that all the corresponding zodiac themes can be present in each phase and crisis point. Huber simply gives a starting point.

It is most likely that for vocational work you will have only clients whose ages lie between the 3rd and the 10th phases. As I have mentioned, a VP is relevant after that but for reasons other than looking for a job, which is often why clients come to you in earlier phases. So I will give you more information on phases 3 to 10 with regards to vocation, and suggest what might be useful at each phase.

Phase 3 • *Ages 12–18 with a critical point between 15–16*

Puberty! This is the Gemini phase. The Hubers write, 'During this period, the child pushes out from the intimate sphere of the parental home and feels most at home with the peer group collective.' Gemini is concerned with forming opinions and learning. In this phase, teenagers learn how to communicate with their own kind

– not their parents. They must rebel somehow against the ideas of their parents so that they can discover what they themselves think. So, there is a warning here if you are asked questions about someone of this age group. Often it is one of the parents who wants to come to you or who wants their child to come. Alarm bells should ring for you if the parent wants to come on their own. A child of this age is usually perfectly capable of discussing which subjects or professions they might want to study. It is not for nothing that the ethical code of the professional group of astrologers of which I used to be a board member and am still a member states: 'In principle an astrologer should not make a horoscope for third parties without permission, with the exception of (own) children under the age of twelve.' Clearly there can be extenuating circumstances in the case of people with severe learning difficulties or other handicaps. But the code acts as a guide.

I ask parents to either send the child on their own or to come with them. Mostly if the parent wants to come alone, I do their chart (not the child's), as it is they who are asking the question. I agree with the Hubers when they say that the crisis is about school, vocational development, parents and authority figures – hence my warning. Of course, parents usually want the best for their children but this sometimes means they ignore their children's ideas and dreams.

What is usually helpful for this group is a vocation and talents session – just one session is usually enough to get someone discussing what they love to do and might be good at. And to get them (and their parents) thinking of possible options. As this is a Mercury-ruled phase, it might be worthwhile looking at communication skills too.

Phase 4 • Ages 18–24 with a critical point between 21–22

This is the Cancer phase, so the main background focus should be about making a nest for yourself. It is the 'leaving home' phase. Of course, many will leave earlier or later but there is still a nest-building energy. However it is done, the family influence must lessen. The Hubers call the critical point 'separation crisis'. I have found age 18 to be very important. In the horoscope it represents the base of the chart, the IC. It is a major turning point, as are the other axes points. It represents the start of a period of gradually having to stand on your own two feet – not wanting to break family bonds but having to go your own way. Often a study path has already been chosen, and even completed, but there is a need to now translate that into paid employment. Someone in this phase might need help with possible real jobs, rather than a study area. Again, talents and vocation are good to explore and also ideas about how to carry out research on companies by looking at advertisements or searching the Internet. It is useful to have some good websites to hand for this that give instructions on how to construct a CV and to look for 'situations vacant'. As this is a Moon-ruled phase, you might want to consider offering an 'ideal environment' session.

Phase 5 • Ages 24–30 with a critical point between 27–28

The Leo phase – and as I write this singer Amy Winehouse has recently been found dead. There has been much media attention on the so-called Club of 27, the group of famous musicians who died at this age and which Amy has now joined. Yes, this phase should be creative and about having fun – it is Leo, after all. But the Hubers call the crisis point 'existential upset or love crisis' in the 'most aggressive time... pursuing the organization of family and family goals'. We do indeed want to be seen and noticed in this phase but the challenge is to be recognized for our own creations. I think that pop stars must struggle with fame, money and others telling them what they should create. Perhaps the 'playing' with drugs is a search for some kind of fun on their own terms. We need to tread carefully with clients in this phase. My suggestion is to encourage their own creativity and what they want to 'produce', be it an invention or a child. 'Should I have children yet?' is a very real question for this group. (Amy was said to have been obsessed by this question and it couldn't have helped to hear that her ex-husband's new partner was expecting a child.) Perhaps this would actually be the perfect time if society hadn't suggested we could do it much later! Leo does love children. A focus on talents would be a good session to offer this group, and perhaps a real discussion on who has influence in their lives. But of course, being a Sun-ruled phase, looking at vocation will always be of interest.

Phase 6 • Ages 30–36 with a critical point between 33–34

A main target group, as I have mentioned. I have often thought I should advertise with the slogan 'Are you 33? Time for a look at your job?' If your client is 33 you need to ask about their work, even if they come to you for something else. I often get mothers of young children in this group struggling with the fact that they are not working. Or they may well be trying to get back into the work force. It's the Virgo phase with, as the Hubers put it, a 'professional crisis'. After Leo, the fun and games are over and we have to get back to the daily grind. Routine, going to work and earning a living – so try to show your client that if work is a necessary evil, it might as well be something she wants to do! Work–life balance is one of the big issues here. Virgo is about serving, so getting this right can be tricky. I have had many people come to me at this age with burn-out, an all too common problem these days, usually caused by over-work and over-responsibility in an area not suited to the heart. If you can do a whole VP trajectory for them, that is great. That is probably the most helpful strategy, but don't underestimate your role as a sounding board. What this group really needs is *information*. Which expert can you send them to in order to help with their issues?

Phase 7 • Ages 36–42 with a critical point between 39–40

Libra is concerned with relationship, so clients will want dialogue and a listening ear. As with the IC (18), 36 is on one of the axes, but this time it is the Descendant and a *major* turning point – very noticeable to most clients. This point is halfway around the cycle so is like a full Moon, turning around to head for a new Moon again. We are now opposite the birth phase, so we will be dealing with the ideas inherent in the Aries phase of getting an identity. But this time we must discover (and, more to the point, stay true to) who we really are both in the 'big bad world' and in our primary relationships, including those at work. If you get clients in this phase with career problems, the issue usually concerns their listening to others too much or asking others for advice. So you need to be careful here that clever clients don't trap you into giving too much advice not based on their chart! This can be very tempting sometimes. In my experience, there is a often a relationship crisis at the critical point, but that may be because I have a lot of clients who follow their partners around the world, and at this stage start wondering: 'What about me and my career?' Life may begin at 40 but you have to get through 39 first and do that well! The Hubers say that the formation of 'character' is not finished until the end of this phase at 42, and I can see what they mean. It takes a long time to get out from under the influence of loved ones. The most help you can offer here, apart from the listening ear, is to remind clients of their dreams, of who they really are and what their real identity actually is. Are they living life for themselves or for others? A vocation session and one on blocks are useful but the environment session, particularly the colleagues session, might prove fruitful – as of course will any of the Venus-related sections on talents, making money and defining norms and values.

Phase 8 • Ages 42–48 with a critical point between 45–46

The big one according to the Hubers – the *life* crisis point. In the research relating to this age that I did for my MA, I can certainly agree that many Scorpio themes come to the fore at age 45. This is indeed the real mid-life crisis, not that Saturn and Uranus oppositions and Neptune squares aren't important (these are often quoted when explaining mid-life crises and occur during the early to mid 40s). But try this theory out on those aged 45. You will be amazed by how many Scorpio themes you will hear if you ask them what is happening in their lives. The question here goes something like 'I'm not really old but it's time to be what I want to be when I grow up, but what is that? Why am I here? I'm not young either so I better get on with it!' In this period, death often visits. In my study one person actually died at this age but many of the rest I studied lost a parent or a close friend. In whichever way death touches us, we realize immortality is not an option. Time is running out so we need to take life seriously and radically change or transform anything that isn't working. Of course, the 8th House also affects emotional relationships and joint possessions, so money and security (in a much bigger way than the opposite 2nd House) are often issues. If a client is in this phase, they will need to talk about deep issues and not trivia, so you need to be able to do that. These are people ready to define their blocks and work on them, and ready to look at what their life is really about. Obviously, the best option here is several sessions, if possible. You may need to refer them to someone else for more work on the blocks.

Phase 9 • Ages 48–54 with a critical point between 51–52

The Sagittarian Archer takes control in this phase, a big relief for many after the previous one. Most people feel a sense of wanting to grow and expand again. Many people I know have gone back to study in this phase, particularly at university where, this time round, they chose a subject because they want to, not because they should. This phase is about finding your own life philosophy, as opposed to the Gemini (opposite) phase of discovering your opinions. Now you want more meaning. The crisis point is what the Hubers call a 'crisis of faith'. The best session to offer here is perhaps the Jupiter-ruled norms session, looking at belief systems and seeing if they need to be worked on. Are they holding your client back? I encourage clients to study what they love and sometimes that takes some convincing, many feeling they are already too old to start again. Frankly, I think that's rubbish, but that's my belief system! Many clients decide to start their own enterprises in this phase. You can help them by doing the image-branding session. That will assist in getting their strategy and marketing in place (both 9th House concepts). Risk-taking should be encouraged in this phase. The faith crisis is often caused by realizing that what you may have believed about the world and life has lost meaning. It may mean casting off the faith or religion you grew up with and creating your own 'manifesto' for life. In your working life, it becomes quite difficult to be employed by a company that goes against your philosophy, hence the fact that many start their own companies or at least start planning for them. Going well, this phase should engender optimism about the future, but of course this needs to be realistic rather than too Jupiterian in the negative sense of over-estimating one's abilities.

Phase 10 • Ages 54–60 with a critical point between 57–58

Finally, at 54 we reach the top of the chart, another turning point that repeats themes of being 18. The prime of life you might say, where everything learned in life can be put to good use and be harvested. Capricorn: ambition achieved, goal reached, authority gained. If all goes well, these are the rewards in this phase. But 57 often brings a huge sense of having failed, of being of no more use in society, or being too old to get another job. In our society this often happens and many who are made redundant in this phase suffer dreadfully from Saturnian problems such as depression, fears of loneliness and of having a 'failed' life. In my experience, men go through this more than women. Women are often ready to take on more responsibility as they are now finally really child-free. Sessions that refocus on missions or goals can be useful, but if someone is suffering you will need to look at their blocks. Clients must see that blaming others or society is not going to help – they need to get real and take responsibility for where they are. All being well, this can be a very productive time and you can help your clients to realign with their life mission. People in this phase want concrete answers and concrete things to do. Offering clients some sort of structure, and perhaps homework, is a good idea. This phase should be a time when being a 'manager' has its rewards, be it literally – by being in a responsible job with authority – or just being a manager of your own life, where you have the authority and responsibility to decide your own actions. At the end of this phase comes a time to step out of positions that require taking responsibility for others. But not a time to step out of society. It's time to get ready for the Aquarius or 'mentor' phase of giving back to society the knowledge you have gained, be it within or outside company life.

Sessions after that

Sessions after 60 often have a different focus, or at least they should have. These are mainly with people who love working after 60 and want to be gainfully employed. The questions are often more about fulfilment, spiritual growth and meaning. Up until 66 is a good time to go your own way in the Aquarius phase – authenticity is the key here, so any sessions that help your clients with that are beneficial. The Pisces phase should be a gestation phase for a new start at 72, so help clients with their dreams. And so you go around again. I love clients who are older than 72. They have indeed been around the clock! They can learn a lot by looking at what happened to them at the same point in the cycle 72 years earlier.

Age *does* matter, but we can all use some help, regardless of how old we are.

This last chapter stresses the importance of offering astrology sessions that are appropriate to age and, as such, it draws on different techniques not covered in the VP trajectory. It also serves as an example of how your own favourite techniques and heavenly bodies can be included in the work of giving career advice and guidance to your clients.

I hope you find my model useful for developing and deepening your own way of working. As astrologers we have all been inspired by different teachers, methods and experiences and our work does and should reflect this. And we keep evolving. That is what makes each of us a unique, authentic astrologer. One who is called to this rich, ancient profession.

---

1. Bruno and Louise Huber, *LifeClock*, HopeWell, 2006, pp. 46-47.

APPENDIX 1

Summary of planets in the Vocational Profile and their effects

	Part of Vocational Profile	Examples of effects on aspected planet
Sun	Vocation, calling, motivation	Attention-grabbing, in spotlight, enthusiastic, delegating, leading, bold, courageous, warm, dramatic, theatrical, enabling, proud, vital, fatherly, playful, fun-loving
Moon	Preferred environment and colleagues	Caring, feeling, encompassing, emotional, creating safety, belonging, welcoming, patriotic, responsive, motherly, nurturing, protective
Mercury	Communication skills	Curious, chatty, inquisitive, quick-thinking, creative with ideas, networking, making connections, communicative, rational, helpful, informative, serving
Venus	Talents, norms, values, colleagues	Discussing, feedback, fair, comparing, valuing, client- or other-orientated, cooperative, sharing, giving, compromising, peace-seeking, mediating
Mars	Style, approach	Quick, assertive, taking action, leading, pioneering, competitive, sales-orientated, enthusiastic, brave, motivating, initiating, encouraging, defending
Ceres	Environment	Practical nurturing, environmental, abundant, cultivating, nutrition, finding the right place, biology, women's issues, passing on knowledge to younger generations, rites of passage, nature's cycles
Jupiter	Beliefs, norms	Strategic, big-picture, overview, visionary, philosophical, enterprising, entrepreneurial, risk-taker, adventurous, confident

Saturn	Blocks	Careful, structured, goal-orientated, managing, mentoring, teaching, authoritative, planning, disciplined, meets deadlines, responsible
Uranus	–	Independent, quirky, out-of-the-box, bright, intellectual, future-orientated, different, questioning status quo, honest, mentoring, advisory
Neptune	–	Conceptual, creative, artistic, compassionate, 'improving the world', helpful, service-orientated, intuitive, spiritual, imaginative, visual
Pluto	–	Passionate, powerful, researching, leading, emotional, deep, decisive, political, persuasive, loyal, good in a crisis, a survivor
Chiron	Blocks	Healing, understanding pain, alternative, bridging, teacher, shaman

APPENDIX 2

Birth Data

Name   Chapter RR   Source*
  Birth data

Prince Albert of Monaco   4   AA   Times Newspaper
  14 March 1958, 10:50 MET, Monte Carlo, Monaco 43n45, 7e25

Buzz Aldrin   9   AA   Birth certificate
  20 January 1930, 14:17 EST, Glen Ridge NJ, USA, 40n48, 74w12

Woody Allen   11   AA   Birth certificate
  1 December 1935, 22:55 EST, Bronx NY, USA, 40n51, 73w54

Jeffrey Archer   11   A   From him
  15 April 1940, 11:45 GDT, London, England, 51n30, 0w10

Giorgio Armani   11   AA   Birth certificate
  11 July 1934, 07:20 MET, Piacenza, Italy, 45n01, 9e40

Julian Assange   11   B   Autobiography
  3 July 1971, 15:00 (or 14:05?) AEST, Townsville, Australia, 19s16, 146e48

Pope Benedict XVI   4   AA   Birth certificate
  16 April 1927, 04:15 MET, Marktl, Germany, 48n15, 12e51

Silvio Berlusconi   4   A   From him
  29 September 1936, 05:40 MET, Milan, Italy, 45n28, 9e12

Tony Blair   4   AA   Birth certificate
  6 May 1953, 06:10 GDT, Edinburgh, Scotland, 55n57, 3w13

Gordon Brown   4   AA   Birth certificate
  20 February 1951, 08:40 GMT, Giffnock, Scotland, 55n48, 4w17

George W. Bush   4   AA   Hospital records
  6 July 1946, 07:26 EDT, New Haven CT, USA, 41n18, 72w55

David Cameron   4   A   From him
  9 October 1966, 06:00 GDT, London, England, 51n30, 0w10

Prince Charles, Prince of Wales   4   A   Palace records
  14 November 1948, 21:14 GMT, London, England, 51n30, 0w10

Jacques Chirac   4   AA   Birth Certificate
  29 November 1932, 12:00 GMT, Paris, France, 48n52, 2e20

Winston Churchill   4   A   Father's letter
  30 November 1874, 01:30 GMT, Woodstock, England, 51n52, 1w21

Helen Clark   4   A   From her electoral office
  26 February 1950, 19:30 NZT, Hamilton, New Zealand, 37s47, 175e17

Bill Clinton   4   A   From his mother
  19 August 1946, 08:51 CST, Hope AR, USA, 33n40, 93w36

Hillary Rodham Clinton   11   DD   Various conflicting data
  26 October 1947, 08:02 CST, Chicago IL, USA, 41n51, 87w39

Francis Crick   9   X   Date from online sites
  8 June 1916, Northampton, England. Time unknown.

Richard Dawkins   9, 11   X   Date from online sites
  26 March 1941, Nairobi. Time unknown.

Princess Diana   4   A   From her mother
  1 July 1961, 19:45 GDT, Sandringham, England, 52n50, 0e30

Benjamin Disraeli   9   AA   Family records
  21 December 1804, 05:30 GMT, London, England, 51n30, 0w10

Albert Einstein   11   AA   Birth record
  14 March 1879, 11:30 LMT, Ulm, Germany, 48n24, 10e00

Queen Elizabeth II   4   A   Palace records
  21 April 1926, 02:40 GDT, London, England, 51n30, 0w10

Roger Federer   9   A   His website
  8 August 1981, 08:40 MEDT, Basel, Switzerland, 47n33, 7e35

Betty Ford   11   AA   Birth certificate
  8 April 1918, 15:45 CST, Chicago IL, USA, 41n52, 87w39

Indira Gandhi   4   A   From her secretary
  19 November 1917, 23:11 IST, Allahabad, India, 25n27, 81e51

Mohandas Gandhi   4   DD   Various conflicting data
  2 October 1869, 07:11:48 LMT, Porbandar, India, 21n38, 69e36

Jane Goodall   7   X   Date from online sites
  3 April 1934, London, England. Time unknown.

Adolf Hitler   4   AA   Baptismal certificate
    20 April 1889, 18:30 LMT, Braunau, Austria, 48n15, 13e02

Barry Humphries   11   A   From him
    17 February 1934, 06:30 AEST, Camberwell, Australia, 37s50, 145e04

David Icke   9   A   From him
    29 April 1952, 19:15 GDT, Leicester, England, 52n38, 1w05

John F. Kennedy   4   A   From his mother
    29 May 1917, 15:00 EST, Brookline MA, USA, 42n20, 71w07

Karl Marx   4   AA   Official records
    5 May 1818, 02:00 LMT, Trier, Germany, 49n45, 6e38

Ludwig Minelli   11   X   Date from online sites
    5 December 1932. Time and place unknown.

Rupert Murdoch   11   B   Newspaper
    11 March 1931, 23:59 AEST, Melbourne, Australia, 37s49, 144e58

Benito Mussolini   4   AA   Birth certificate
    29 July 1883, 13:10 GMT, Dovia Il Predappio, Italy, 44n13, 12e02

Rafael Nadal   9   AA   Birth certificate
    3 June 1986, 18:20 MEDT, Manacor, Spain, 39n34, 3e12

Martina Navratilova   9   A   From her
    18 October 1956, 16:40 MET, Prague, Czech Republic, 50n05, 14e26

Florence Nightingale   9   DD   Various conflicting data
    12 May 1820, 14:00 LMT, Florence, Italy, 43n46, 11e15

Barack Obama   4   AA   Birth certificate
    4 August 1961, 19:24 AHST, Honolulu HI, USA, 21n18, 157w51

Emmeline Pankhurst   9   A   From her
    14 or 15 July 1858, 21:30 GMT, Manchester, England, 53n30, 2w15

Christopher Reeve   9   A   From him
    25 September 1952, 03:12 EDT, Manhattan NY, USA, 40n46, 73w59

Franklin D Roosevelt   4   AA   Family records
    30 January 1882, 20:45 LMT, Hyde Park NY, USA, 41n47, 73w56

Nicolas Sarkozy   4   AA   Birth certificate
    28 January 1955, 22:00 MET, Paris, France, 48n52, 2e20

Harrison H. Schmitt   9   A   From him
    3 July 1935, 23:02 MST, Santa Rita NM, USA, 32n48, 108w04

Rupert Sheldrake   9   A   From him
  28 June 1942, 18:00 GDWT, Newark upon Trent, England, 53n05, 0w49

Sir Charles Kingsford Smith   11   A   From him
  9 February 1897, 4:30 AEST, Brisbane, Australia, 27s28, 153e02

Dame Joan Sutherland   9   C   No source
  7 November 1926, 17:30 AEST, Sydney, Australia, 33s52, 151e13

Margaret Thatcher   4, 9   A   From her secretary
  13 October 1925, 09:00 GMT, Grantham, England, 52n55, 0w39

Oscar Wilde   11   AA   Baptismal certificate
  16 October 1854, 03:00 LMT, Dublin, Ireland, 53n20, 6w15

Harold Wilson   4   A   From him
  11 March 1916, 10:45 GMT, Huddersfield, England, 53n39, 1w47

Amy Winehouse   15   A   From her mother
  14 September 1983, 22:25 GDT, Enfield, England, 51n40, 0w05

* The source is given here for completeness however I refer you to the Astrodatabank site (www.astrodatabank.com) for more information, as sometimes there are various times given. The site contains data for most of the people mentioned.

APPENDIX 3

Bibliography, useful books and other resources

Astrology books

There are many good astrology books – far too many to list here. Below is a list of books I have either quoted from or have found to be useful in deepening astrological knowledge when defining a VP. Note that they are listed by author, so all their books can be grouped together.

Addey, John, *Harmonics in Astrology*, L N Fowler, 1976

Arroyo, Stephen, *Exploring Jupiter, Astrological Key to Progress, Prosperity and Potential*, CRCS Publications, 1990

Bell, Lynn, Costello, Darby, Green, Liz and Reinhart, Melanie, *The Mars Quartet: Four Seminars on the Astrology of the Red Planet*, CPA Press, 2001

Brady, Bernadette, *Star and Planet Combinations*, The Wessex Astrologer, 2008

Burt, Kathleen, *Archetypes of the Zodiac*, Llewellyn Publications, 1988

Clark, Brian, *The Sibling Constellation*, Arkana, 1999

Clark, Brian, *Vocation: The Astrology of Career, Creativity and Calling*, Astro*Synthesis, 2016

Clifford, Frank C, *The Midheaven: Spotlight on Success*, Flare, 2016

Costello, Darby, *Earth and Air*, CPA Press, 1999

Costello, Darby, *Water and Fire*, CPA Press, 1998

Cunningham, Donna, *Moon Signs; The Key to Your Inner Life*, Ballantine Books, 1988

George, Demetra and Bloch, Douglas, *Asteroid Goddesses*, Ibis Press, 2003 (for Ceres)

Goodman, Linda, *Linda Goodman's Sun Signs*, Pan Books, 1972

Greene, Liz, *Saturn: A New Look at an Old Devil*, The Aquarian Press, 1983

Greene, Liz and Sasportas, Howard, *The Luminaries: The Psychology of Sun and Moon in the Horoscope*, Samuel Weiser Inc, 1992
Greene, Liz and Sasportas, Howard, *The Inner Planets: The Building Blocks of Personal Reality,* Samuel Weiser, 1993

Greene, Liz, *The Art of Stealing Fire: Uranus in the Horoscope*, CPA Press, 2004

Greene, Liz, *The Astrological Neptune and the Quest for Redemption*, Samuel Weiser, 2000

Guttman, Ariel and Johnson, Kenneth, *Mythic Astrology: Archetypal Powers in the Horoscope*, Llewellyn Publications, 1993

Hamaker-Zondag, Karen, *The Twelfth House: The Hidden Power of the Horoscope*, Red Wheel/Samuel Weiser, 1992

Hamblin, David, *Harmonic Charts*, The Aquarian Press, ed. 1987

Hand, Robert, *Horoscope Symbols,* Para Research Inc, 1981

Harding, Michael and Harvey, Charles, *Working with Astrology: The Psychology of Harmonics, Midpoints and Astro*Carto*Graphy,* Arkana, 1990

Hopewell, Joyce and Llewellyn, Richard, The *Cosmic Egg Timer*, HopeWell, 2004

Huber, Bruno and Louise, *LifeClock*, HopeWell, 2006

Jayne, Vivia, *Aspects to Horoscope Angles*, Astrological Bureau, 1975

Marks, Tracy, *Your Secret Self: Illuminating the Mysteries of the Twelfth House*, CRCS Publications, 1989

Reinhart, Melanie, *Chiron and the Healing Journey*, Starwalker Press, 2009

Rodden, Lois M, *Money: How to Find it with Astrology*, AFA, 2006

Sasportas, Howard, *The Twelve Houses*, Flare Publications, 2007

Sasportas, Howard, *Direction and Destiny in the Birth Chart*, CPA, 2002

Tarnas, Richard, *Prometheus the Awakener*, Spring Publications, 1998

Tompkins, Sue, *The Contemporary Astrologer's Handbook*, Flare Publications, 2006

Tompkins, Sue, *Aspects in Astrology*, Element Books, 1989

Other books

Bolen, Jean Shinoda, *Gods in Everyman: A New Psychology of Men's Lives and Loves*, Harper & Row, 1989

Bolen, Jean Shinoda, *Goddesses in Everywoman: A New Psychology of Women*, Harper & Row, 1985

Bolles, Richard N., *What Color Is Your Parachute? 2012: A Practical Manual for Job-Hunters and Career-Changers*, Ten Speed Press, 2011

Bradshaw, John, *Homecoming: Reclaiming and Championing your Inner Child,* Bantam Books, 1992

McTaggart, Lynne, The Field, Harper Paperbacks, 2003

Ofman, Daniel, *Core Qualities: A Gateway to Human Resources*, Scriptum Publishers, 2002

Sheldrake, Rupert, *The Science Delusion*, Coronet, 2012

Sturman, Gerald M, *If You Knew Who You Were, You Could Be Who You Are,* Bierman House, 2010 Ten Dam, Hans, *Exploring Reincarnation: The Classic Guide to the Evidence for Past-Life Experiences*, Rider Books, 2003

Other resources

My own online articles are available on my Amsterdam School of Astrology site www.asastrology.nl and my blog is at www.fayeblake.nl/faye_blog which has an archive. You can subscribe to this free blog through the site.

Vocational horoscope – written by Liz Greene – available to order through www.astro.com – sample online.

Studyshops from Astro Logos (all on CD)
Brady, Bernadette, *Profession and Money in the Natal Chart*
Greene, Liz, *Neptune*
Greene, Liz, *Pluto and the Inner Planets*
Harvey, Charles, *Mercury the Translator*

Data and charts for further study

Rodden database www.astro.com/astro-databank/Main_Page

Clifford, Frank C, *The Astrologer's Book of Charts*, Flare Publications, 2009

ABOUT FAYE

A groundbreaking astrologer of long experience, Faye Blake brings to this book a unique blend of knowledge in business and human resources, practice in therapy, and generosity of spirit. As a teacher, therapist, writer and company owner, she has worked in her native New Zealand, Australia, Fiji, the UK, Belgium, Norway, the USA and of course throughout the Netherlands, where she has been resident for over 30 years.

One of the first MA graduates in Cultural Astronomy & Astrology from Bath Spa University (UK), Faye combines academic training and thorough research with her wealth of hands-on, practical experience with hundreds of individual and business clients. Her results-oriented approach is eminently useful in business and gives a unique balance to her work. As one client testifies, a vocational session with Faye really helped her to get her life in perspective, both personally and at work, and brought unanticipated, concrete results.

As part of the MA program, Faye wrote four papers (available directly from her): *Three Histories of Uranus, The Sun and Authority, Astrology and Past Lives* and *Astrological Research*. Her dissertation, called the *Company Clock*, researched the use of the Huber Age Point in companies. She also wrote a chapter entitled *The Business of Place and the Place of Business: Making Astrolocality Techniques Useful* for the book *From Here to There: An Astrologer's Guide to Astromapping*, edited by Martin Davis, and a chapter for *Transpersonal Astrology: Explorations at the Frontier* entitled *Is the Transpersonal Becoming Personal? The Planets as a Guide to Conscious Evolution*.

The Vocational Astrology Approach

Unconventional and revolutionary – as befits an Aquarian! – Faye's approach is always client-centred, and is based on active dialogue, rather than a more static, chart-based 'reading'. She shows students in astrology how to involve the client with their own chart, engaging them in their own process. It may not be what clients expect from an astrologer, but the impact of this interactive, businesslike orientation is, quite simply, practical results. There is nothing complicated about Faye's method: its very simplicity allows conversation to penetrate further into the client's situation, leading to a deeper understanding of the forces underlying their experiences, and the potential to better navigate them. As her client in this book remarks:

Maybe the biggest impact of my sessions with Faye has been getting clear about how I came to be, who I am, and what next is in store for me… I could better see what I'm working with, where I'm holding myself back, where natural forces are pulling me to. The write-ups make it dead easy to whip out cover letters and tailor my CV's profile depending on the job I'm applying for. I don't have to start from scratch, which can deter me from starting at all.

Training

Faye offers an online apprenticeship using this book as a basis, helping students to set up their own practice and leading them though a process of working with their own clients in the vocational profiling process.

In addition to learning simple, deep and effective techniques, Faye's training course offers students the opportunity to practise on each other in a safe environment, and receive feedback on their work with a practice client of their own. As one participant comments:

If I were to sum up, in one word, what this method did for me, I would say it gave me confidence. Doing the course (and having chapters from the book to refer to) gives me a clear structure from which to work. I can give clients a time frame within which we will work. I start by telling clients that they will have to do homework as part of the work we would do together. The biography and CV that they provide at the outset gives me information from which I can generate questions. It helps me to articulate my thinking and, because of its conversational style, makes working with clients feel more collaborative. My current client says it has given her time to just focus on herself, and I can see the way she has blossomed. (Sharon Bond, London)

Together with a colleague, Faye also runs a basic Vocational Astrology course online for Kepler College. For more details, see www.keplercollege.org

Contact

Faye's firm belief is that the work of astrologers is to help clients to be authentic and happy. To this end, she has developed a method that offers concrete results. Faye is open to questions about her approach to vocational astrology described in this book, and about her training courses.

Visit her website at www.fayeblake.nl, where she offers a free blog called *The Monthly Planet*, or the Amsterdam School of Astrology website at www.asastrology.nl

Faye's consultancy site for business is www.juxtaposition.nl

Faye can be contacted at: faye@asastrology.nl

A complete guide to horoscope synthesis – designed to help astrologers identify, prioritize and synthesize the components, themes and storylines of any chart. Packed with original ideas and observations, this textbook includes 150 horoscopes and profiles showing astrology in action.	14 essays on psychological, traditional, mundane and evolutionary astrology from a new wave of astrologers that includes Gary Caton, Frank Clifford, Rebecca Crane, Nick Dagan Best, Maurice Fernandez, John Green, Tony Howard, Mark Jones, Keiron Le Grice, Eric Meyers, Wendy Stacey and Branka Stamenkovic	In *From Symbol to Substance: Training the Astrological Intuition* learn to: develop creative and spontaneous interpretations for any placement; enhance intuitive faculties when analysing charts; and think creatively when exploring symbolism and correspondences.

Sue Tompkins (*Aspects in Astrology*) presents an authoritative guide to chart interpretation with an in-depth exploration of the planets, zodiac signs, houses and aspects. Included are biographies and step-by-step instructions for synthesizing the main horoscope factors.	From an award-winning psychological astrologer comes the definitive book on the astrological houses. This new edition of the best-selling handbook remains a firm favourite among students and professionals. With a new foreword by Dr. Liz Greene and tribute essays from astrologers.	Based on over 30 interviews with researchers and leading astrologers, this landmark, thought-provoking volume examines the lives and work of contemporary astrologers, and considers many of the issues facing this ancient and systematic art.

Join two international
astrologers and lecturers
as they examine (in
four new essays):
potential traps for the
counselling astrologer; the
importance of Mercury
in consultation; the
transformational potential
of astrology; and the tools
to use when preparing for
a chart analysis.

The Midheaven
is associated with
success, achievement
and recognition. It has
much to say about our
reputation and public
image, as well as early
parental messages. This
absorbing volume offers
many original insights
from the author's years of
research.

All you'll ever need to
know about Solar Arc
Directions is packed
inside this informative
and popular manual,
presented clearly and
concisely. There are
numerous examples
and an intro to Shadow
Transits, an indispensable
new method that connects
directions to transits.

An exceptionally handy
booklet packed with info
including: mind maps
for the signs, planets
and aspects; Mercury
Retrograde advice; a
history of the outer
planets through the
signs; an outer planet
ephemeris; and easy-to-
use Ascendant and MC
calculators.

In *Horoscope Snapshots*,
discover: he deeper,
hidden sides to your
Sun sign; how your Sun,
Moon and Ascendant
signs differ; the real
nature of Jupiter;
parental significators;
planetary types;
vocational indicators;
the role of Pluto in
America.

This acclaimed, fully
illustrated textbook
offers immediate access
to the mysteries of
the hand. In 4 easy-
to-follow-steps, this
innovative, fully revised
edition presents: The
Palm Detective; Timing
Techniques; Love,
Health and Career; and
Palmistry in Action.

www.flareuk.com

The London School of Astrology

– the students' choice in contemporary astrological education –

• Accredited Foundation courses for beginners in central London
• Accredited Diploma courses for those with more experience
• Saturday seminars, residential courses and other events
• Short courses in tarot and palmistry (modern hand analysis)
• A distance learning course in palmistry

Learn astrology, palmistry and tarot in a fun, supportive environment
with the UK's most experienced astrologers/tutors

To find out more
Visit our website www.londonschoolofastrology.co.uk
Email: admin@londonschoolofastrology.co.uk

London School of Astrology
BCM Planets, London WC1N 3XX

Telephone: 020 8402 7772

Fun, self-knowledge, spiritual development, vocational training

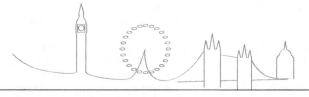